GUIDE TO THE EUROPEAN UNION

OTHER ECONOMIST BOOKS

Guide to Analysing Companies
Guide to Business Modelling
Guide to Business Planning
Guide to Economic Indicators
Guide to Financial Management
Guide to Financial Markets
Guide to Hedge Funds
Guide to Investment Strategy
Guide to Management Ideas and Gurus
Guide to Organisation Design
Guide to Project Management
Guide to Supply Chain Management
Numbers Guide
Style Guide

Book of Obituaries
Brands and Branding
Business Consulting
The City
Coaching and Mentoring
Dealing with Financial Risk
Economics
Emerging Markets
The Future of Technology
Headhunters and How to Use Them
Mapping the Markets
Marketing
Successful Strategy Execution
The World of Business

Directors: an A–Z Guide
Economics: an A–Z Guide
Investment: an A–Z Guide
Negotiation: an A–Z Guide

Pocket World in Figures

GUIDE TO THE EUROPEAN UNION

Dick Leonard
with assistance from Leo Cendrowicz

10th edition

THE ECONOMIST IN ASSOCIATION WITH

PROFILE BOOKS LTD

Published by Profile Books Ltd
3A Exmouth House, Pine Street, London EC1R 0JH
www.profilebooks.com

First published in 1988 as *Pocket Guide to the European Community*;
reprinted 1988; revised editions 1989, 1992, 1994, 1994, 1997, 1998, 2000,
2002, 2005, 2010

Typeset in EcoType by MacGuru Ltd
info@macguru.org.uk

Printed in Great Britain by
Clays, Bungay, Suffolk

A CIP catalogue record for this book is available
from the British Library

ISBN 978 1 84668 172 1

The paper this book is printed on is certified by the © 1996 Forest Stewardship
Council A.C. (FSC). It is ancient-forest friendly. The printer holds FSC chain of
custody SGS-COC-2061

FSC
Mixed Sources
Product group from well-managed
forests and other controlled sources

Cert no. SGS-COC-2061
www.fsc.org
© 1996 Forest Stewardship Council

Contents

List of figures

List of tables

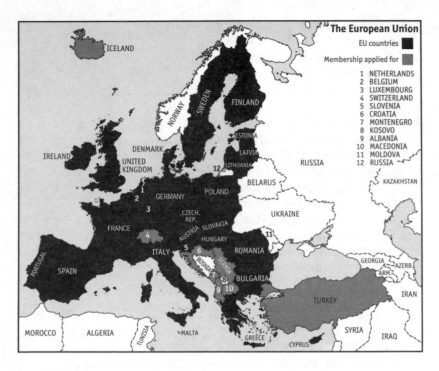

The European Union

EU countries

Membership applied for

1 NETHERLANDS
2 BELGIUM
3 LUXEMBOURG
4 SWITZERLAND
5 SLOVENIA
6 CROATIA
7 MONTENEGRO
8 KOSOVO
9 ALBANIA
10 MACEDONIA
11 MOLDOVA
12 RUSSIA

Membership

1958 Belgium
France
Germany[a]
Italy
Luxembourg
Netherlands
1973 Denmark
Ireland
United Kingdom
1981 Greece
1986 Portugal
Spain

1995 Austria
Finland
Sweden
2004 Cyprus
Czech Repulic
Estonia
Hungary
Latvia
Lithuania
Malta
Poland
Slovakia
Slovenia
2007 Bulgaria
Romania

Applications for membership

Turkey[b]
Croatia[b]
Macedonia
Montenegro
Albania
Iceland
Serbia
Switzerland[c]

a East Germany joined as part of unified Germany in 1990.
b Negotiations began in 2005.
c Not currently (2010) proceeding.

Introduction

Now, well into its sixth decade, following the signing of the Treaty of Rome in 1957, the European Union (EU) has established itself as a major force in the world, and its activities now impinge more and more on the lives of the citizens of its different member states. The coming into force of the Treaty of Lisbon, on December 1st 2009, should make it a more effective, transparent and accountable institution. Yet the extent of public knowledge of the EU has lagged some way behind.

Many excellent books have been written about the EU. The majority of these have been addressed to specialists, or are concerned with one particular aspect of the Union's role. The purpose of this book is rather different. It is addressed specifically to lay people, and is intended to give a simplified account of the origin, history, institutions and functions of the Union in a form accessible to the intelligent reader with no previous knowledge of the EU.

The book is divided into four parts. Part 1 contains an account of the origins of the European Community (EC; later the EU), followed by a historical account of its development up to the beginning of 2010. Part 2 describes in some detail the institutions of the EU, such as the Council of Ministers, the European Commission, the Court of Justice, and so on. Part 3 deals with its competences, from agriculture to technological research. Part 4 considers some specific problems, including enlargement and the continuing difficulties which the UK has experienced in adapting to EU membership, and concludes with an assessment of future prospects. A series of appendices provide reference material on the Union and its institutions. Lastly, there are suggestions for further reading for those who wish to pursue the subject further.

The source of most of the figures and much of the factual information contained in this book is the European Commission. Permission to reproduce this information is gratefully acknowledged, as is the help of Leo Cendrowicz in preparing this tenth edition.

I would like to dedicate this book to the memory of Dr Gertrud Heidelberger, my mother-in-law, an indomitable lady who represented all that is best in European culture.

Dick Leonard
January 2010

1
THE BACKGROUND

1 The origins

Hitler was the catalyst

Adolf Hitler was the main catalyst of the European Economic Community (EEC), although none of its leaders would readily admit him as a founding father. Like Charlemagne and Napoleon before him, Hitler brought together, by the sword, virtually the entire land area of the original EEC, destroying in the process the self-confidence of the nation states from which it sprang.

These were recreated in 1945, but no longer saw themselves as autonomous actors on the world stage. The governments of the three smallest – the Netherlands, Belgium and Luxembourg – decided in 1944, before the liberation of their territories had been completed, that their economic futures were inextricably intertwined. The Benelux Union came into force on January 1st 1948 as a customs union, with the intention of progressing to a full economic union at a later stage.

The Marshall Plan

The United States and the Soviet Union each gave the nations of western Europe a strong shove in the direction of unity, one with apparently benign, the other with malign intentions. The Organisation for European Economic Co-operation (OEEC) was set up in 1947 in order to divide up among the member states the flow of US aid under the Marshall Plan. The aid programme was completed over three years, but the OEEC continued as a forum for promoting economic co-operation and freer trade among west European countries. It later widened its membership to include all the advanced industrial nations of the non-communist world, and changed its name in 1961 to the Organisation for Economic Co-operation and Development (OECD).

Fear of the Soviet Union

If the United States, partly no doubt through self-interest, had contributed hope, the Soviet Union contributed fear. Its brutal suppression of the countries of eastern Europe, culminating in the communist takeover of Czechoslovakia in February 1948, forced several west European countries to come together for self-preservation. As early as March 17th 1948 the Treaty of Brussels was signed, providing for a 50-year agreement between the UK, France, Belgium, the Netherlands and Luxembourg known as the Western European Union (WEU). This provided "for collaboration in economic, social and cultural matters and for collective self-defence". In practice the WEU was largely superseded by the creation of NATO in 1949, although it remained in existence and its five original members were joined by West Germany and Italy in 1954.

And fear of Germany

Fear of the Soviet Union in the post-war years was matched by fear of Germany, which had tried to overrun western Europe in the second world war, and had also fought three ferocious wars with France over a period of 70 years. How to prevent a recurrence of these wars in the future occupied many minds in western Europe, as elsewhere in the world, in the immediate post-war period. Two possible solutions presented themselves. The first was to ensure that Germany should not only remain divided (which the division of Europe between East and West seemed likely to secure, in any event), but that it should also be reduced to a permanent state of economic backwardness. Apart from intrinsic improbability, this solution had the serious disadvantage of conflicting with another west European priority: resisting the advance of Soviet communism. This pointed to the need not only for a German military contribution to western defence, but also for a strong economy which would help to satisfy the rapidly rising material expectations of West Europeans. It was this consideration which tipped the balance decisively towards the second proposed solution to "the German problem". This was that Germany (or West Germany at least) should be linked so organically with its neighbours, and that the link should appear so evidently in the self-interest of both Germans and all the other nationalities, that another war between the nations of western Europe would become impossible.

Monnet's decisive role

The continental country most resistant to this concept was France, and it was fortunate that the most clearsighted and persuasive advocate of this approach was a Frenchman, Jean Monnet. If Hitler provided the impetus towards European unity, Monnet was indisputably its principal architect.

He had a remarkable career, almost all of it devoted to international co-operation of a genuinely practical kind. Originally a salesman in the UK for his family firm of brandy distillers, he spent the first world war as a temporary civil servant co-ordinating the contributions of the French and UK economies to the joint war effort. Between the wars he acted as deputy secretary-general of the League of Nations, but in 1939 he was recalled to resume his role as an Anglo-French co-ordinator. It was his plan for a Franco-UK Union which Churchill put forward in 1940 in a vain attempt to forestall the French surrender to the Germans. Monnet spent the rest of the war years in London and Washington, once again co-ordinating the economic warfare of the allied nations.

He returned to France as a member of de Gaulle's government, and subsequently became head of the French planning organisation. In 1950 his moment of destiny came: it was his proposal that paved the way for the Franco-West German reconciliation which has been the essential condition for all subsequent progress towards European unity. The occasion was the Franco-West German dispute over the Saarland, which was largely fuelled by French fears that if its iron and coal industries were integrated with those of the rest of West Germany it would once again dominate the economy of Europe. France had tried unsuccessfully to annex the Saarland, which was overwhelmingly German in population, and, as in the post-1919 period, this attempt had poisoned relations between the two countries.

The Schuman plan

Monnet succeeded in capturing the ear of the French foreign minister, Robert Schuman, a man whose own personal history (as an Alsatian born in Luxembourg) had predisposed him to the advantages of European integration. Monnet's proposal, which was put forward by the French government as the Schuman Plan, was that the West German and the French coal and steel industries should be placed under a single High Authority which should supervise their development. "The solidarity between the two countries established by joint production will show that a war between France and Germany becomes not only unthinkable but materially impossible," Schuman said in launching his plan on May 9th 1950.

Other European countries were invited to join the plan, which was instantly accepted by Chancellor Konrad Adenauer on behalf of the West German government, which rightly saw it as the way to rejoin the European comity of nations on equal terms. Italy and the Benelux countries also quickly responded, and the Treaty of Paris, signed on April 18th 1951, formally established the European Coal and Steel Community (ECSC), which came into being on August 10th 1952. Jean Monnet was its first president.

The UK stands aloof

One notable absentee was the UK, which had been invited to join but declined to do so after giving the matter little serious thought. The decision was taken by Clement Attlee's Labour government, but was confirmed by the Conservative government under Winston Churchill, elected in October 1951. The UK did not then regard itself primarily as being a European nation, and adopted a superior attitude to the new organisation, as evidenced by the private remark of Churchill to his doctor in January 1952, "I love France and Belgium, but we must not allow ourselves to be pulled down to that level."[1]

The absence of the UK facilitated the construction of a community that was different from the many other international organisations established during this period, such as the Council of Europe, the North Atlantic Treaty Organisation (NATO) or the General Agreement on Tariffs and Trade (GATT). Each of these bodies established a permanent secretariat; however, there was no question of it having any more than an administrative role. Decision-making was reserved for meetings of representatives of each of the member states. The ECSC was unique in being provided with a supra-national High Authority which was given wide powers to determine the direction of two key industries throughout the member states. There was provision for a Council of Ministers, a purely advisory Assembly (or indirectly elected Parliament) and a Court of Justice, but the High Authority was, and was intended to be, the main organ of decision-making.

The constitution of the ECSC, as spelled out in the Treaty of Paris, closely reflected the views of Monnet, who wrote in his memoirs of the necessity of providing a firm institutional base to give effect to political intentions: "Nothing is possible without men: nothing is lasting without institutions."[2] He had intended that the ECSC would be paralleled by a common European defence force, which would supersede national armies and facilitate the rearming of West Germany without creating a specifically West German force. The same six governments – France, West Germany, Italy, Belgium, the Netherlands and Luxembourg – signed a treaty in May 1952 providing for the creation of a European Defence Community (EDC), for this purpose, but the French National Assembly in August 1954 declined to ratify the treaty.

Towards an economic community

The failure of the EDC had two significant consequences. West German rearmament proceeded on a national basis, and West Germany was admitted as a full member of NATO in October 1954. For his part, Monnet concluded that the path towards European unity lay through economic rather than military co-ordination. When his first term of office as president of the High Authority came to an end, in February

1955, he declined to accept a further term. Instead, he left to head a high-powered pressure group, the Action Committee for the United States of Europe (ACUSE), which included leading figures from the Socialist, Christian Democratic and Liberal parties of all the six member states.

ACUSE did not have to wait long for the first fruits of its activities. The foreign ministers of the Six (as the founder members of the Community were known) met in Messina in June 1955 and appointed a committee under the chairmanship of the Belgian foreign minister, Paul-Henri Spaak, to investigate establishing a common market. This committee produced a report which was the basis of the Treaty of Rome, signed on March 25th 1957, establishing the EEC. A separate treaty, signed in Rome on the same day, established the European Atomic Energy Community (Euratom). All six parliaments ratified the treaties, which came into effect on January 1st 1958, with a West German, Walter Hallstein, as first president of the EEC Commission.

The EEC's constitution paralleled that of the ECSC, but the supra-national element was significantly less. The EEC Commission, which was the counterpart of the High Authority, had substantially less power, and the Council of Ministers substantially more, than under the Treaty of Paris. In the early years of the EEC this difference was hardly apparent, as the confident and decisive Hallstein dominated the development of the Community. But in 1965–66 his authority was successfully challenged by France's President Charles de Gaulle (see page 11), and he subsequently resigned. None of his successors has wielded as much power as he had done, and since his departure the supremacy of the Council of Ministers (the representatives of the different member states) over the supra-national commission has been evident.

Amalgamation

The three communities – the ECSC, Euratom and the EEC – were formally amalgamated on July 1st 1967. They became jointly known as the European Community (EC), or sometimes the European Communities, although the abbreviation EEC remained in common use to denote the combined organisation. Since November 1993, when the Treaty of Maastricht came into force, the EC has been known as the European Union (EU).

Note

1   Alfred Grosser, *The Western Alliance: European-American Relations since 1945*, London, Macmillan, 1980, page 121.
2   Ibid, page 102.

2 Evolution – 1958–2010

The EEC might have broken up during its first year of operation. On June 1st 1958, five months after its foundation, General Charles de Gaulle became prime minister (and subsequently president) of France. His followers had bitterly opposed its creation; however, de Gaulle saw it as a useful means of extending French influence, and during his early years in power he encouraged its development.

Three months after coming to power he had a momentous meeting with the West German chancellor, Konrad Adenauer, which, in the words of a French historian, Alfred Grosser, turned out to be a case of "love at first sight".[1] Grosser quotes de Gaulle as writing in his memoirs: "From then until mid-1962, Konrad Adenauer and I were to write to each other on some 40 occasions. We saw each other 15 times ... we spent more than 100 hours in conversation." From this mutual attraction sprang an enduring alliance which has proved to be the mainspring of the Community ever since. It was formalised in the Franco-West German Treaty of January 22nd 1963, which provided for the co-ordination of the two countries' policies in foreign affairs, defence, information and cultural affairs.

This co-ordination has been spasmodic, but whenever France and West Germany have acted together within the Union their influence has been enormous and they have generally been able to achieve their objectives. Where they have not done so, the Union has drifted and has found it difficult or impossible to agree on a course of action. For many years West Germany, although the stronger of the two powers economically, was content to play a subordinate role. When West German leaders' views differed from those of France, they were often willing to defer to their partners, or at least refrain from carrying their opposition to extremes.

An encouraging start

With the background of the Franco-West German entente, the benefit of strong economic growth in all six member states and the enthusiastic encouragement of the United States, the Community got off to a tremendous start in the first years after 1958. Intra-Community trade leapt ahead, increasing by 28.4% annually during the first ten years of the EEC, and the average increase of imports from third countries was 10%.

The timetable for removing all internal tariffs and quota restrictions was originally intended to be completed in successive stages by December 31st 1969. It was, however, twice accelerated, and the process was completed 18 months ahead of schedule, on July 1st 1968. Simultaneously with the removal of internal tariffs, a common external tariff was erected, based on an average of the duties previously levied by the member states, with some downward adjustment. This, too, was completed 18 months early, and the Community collaborated with the United States in the Kennedy round of the GATT, which resulted in a further 35% cut, on average, in its external tariff.

The other economic objective spelled out in considerable detail in the Rome treaty was the development of a common agricultural policy (CAP), based, however, on protectionism rather than free trade. In fact the two major prongs of the EEC were widely regarded as offering quid pro quos to West Germany and France. Free trade for industry accorded with the interests of West German manufacturers, and a guaranteed market for agricultural produce with those of French farmers. Despite the provisions in the Rome treaty, the CAP proved much more difficult to launch than the customs union, but in January 1962, after what a commission publication describes as "lengthy and often bitter negotiations and the longest negotiating marathon in the Community's history",[2] the Council of Ministers adopted the basic regulations for a common market in agriculture.

Foreign policy gap

The economic progress made by the Six soon showed up a glaring omission in the Rome treaty, in that no mention was made of political co-operation. At a summit meeting in February 1961, the heads of government of the Community agreed that a political union should be set up between the Six. A committee chaired by a French politician, Christian Fouchet, produced two successive plans to bring this into effect. But neither the Fouchet Plan nor the Second Fouchet Plan was approved, owing to a basic difference between the larger and smaller member states. The larger states, particularly Gaullist France, thought that they should effectively direct the foreign policy of the Six. The smaller Benelux countries, on the other hand, fearing the prospect of domination, wanted a more equal say. In the end nothing came of the proposal, except that the heads of government agreed to hold regular meetings for general political consultation. Despite this decision, no further summit was held until six years later, and it was only after December 1974, when the European Council (see page 68) was formalised, that the heads of government began to meet regularly on a three times a year basis (reduced to twice a year in 1986).

Other European countries began to take note of the economic success of the Community. Greece and Turkey both applied to become associated states during 1959, while the UK government, whose earlier attempt to negotiate a wider free trade area within the OECD had ended in failure, became alarmed at the prospect of being left out in the cold. It took the initiative in organising the European Free Trade Association (EFTA), which linked it much more loosely with six of the smaller west European states. Together with Austria, Denmark, Norway, Portugal, Sweden and Switzerland,[3] it signed the Stockholm Convention, establishing EFTA, on January 4th 1960.

The UK knocks at the door

Yet no sooner had this Convention been signed than the UK government, led by Harold Macmillan, reappraised its position once again and decided that EFTA was much too small a grouping to meet its trading interests (it had a combined population of no more than 90m compared with 170m in the Six). In July 1961 the UK applied for full membership of the EEC, and was followed shortly afterwards by Ireland, Denmark and Norway.

The application was welcomed by five of the Six, but it soon transpired that President de Gaulle was lukewarm if not actually hostile to the entry of an "Anglo-Saxon" nation. Detailed accession negotiations began in November 1961, but soon became bogged down as the UK negotiators strove, perhaps ill-advisedly, to achieve a mass of detailed concessions on agriculture, Commonwealth trade and future relations with the other EFTA countries. Meanwhile, de Gaulle bided his time, but in January 1963, following Macmillan's Nassau agreement with President Kennedy on the supply of Polaris missiles which confirmed the French president's view that the UK's links with the United States took priority over any European commitment, he promptly vetoed the UK application at a press conference in Paris. The other three applicant countries accordingly withdrew their own applications.

The other five members states were aghast at the French action, but were unwilling to bring matters to a head. The EEC without the UK was a misfortune, in their view; without France it would be an impossibility. So they reluctantly acquiesced in de Gaulle's action, and only one week later the Franco-West German Treaty was signed. Three years later a UK

Labour government, under Harold Wilson, made a renewed attempt to secure entry, but once again de Gaulle applied a veto, and once again his EEC partners submitted to his will.

Hallstein versus de Gaulle

At the head of the European Commission during the first nine years was Professor Walter Hallstein, formerly a close aide and confidant of Adenauer, whose name was previously associated with the so-called Hallstein doctrine, under which West Germany refused to have diplomatic relations with any government which recognised the East German regime. Hallstein had been the leader of the West German delegation to the Schuman Plan conference in 1950, and he enjoyed a large fund of French as well as West German goodwill at the outset of his presidency which greatly helped him to keep up the momentum. After several years, however, the gap between his own beliefs in a supra-national Europe and the more nationalistic approach of President de Gaulle became more and more apparent, and it was probably only a matter of time before a clash would occur.

The occasion might have been a difference over foreign policy or the rejection of UK membership. In the event, it was the decision-making process within the Council of Ministers which led to the break. During the early years of the Community most decisions within the council needed to be taken, under the terms of the Rome treaty, by unanimity. From 1966 onwards, when the transitional period came to an end, a wide range of decisions should have been reached by qualified majority voting. President de Gaulle was not willing to contemplate the possibility of France being outvoted on major issues and when, in June 1965, France found itself in a minority of one against commission proposals on the financing of the CAP, the provision of its own financial resources and extending the budgetary powers of the European Parliament, he refused to allow decisions to be taken. For the next six months France boycotted all meetings of the Council of Ministers, and its "empty chair" policy was not abandoned until January 1966, when the so-called Luxembourg compromise (see page 64) was reached. This effectively gave all member states a right of veto when their "very important interests" were concerned. Not long afterwards Hallstein, who rightly concluded that the Luxembourg compromise had severely undermined the role of the commission as the principal initiator of policy, submitted his resignation.

The transformation of farming

One of the most profound changes within the Community during the 1960s and 1970s was the transformation of its agriculture. Not only did productivity and production shoot up, making the Community more than self-sufficient in most temperate products, but the number of people working on the land fell sharply, from 15.2m in 1960 to 5.8m in 1984 in the original six member states. The process would have gone even further if the Mansholt Plan, named after Dr Sicco Mansholt, the agricultural commissioner and later president of the commission, had been adopted. This plan, put forward in 1968, would have provided generous financial inducements for increasing the size of holdings, mechanising farming operations and taking some 5m ha of poorer land out of cultivation. A much watered down programme was eventually approved by the Council of Ministers in 1972, but unfortunately it did nothing to cure the emerging problem of structural surpluses nor to lighten the burden on the Community's funds of production guarantees.

Another significant development was the conclusion, in 1963, of the Yaoundé Convention, signed in the capital of Cameroon with 18 African states which were former dependent territories of EEC member states. The convention provided for the duty-free access of all their exports, except for certain products covered by the common agricultural policy, and for financial aid to be provided through the European Development Fund and the European Investment Bank. The first Yaoundé Convention was replaced in 1969 by Yaoundé II, and subsequently by four successive conventions bringing in many of the developing countries of the Commonwealth, signed at Lomé (Togo) in 1975, 1979, 1984 and 1989 (see Chapter 35). Lomé IV, signed by 70 African, Caribbean and Pacific states (the ACP states), continued the programme until 2000, when it was replaced by the 20-year EU–ACP Agreement, signed in Cotonou (Benin) by 78 ACP states and the then 15 states of the EU.

An EC summit conference at The Hague, in December 1969, marked an important step forward. The conference finally approved the proposals for financing the common agricultural policy, the creation of the Community's own financial resources (see page 103) and the extension of the European Parliament's budgetary powers, which had earlier been blocked by France. It agreed that the Community should proceed to the establishment of an economic and monetary union to be completed by 1980 (which proved to be a wildly over-optimistic target date), and it commissioned a report on ways of improving foreign policy co-ordination between member states. This report, written by Belgian diplomat, Etienne Davignon (later an influential commissioner), was approved ten months later. Since then the foreign ministers of the member states have met "in political co-operation" at frequent intervals, as have senior officials of the different foreign ministries, the idea being to discuss and if possible harmonise foreign policy opinions and activities (see Chapter 36).

Enter Denmark, Ireland and the UK

President de Gaulle's resignation in 1969, followed by his death the following year, removed the main obstacle to UK accession. His successor, Georges Pompidou, was less inflexible and the new West German chancellor, Willy Brandt, strongly urged him to agree to an enlargement of the Community. The Danish, Irish, Norwegian and UK governments all renewed their applications and, after much hard bargaining, treaties of accession were signed in Brussels on January 22nd 1972. Norway narrowly rejected the treaty terms (by 53% to 47%) in a referendum in September 1972, but the other three countries formally became members on January 1st 1973.

Denmark and Ireland also held referendums on EC accession, which produced majorities in favour of, respectively, 83% and 63%. The UK did not initially do so, although the issue of accession was highly divisive. The prime minister, Edward Heath, pursued the objective of UK membership with great determination, and succeeded in rallying a large majority of the Conservative Party behind him. The Labour Party, however, was badly split on the issue, with the majority coming down decisively against. A defiant minority of 69 Labour members of Parliament, led by Roy Jenkins, insisted on voting against a three-line whip, in favour of the terms that Heath had negotiated, in a House of Commons vote in October 1971. The Labour Party subsequently resolved to hold a retrospective referendum on continued UK membership if it won the next general election.

The government of Harold Wilson, which came to power in 1974, first as a minority government, later with a tiny majority, fulfilled this undertaking in June 1975 after having "renegotiated" the terms of entry. The main change secured was the institution of a "corrective mechanism" which was intended to prevent excessive UK contributions to the EC budget. The mechanism was later to prove inoperative, but the referendum produced a decisive vote (67%) in favour of continued UK membership, and it seemed as though the controversy was at an end.

Denmark and the UK left EFTA on their accession to the EC, but were not required to sever their trading links, as the remaining members of EFTA negotiated industrial free trade agreements with the Community and formed a sort of "outer ring", sharing in the benefits of tariff-free trade, except for agricultural produce, without having to accept any of the obligations of EC membership.

Problems of enlargement

The 1973 enlargement, which increased the Community's membership from six states to nine, and its population from 191m to 255m, was expected to give it a fresh wind and enable it to develop further and faster during the 1970s. These hopes were largely unfulfilled. In part, this was because the enlarged EC lacked an agreed programme for its medium-term development, which the Rome treaty, with its precise timetable for progressing to a customs union and its outline of the basic constituents of a common agricultural policy, had provided in the first years of the Community. Moreover, the nine members formed a less cohesive grouping than the original six, and the persistence of hostility to the EC among large sections of the population in the UK and Denmark made it difficult for these two countries to accommodate themselves to the essential process of compromise and "give and take" that the smooth operation of the Community required.

The biggest blow to the Community's development, however, was undoubtedly the prolonged economic recession which followed the Yom Kippur war of 1973, and the consequent quadrupling of petroleum prices. All the member states suffered from mounting inflation and unemployment, and most of them saw their balance of payments slide into severe deficit. Moreover, efforts to co-ordinate energy policies of the member states proved elusive, as did attempts to find a common economic strategy to enable the Community to hoist itself out of the recession. The member governments all felt constrained, to varying degrees, to implement austerity policies in their own countries, and it became increasingly difficult to persuade them to release resources for the introduction of new common policies under the aegis of the Community.

Yet at the Paris EC summit in December 1974 agreement was reached on the establishment of the European Regional Development Fund (ERDF, see pages 170–3), whose purpose was to help close the gap between the most disadvantaged and the more favoured regions within the Community. Although the ERDF provided assistance to all the member states, its main beneficiaries during its first ten years of operations were the UK, Ireland and Italy.

The European Council

The same summit conference took three other important decisions. It resolved that henceforth the heads of government should consult among themselves much more frequently, and instituted the European Council (see Chapter 6), which should meet three times a year and consider important foreign policy questions as well as the affairs of the Community. It decided that the European Parliament should be elected by direct universal suffrage from 1978 onwards (later postponed until 1979). And it appointed Leo Tindemans, the then Belgian prime minister, to compile a report on European union by the end of 1975.

Tindemans duly reported one year later, proposing a series of measures, including a common foreign policy, an economic and monetary union, European social and regional policies, joint industrial policies as regards growth industries, policies affecting EC citizens and a substantial reinforcement of Community institutions. The report was discussed on several occasions by the European Council but no action was taken on it, an outcome which reflected the general lowering of the horizons of west European leaders so far as European union was concerned.

The appointment of Roy Jenkins as president of the commission, for four years from January 1977, was seen as a most encouraging development. A senior political figure, who had been deputy leader of the Labour Party as well as chancellor of the exchequer and home secretary, he had (together with Edward Heath) been the most energetic and consistent campaigner for UK adhesion to the EC. His admirers from many member states hoped that his arrival in Brussels would give the Community the added momentum which the enlargement four years earlier had failed to provide.

Jenkins proved a resourceful and diligent president but, partly because of lack of support from the UK government, first under James Callaghan and then under Margaret Thatcher, his presidency did not quite match up to expectations. He did, however, have two undoubted achievements to his credit. He established the right of the president of the European Commission to attend the annual Western economic summits as the representative of the Community, despite stubborn resistance from President Valéry Giscard d'Estaing and only lukewarm support from Callaghan. He was also one of the architects of the European Monetary System (EMS, see pages 136–7), which came into effect in March 1979.

The European Monetary System

The European Monetary System (EMS) compensated, to some extent, for the failure of the earlier aspiration to achieve a full economic and monetary union by 1980. Based on a European currency unit (the ecu), the EMS comprised an exchange and intervention mechanism, credit facilities and a vehicle to ease the path of the less prosperous Community countries. Proposed by Jenkins in a speech in Florence, it was taken up by the West German chancellor, Helmut Schmidt, who, in conjunction with Giscard d'Estaing, was able to secure its acceptance by the European Council during three successive meetings in 1978. Despite the UK's refusal to join its exchange rate mechanism during its first 11 years, it was credited with having done a great deal to dampen down currency fluctuations and to encourage co-operation in financial policies between member states.

International trading relations developed continuously through the 1970s. The centrepiece was the Tokyo round of GATT negotiations between the European Community and 99 other participants. Given the background of world recession and rising unemployment (which had already reached 10m in the Community as a whole, and was subsequently to rise to 16m), the results of the round were remarkable, leading as they did to further cuts in customs duties, averaging about one-third, which came into effect from 1980.

The Community greatly extended its network of bilateral trade and aid agreements with developing countries. Agreements with the Maghreb countries (Tunisia, Algeria and Morocco), signed in 1976, were followed by others with the Mashreq countries (Egypt, Syria, Jordan and Lebanon) in 1977. An agreement had been reached with Israel in 1975, and one with Yugoslavia was concluded in 1980, which enabled the Community to implement a global Mediterranean policy. In Asia more limited agreements were made with Sri Lanka (1975), Bangladesh and Pakistan (1976), and India (1981), while a co-operation agreement was reached with the five ASEAN countries in 1981.

In Latin America agreements with Uruguay (1973), Mexico (1975) and Brazil (1980) were followed by a co-operation agreement with the five-nation Andean Pact in 1983. The third Lomé Convention, concluded in December 1984, covered trade with 66 African, Caribbean and Pacific countries, and provided aid worth 8,500m ecus for the period 1985–90 (see Chapter 35).

Attempts to secure a framework for the expansion of trade with communist countries made little progress. Talks with Comecon, the Soviet-dominated organisation for economic co-operation, continued from 1977 to 1980 but no agreement was reached, and the dialogue was only resumed in 1986, following Gorbachev's rise to power. Trade agreements were, however, concluded with China and Romania, and sectoral agreements with some other communist states (see pages 116–7).

Greece enters the Community

Meanwhile, further enlargements of the EC appeared on the agenda when three countries which had recently emerged from dictatorial or military rule applied to become full members. Greece tabled its application in 1975, and Portugal and Spain in 1977. The negotiations with Greece proceeded relatively smoothly, partly because the Greek government took the view that it had to secure entry at all costs and therefore did not haggle much over the terms, taking the view that its bargaining power would be greatly increased once it was inside the Community. It duly became a member on January 1st 1981.

The negotiations with Spain and Portugal were much more difficult, and not only because these two countries adopted a more stringent negotiating stance than Greece. There was far more opposition from within the Community itself, particularly in France, to their accession, largely because farmers in southern France, and also in Italy and Greece, feared competition from their Spanish rivals. There was a lively apprehension that France would again veto a membership application, and although this did not happen, President Giscard d'Estaing, in 1980, deliberately set out to slow down the negotiations.

Although Giscard d'Estaing played a negative role in this context, his overall influence on the Community was a positive one. Throughout his seven years as president he worked in close partnership with the West German chancellor, Helmut Schmidt, with whom he shared a considerable commonality of views, despite their different political backgrounds. Able to converse freely to each other in English, they sat side by side at meetings of the European Council and were often able to steer it in the direction in which they both wanted to go. In so far as anybody provided leadership to the Community during those seven years it was Schmidt and Giscard.

In 1981–82 both lost power and their successors, who were François Mitterrand and Helmut Kohl, signally failed to reproduce the Schmidt–Giscard relationship. Accordingly a vacuum appeared at the apex of the Community, and for several years it drifted helplessly, seemingly unable to tackle the mounting problems that it faced. A contributory factor was that Jenkins's term as president of the commission ended at about the same time, and his successor, a Luxembourger, Gaston Thorn, carried insufficient weight to be able to fill the gap.

A maze of problems

As the 1980s began, the Community was faced by a series of distinct problems which became increasingly entwined as the years went by; no solution was found until 1984. The issues were as follows:

- The prospect of disproportionately high UK payments to the budget.
- The threatened exhaustion of budget resources, allied to the need to curb the amount spent on the CAP.
- The need to reform the Community's institutions in order to speed up decision-making and to make them more accountable.
- The need to respond to the technological challenge of the US and Japan if Europe was not to become an industrial backwater.
- The need to remove internal barriers within the Community.
- The enlargement negotiations with Spain and Portugal.

The UK budget problem for several years proved the most intractable, partly because of the personalities involved, including Margaret Thatcher, whose combativeness was an unwelcome revelation to her fellow heads of government. The fact that the UK was liable to pay an unacceptably high net contribution, once its transitional stage had come to an end, came to light during the closing months of James Callaghan's Labour government in 1979. The basic reason for this was that despite indications given during the negotiations and renegotiations for membership, agriculture continued to take the lion's share of the Community's budget. As a large importer of food, the UK was paying a disproportionately high amount in import levies, but as a small food producer it was getting much less than its proportionate share back in payments under the CAP.

When Mrs Thatcher became prime minister in 1979 she took an extremely robust line in defence of UK interests, and managed to obtain from the other member states in May 1980 a temporary agreement limiting UK contributions for 2–3 years while a longer-term solution was sought. An unfortunate by-product of Mrs Thatcher's hard-hitting campaign was to rekindle anti-EC feeling within the Labour Party, whose annual conference in 1980 passed a resolution calling for UK withdrawal. Under the leadership of Michael Foot, this then became part of Labour's manifesto for the 1983 general election.

The search for a long-term solution went on until 1984, practically monopolising the agenda of several meetings of the European Council before a settlement was reached, which, in the opinion of many, could have been obtained a great deal earlier if cooler counsels had prevailed.

Budgetary crisis

The UK budget dispute inevitably got bound up with the looming crisis in the general budgetary affairs of the Community, in that its "own resources" were proving inadequate to meet the many demands on its budget. The proceeds of customs duties and agricultural levies were declining each year, and the day was fast approaching when the EC's only other resource – a maximum take equal to a 1% rate of VAT throughout the Community – would be exhausted. The member states were divided between those that were prepared to raise the VAT limit and those (including especially the UK) that were more interested in budget-cutting, particularly in the large part of the budget (around 70%) devoted to agriculture.

Those that wished to expand the budget pointed to the desirability, which the commission was repeatedly asserting, of a major expansion of Community expenditure on technological research to enable European firms to obtain a share in world markets that would otherwise be monopolised by US and Japanese suppliers of "third industrial revolution" products. In parallel with this was a growing realisation that, in order to compete at all, western Europe must turn itself into the "common market" it was supposed to be, and rid itself of the innumerable barriers to free trade which still existed a quarter of a century after the Community had been established.

Progress towards removing these barriers in the internal market was being thwarted by the failure of the Council of Ministers to agree on a vast number of proposals for liberalisation which had been tabled over the years by the commission. The backlog, largely resulting from the council's unwillingness to apply the majority voting rules of the Rome treaty, acted as a spur to proposals to speed up and democratise the decision-making process which emanated, in particular, from the European Parliament. Lastly, frustration was growing dangerously in both Spain and Portugal at the slowness of their entry negotiations, and there was a widespread feeling within the Community itself that these two newly democratic countries were not receiving the encouragement that they deserved.

Mitterrand's initiative

Like his predecessors, as president of France François Mitterrand eventually made his own considerable mark on the history of the EC. After all the above-mentioned problems had been incessantly argued for several years, to no measurable effect, he apparently determined that solutions to several of them should be reached during the French presidency of the Council of Ministers, in the first half of 1984. In order to achieve this he had to rise above narrow French interests, so far as Spanish entry and the size of any budget rebate for the UK was concerned. This he succeeded in doing, and at the Fontainebleau summit, in June 1984, agreement was reached on the UK budget issue, on increasing the Community's own resources, on restraining agricultural spending and on clearing the way for the admission of Spain and Portugal.

The settlement for the UK was based on a yearly rebate of 66% of the difference between its VAT contribution and its share of EC expenditure. In exchange for this, Mrs Thatcher agreed that the general limit of VAT contributions should be raised from 1% to 1.4%. It was also agreed that in future agricultural spending would rise in each year by a smaller proportion than the overall rise in expenditure, which should have meant that the percentage of the budget devoted to the CAP would decline year by year.

The 1992 programme

A year later, at the Milan summit, progress was made on two other issues: a seven-year timetable was agreed for removing 300 barriers to the internal market (see Chapter 16); and it was agreed to hold an intergovernmental conference to discuss amendments to the Rome treaty and other ways of speeding up and democratising the decision-making process. This led to the Single European Act, adopted in Luxembourg in December 1985 and implemented, after ratification by all 12 national parliaments (which involved referendums in Denmark and Ireland), in July 1987 (see page 46).

The programme for the completion of the EC's internal market became known either as the 1992 programme or, in some member states, the 1993 programme. The ambiguity arose from the target date of December 31st 1992 by which time all 300 measures were intended to be implemented. The original idea came from Jacques Delors, but credit for the detailed planning and the enthusiastic way in which the programme was launched should go to the then UK commissioner for internal market affairs, Lord Cockfield. Despite initial scepticism, it soon became clear that the programme would be substantially completed within the timetable laid down and that it would bring considerable economic benefits to all the member states. Beyond this, it gave a new sense of purpose to the Community and helped to create the atmosphere in which further initiatives to broaden and deepen the EC appeared both practical and desirable. By the end of December 1992 almost 95% of the programme had in fact been legislated.

Meanwhile, agreement was reached on launching several EC research programmes (see Chapter 21), as well as the Eureka programme which also involved several non-EC European countries, although the budgets agreed for them were substantially less than the commission would have liked. It seemed that the EC had woken from its slumbers, and at last was tackling the most urgent problems on its agenda. Unfortunately, however, new obstacles arose to imperil some of the agreements reached. The Spanish and Portuguese entry negotiations were successfully terminated, but at the last moment their ratification was put in doubt by a stratagem of the Greek government. It refused to endorse the entry terms unless Greece received more economic aid from the Community. Greece was eventually bought off by the institution of the Integrated Mediterranean Programmes, which provided for 6,600m ecus to be spent over seven years (1986–92). Most of this sum was applied to the modernisation of the Greek economy, but Italy and southern France were also beneficiaries.

Enter Spain and Portugal, and a new budget crisis

No sooner had Spain and Portugal taken their places in the Community in January 1986 than the budgetary measures agreed at Fontainebleau began to come unstuck. In the face of falling world prices, and the steep decline in the value of the dollar in 1986 and 1987, the cost to the EC of export refunds for its food exports rose dramatically. It became politically impossible to adhere to the guidelines for agricultural expenditure, and within a year of the VAT limit being raised from 1% to 1.4% the available funds for the Community budget were once again exhausted. By the beginning of 1987 it was clear that the Community would face a budget deficit for the year of 5 billion–6 billion ecus, with agricultural expenditure greatly exceeding the planned appropriations, and with no prospect in sight of reconciling the EC's political and financial objectives within the existing budgetary framework. Under the leadership of Jacques Delors the commission then produced a programme which became known as the "Delors package", designed to put the funds of the

Community on a more assured basis, while reinforcing control over farm spending and releasing resources for priority objectives including, especially, research and the expansion of the so-called structural funds (the regional and social funds and the guidance section of the EAGGF[4]), which the commission argued should be doubled, in real terms, by 1992.

A new beginning

It took three meetings of the European Council to reach agreement on the Delors package, partly because of the reluctance of Margaret Thatcher to accept proposals for controlling future expenditure which she regarded as less than watertight, and partly because of her determination that any new basis for budgetary contributions should include arrangements for abating the UK share which would be at least as generous, and as secure, as those agreed at Fontainebleau in 1984. Finally, however, at an emergency summit meeting in Brussels in February 1988, she agreed with the other 11 national leaders on proposals largely based on those put forward by Delors one year earlier.

The Brussels agreement meant that the Community could make a new start. A new budget limit was set at 1.2% of the total GNP of the Community, equivalent to 1.9–2.0% of VAT contributions as calculated on the previous basis. This enabled a budget of 43.8 billion ecus to be agreed for 1988, compared with actual expenditure of 37 billion ecus the previous year. By 1991 the budget had increased to 55.6 billion ecus. Under the agreement reached, a fourth resource based directly on the national share of GNP was added to the three main existing sources of revenue. The Fontainebleau agreement, under which 66% of the UK's net contribution is refunded, was written into the new dispensation.

The other main features of the agreement were that the structural funds were to be doubled, in real terms, by 1993, with more focus on economically backward areas, while much stricter control was to be applied to agricultural spending. In future this was not to grow by more than 74% of the annual growth rate of GNP, and so-called "stabilisers" would be applied progressively to reduce the level of subsidy for products in excess supply. Moreover, "set-aside" payments would be made to encourage farmers to take less fertile land out of production.

EMU back on the agenda

With this settlement under their belts, the EC leaders felt free to seek to revive the dormant project for economic and monetary union. At the Hanover summit of June 1988, which reappointed Jacques Delors for a further two years from January 1989, a committee was set up under his chairmanship with a mandate to study and report on means of preparing for monetary union. The summit noted that progress made towards achieving the 1992 programme for completing the internal market was now "irreversible" and that the Single European Act had succeeded in its objective of speeding up decision-making. At the subsequent Rhodes summit, in December 1988, it was noted that almost half the legislation involved in the 1992 programme had been adopted by the Council of Ministers, and the meeting reasserted the importance of the social aspects of the single market. The commission drew up proposals for a Community charter of fundamental social rights, which it hoped to have approved at the Madrid summit in June 1989. In the meantime, however, the Community had been treated to yet another example of UK reluctance to commit itself to progress towards closer European integration. The new crisis, if crisis it was, was caused by Mrs Thatcher's strident attack on the European Commission during a highly publicised speech to the College of Europe at Bruges in September 1988, accusing it of accumulating power for its own sake and of trying to create an "identikit European personality".

Mrs Thatcher's speech (which was widely characterised as "Gaullist") was followed by a deliberate policy of nit-picking over commission proposals, which was ill-received not only in other member states but in the UK as well, particularly when it was perceived as directly contrary to specific UK interests. One such case was the rejection, on legalistic grounds, of the Lingua programme of support for foreign language teaching, of which the UK was likely to be the principal beneficiary. Mrs Thatcher's campaign, which clearly embarrassed several of her own ministers, reached its climax in the third election to the European Parliament in June 1989 when, on her initiative, the Conservative Party's appeal was couched in narrow nationalistic terms.

The poor showing of the Conservatives in that election, and the strong support received both by the Labour Party and the Greens, seems to have had a chastening effect on the UK prime minister. This certainly appeared to be the case at the Madrid summit, which followed one week later. The main item on the agenda was the report of the Delors Committee on monetary union. This committee, composed mainly of the 12 central bankers of the member states, had proposed a three-stage process, leading to full currency union and a European system of central banks. It was agreed that the first stage, which involved all 12 member states adhering to the exchange rate mechanism of the EMS, should begin on July 1st 1990 while preparations should be made for an inter-government conference which would prepare the two subsequent stages and agree necessary amendments to the Rome treaty. While predicting that the UK would vote against the holding of such a conference, but would nevertheless go along with it, Mrs Thatcher acquiesced in these decisions and confirmed that the UK would join the exchange rate mechanism once certain conditions had been met. She declined, however, to endorse the Social Charter approved by the other 11 leaders, which was signed by them later in the year.

Downfall of communism

Meanwhile, momentous changes were occurring in eastern Europe which were to have a profound effect on the European Community. By the summer of 1989 both Poland and Hungary were well on the way to a peaceful transition from communism to democracy, and in the following months hardline communist rule crumbled in East Germany, Czechoslovakia, Bulgaria and, after violent resistance, in Romania. The newly liberated states instinctively looked to the Community not only as a source of economic assistance, but also as a potential guarantor of their democratic development.

The Community responded with emergency aid and loans to Poland and Hungary, and at the Western economic summit in July 1989, the European Commission was asked to co-ordinate a much wider Western aid operation involving 24 donor nations (the members of the OECD). This programme was later opened up to include Czechoslovakia, Bulgaria, Romania and Yugoslavia, and all of these countries signed trade and co-operation agreements with the EC, as did the Soviet Union itself in December 1989.

A similar agreement was negotiated with the communist government of East Germany, but before it came into effect Germany was united on October 3rd 1990. Six months before, the EC heads of government, at an emergency summit in Dublin, agreed that, subject to transitional arrangements, the territory of the former German Democratic Republic should be integrated into the Community without any revision of the treaties, as soon as unification was legally established. So East Germany joined the EC, as part of the Federal Republic, without any of the long-drawn-out negotiations which had preceded earlier enlargements of the Community.

Central and eastern Europe

No such quick transition awaited the other countries of central and eastern Europe, although all their leaders, including those of Yugoslavia and, in early 1991, of Albania, declared that their long-term objectives would be membership of the Community. Instead, ten-year association agreements, involving trade concessions, financial assistance and co-operation over a wide range of activities, were signed with Poland, Hungary and Czechoslovakia in December 1991. These agreements specifically acknowledged that the countries involved would eventually be eligible for full membership. Negotiations for similar agreements followed soon after with Romania, Bulgaria, Albania and the three Baltic states of Estonia, Latvia and Lithuania, whose independence was recognised in September 1991. By early 1994 so-called Europe Agreements had been signed with each of these countries, as well as the Czech Republic and Slovakia, to replace the earlier agreement reached with Czechoslovakia. Ukraine signed a partnership agreement with the EU in March 1994, by which time negotiations were well advanced for comparable agreements with Russia and the former Soviet republics of Belarus, Kazakhstan and Kyrgyzstan. Unlike those with east European countries, these agreements did not hold out the prospect of eventual membership. By contrast, this was implied in a Trade and Economic Co-operation Agreement signed with Slovenia in April 1993.

The EC was, in fact, deeply involved almost from the outset in trying to achieve a peaceful settlement to the warfare which broke out following the declaration of independence by Slovenia and Croatia in June 1991. The European Council, meeting in Luxembourg on June 28th–29th, immediately dispatched a team of foreign ministers to try to arrange a ceasefire, and subsequently a peace conference opened in The Hague, under EC auspices, in September 1991 under the chairmanship of Lord Carrington, a former UK foreign secretary. Teams of EC monitors were sent to Yugoslavia to see that the ceasefire was respected. It held in Slovenia but not in Croatia, where over a dozen further ceasefires broke down, a third of the country was overrun by Serbian forces and the federal Yugoslav army, and great death and destruction was caused before, following diplomatic intervention by the UN, a peace of exhaustion set in, reinforced by the arrival of a large UN peace-keeping force in March 1992. This was the first time that the EC had attempted to play an international mediating role beyond its own boundaries. Later in 1992 a similar scenario was played out in Bosnia-Hercegovina, although the EC role was more marginal and the UN intervened, if ineffectively, at an earlier stage.

The EC was heavily engaged in humanitarian aid and in monitoring activities, but the major role of attempting to contain the conflict was undertaken by NATO, at the request of the UN. It was, however, only after the decision to use decisive air power against the Bosnian Serbs, in August 1995, that an end to hostilities was achieved, leading to the signing of the Dayton peace agreement. The EU assumed the predominant role in providing reconstruction aid, and was directly involved in providing a temporary administration for the town of Mostar, the scene of bitter conflicts between Croats and Muslims. Similarly, following the Kosovo conflict in 1999, the EU, in co-operation with the World Bank, undertook the major financial responsibility for rebuilding the shattered territory, establishing the European Agency for Reconstruction, which assumed direct control of the construction effort.

The EC also became involved in Western efforts to provide material assistance to the former Soviet Union. Already in June 1990 the EC heads of government had asked the commission to consult with the Soviet government and to prepare proposals for short-term credits and longer-term support for structural reform. In December 1990 aid programmes of 750m ecus for food and 400m ecus for technical assistance during 1991 were approved, although the latter programme was temporarily suspended as a protest against Soviet repression in the Baltic states.

After the unsuccessful coup in August 1991 a more extensive aid programme was initiated, which, following the dissolution of the Soviet Union in December 1991, was widened to include assistance not only to Russia but also to all the other former Soviet republics. Six of these claim to be European states: Armenia, Azerbaijan, Belarus, Georgia, Moldova and Ukraine. Several soon indicated an interest in eventual membership of the EU, but none is likely to be a viable candidate until the second decade of the 21st century, at the earliest.

Meanwhile, the EC had taken the initiative in setting up the European Bank for Reconstruction and Development (EBRD), with an initial capital of $10 billion subscribed by 40 countries. Its purpose is to help the former communist countries to develop into free-market economies (see pages 93–4).

Inter-governmental conferences

The rapid completion of German unification proved possible only because other states were convinced of West Germany's peaceful intentions and the solidity of its democratic institutions. Nevertheless, Chancellor Helmut Kohl, who took the lead in pushing the process through, was convinced that only if a unified Germany was firmly entrenched in a more democratised European Community would it be acceptable to its neighbours. Accordingly, on the eve of the Dublin EC summit of April 1990, in conjunction with France, the German government launched an initiative to ensure that new and decisive steps should be taken towards closer European unity. The following June a further summit meeting in Dublin agreed to establish a second intergovernmental conference (IGC), to run parallel with that on economic and monetary union (EMU), to recommend changes which would lead to "political union" within the Community. It was agreed that both the conferences would be convened in December 1990, with a view to completing their work in time for the member states to ratify their proposals by the end of 1992.

Although all the member states agreed to the establishment of the two IGCs, it was evident that the UK government, still led by Margaret Thatcher, was the least enthusiastic and was unlikely to accept the far-reaching proposals for change which other member states, with France and Germany in the lead, were putting forward with increasing urgency. Although Mrs Thatcher finally agreed in early October 1990 to let the pound enter the exchange rate mechanism of the EMS, 11 and a half years after it was first established, her hostility towards EMU remained unabated. Three weeks later, at a summit meeting in Rome, she was outvoted by 11 to 1 on the starting date for the second stage of EMU. Her intemperate reaction to this rebuff triggered the challenge which led to her replacement as prime minister by John Major at the end of November.

Major lost no time in mending fences with his fellow EC leaders at the second Rome summit, which followed on December 14th–15th 1990. It was then that the two IGCs, which were manned respectively by the finance and foreign ministers of the 12 member states, were formally convened. As their work proceeded over the following months it became evident that there was no longer a serious risk of the UK being totally isolated in both conferences. It seemed more likely that compromises would be reached, involving rather slower progress towards EMU than had originally been proposed, while the changes effected by political union would be less radical than France and Germany had been seeking.

Maastricht treaty

So it proved when the European Council met at Maastricht in December 1991 to consider a draft treaty based on the work of the two IGCs. After two days of hard bargaining the Treaty on European Union was approved, but only after John Major had insisted on two opt-out clauses so far as the UK was concerned. They symbolised once again that the UK, or at least the UK government, still did not feel thoroughly at ease within the European family.

The Maastricht treaty is described in some detail in Appendix 8, and is discussed in Chapters 18, 23 and 36. It undoubtedly represented the most important development in the EC's history since the signing of the Treaty of Rome. Not only did it set out a detailed timetable for achieving economic and monetary union, at the latest by 1999, and provide for the development of common foreign and defence policies, but it also introduced a new concept of EC institutions. A protocol signed by 11 member states, from which the UK excluded itself, opened the way to the implementation of Social Charter legislation in those 11 countries. Lastly, the treaty committed the EU to establish a further IGC conference in 1996 to review the working of the Maastricht changes and to set the ground rules for the Union well into the 21st century.

Question marks began to appear against the Maastricht treaty in June 1992, when a referendum in Denmark narrowly went against ratification (50% to 49.3%). Although a further referendum in Ireland, later the same month, produced a strong majority in favour, the alarming prospect arose that French voters would turn the project down in a closely contested ballot in September 1992. Although closer European integration was widely supported in France, there was a serious risk that voters would take the opportunity to administer a rebuff to the unpopular Socialist government which had, quite unnecessarily, called the referendum. In the event a narrow majority (51.05% to 48.95%) approved the treaty.

There were also serious difficulties in securing ratification in the UK, where the prime minister, John Major, had great trouble in overcoming opposition within his own Conservative Party. As he was unwilling to renounce the opt-out that he had secured on the Social Charter, he was unable to count on consistent support from the opposition Labour Party and the Liberal Democrats to get the treaty through the prolonged procedures required for ratification by the House of Commons. After considerable delays, which tried the patience of the UK's European partners, the ratification bill was finally approved by the House of Commons on May 20th 1993, and by the House of Lords on July 20th, enabling the UK instrument of ratification to be deposited in early August.

Nine months earlier, at the Edinburgh summit in December 1992, concessions had been made to the Danish government enabling Denmark to opt out of a single European currency, on a similar basis to that agreed for the UK, and a number of other – largely cosmetic – interpretations of the treaty were agreed in order to encourage Danish voters to reconsider their earlier rejection. Consequently, in a further referendum in May 1993, the Danes approved the treaty by 56.7% to 43.3%.

There was yet another delay when German opponents of the treaty sought a ruling declaring it incompatible with the German constitution, despite its having been adopted by an enormous majority in the German Parliament. This attempt was overruled by the German Constitutional Court on October 12th 1993, and the German instrument of ratification was deposited on the same day. This removed the last obstacle, and the treaty finally came into force on November 1st 1993, ten months later than planned. Since then the European Community has been generally known as the European Union (EU).

The difficulties over securing ratification in Denmark, France, Germany and the UK were widely seen as a demonstration that EC political leaders had moved too far ahead of public opinion in their own countries in deciding to push ahead towards closer European integration. The former UK prime minister, Margaret Thatcher, characterised it as a "treaty too far". There was some force in this criticism, and it is true that public knowledge of the provisions of the Maastricht treaty was not extensive, but it is more likely that the undoubted tailing off of enthusiasm for the EU was due to three other factors. These were the economic recession, which struck virtually all European countries, though with varying force, between 1990 and 1994; turmoil in the currency markets which led to UK and Italian withdrawal from the exchange rate mechanism in September 1992, and the abandonment of the narrow bands within the ERM ten months later; and dismay at the apparent failure of EU efforts to bring peace to former Yugoslavia.

New enlargement

In January 1995 three of the EFTA countries – Austria, Finland and Sweden – became full members of the EU. This was the culmination of a process which began with the launching of the 1992 programme in 1985. All seven EFTA countries, anxious not to be excluded from the development of a single market of more than 370m people, sought means by which they could share in the expected benefits. On the initiative of Jacques Delors, the EC offered to negotiate to set up a European Economic Area (EEA), which would permit the EFTA states to join in the 1992 programme at the price of accepting many of the obligations of the EC member states.

The EEA treaty was signed in 1992, but was rejected in a referendum in Switzerland. When it finally came into force in January 1994 it included only Iceland, in addition to Austria, Finland, Sweden and Norway, which were already well advanced in negotiations for full membership of the EU. The door was left open for Liechtenstein to join at a later date, when it had revised its economic relationship with Switzerland. Switzerland had also applied for full membership, but its application was held in abeyance following the referendum decision on the EEA. The four other applicant states completed their negotiations in March 1994, and the membership terms were approved later in the year in referendums in Austria, Finland and Sweden, permitting the three countries to take their place in the Union. The referendum in Norway produced a negative result, and Norwegians will remain outside the Union for the foreseeable future, although they remain members of the EEA.

The prospect was, however, that the Union would take in up to a dozen new member states in the early years of the 21st century. No sooner had the negotiations with the EFTA states been concluded than Hungary and Poland tabled applications to join. They were followed over the next two years by Romania, Bulgaria, Slovakia, the Czech Republic, Slovenia and the three Baltic states. Cyprus and Malta had already applied some time earlier, and at the European Council meeting in Madrid in December 1995 it was agreed that negotiations with all 12 states could begin within six months of the conclusion of the intergovernmental conference that opened in Turin in March 1996 and completed its work at Amsterdam in June 1997. Meanwhile, the newly elected Labour government in Malta announced that it would not proceed with its application.

In May 1995 the commission issued a white paper setting out detailed guidelines for the applicant states regarding the modifications in their economies and in their legal and administrative systems that would be required for them to qualify for membership. It was also made clear that the introduction of a free market, and firm guarantees of democratic and human rights, would be necessary conditions for their admittance. Shortly after the Amsterdam summit, the commission recommended that membership negotiations should begin in March 1998 with six of the candidate members – Cyprus, the Czech Republic, Estonia, Hungary, Poland and Slovenia. The remaining applicants, it advised, had not yet fulfilled the conditions necessary for talks to begin, but they should continue to be assisted in their preparations and the position should be kept under continuous review. The Luxembourg summit, in December 1997, accepted this recommendation, but decided that all 11 applicants (plus Turkey) should be invited to annual European conferences, the first to be held in March 1998. The Turkish government, which was offended that, unlike the other five candidates (Bulgaria, Latvia, Lithuania, Romania and Slovakia), it had not been given an assurance of eventual membership, decided to boycott the conference.

Negotiations with the six favoured candidates duly commenced in March 1998, and in February 2000 with the remaining five plus Malta. Meanwhile, at the Helsinki summit in December 1999, the status of Turkey as a valid candidate was finally recognised, although negotiations would not begin until certain pre-conditions had been met. By the summer of 2002, negotiations with ten of the 12 active candidates – all but Bulgaria and Romania – were sufficiently advanced to give a reasonable hope that they would be concluded by the end of the year, with the prospect of membership on May 1st 2004.

Turin inter-governmental conference

The inter-governmental conference that opened in Turin in March 1996 was originally conceived as a review conference on the operation of the Maastricht treaty. Long before it met, however, it became clear that its agenda would be far wider than anticipated. The IGC would have to make a fundamental reassessment of the institutional arrangements of a Union originally designed for six members, now enlarged to 15, with the prospect of increasing to 27 or more over the next decade. In particular, it needed to examine the following questions:

◪ Should there be more majority voting in the Council of Ministers, given the increasing difficulty of obtaining unanimity with an ever-increasing membership?

◪ Should there be a reweighting of votes in the Council of Ministers to safeguard against the possibility of the larger member states being outvoted by combinations of small countries whose collective population was far smaller? Should there, in particular, be a firming up of the provisions for a blocking minority?

◪ How large should the commission be in future, and should every member state, however small, continue to be entitled to have a commissioner?

◪ Should powers under Pillar Three (on justice and home affairs) continue to be dealt with on an inter-governmental basis rather than coming under the jurisdiction of all the EU institutions?

◪ How could the common foreign and security policy, under the inter-governmental Pillar Two, be made more effective?

As the IGC got under way, it was clear that there were significant differences between the member states on all of these issues. In particular, the interests of the larger and smaller states were seen to conflict, but it was also evident that there was a strong will to succeed and to reach a consensus on all the principal issues. There was, however, one notable exception: the then UK government had set its face against any increase whatever in the EU's powers and was adamantly opposed to any increase in majority voting. The IGC, which might otherwise have been expected to conclude in the spring of 1997, was consequently stalled. The other member states agreed informally among themselves to wait until after the UK general election on May 1st 1997 to see whether the new government would be more willing to reach a compromise agreement with its partners.

UK isolation ended by Blair's election

The unco-operative attitude of the UK government in the IGC was the culmination of a series of events which had progressively alienated the UK from the European mainstream. The events of the Thatcher period have already been recounted, but – despite the early hopes that the Major government would heal the rift – the reverse seems to have occurred. At the root was the difficulty that John Major experienced in getting his own Conservative MPs to back the ratification of the Maastricht treaty. This led him to the conclusion that only by adopting an increasingly hostile attitude to his EU partners could he hope to contain the pressure from the growing number of Eurosceptics within his own party. This was a serious misjudgment. Every concession he made to their demands only whetted their appetite to ask for more, while progressively undermining the influence that the UK government could exert within the EU.

Some of Major's actions were patently irrational. At the Corfu summit in June 1994, he vetoed the nomination (supported by all the other member states) of the Belgian prime minister, Jean-Luc Dehaene, to become president of the commission in succession to Jacques Delors. This he justified on the grounds that Dehaene was a European federalist who wanted to turn Europe into a super-state. However, a few weeks later he agreed to the appointment of the Luxembourg prime minister, Jacques Santer, who publicly stated that his own views were identical to those of Dehaene. Then in April 1996 he adopted a policy of non-co-operation in the Council of Ministers (reminiscent of de Gaulle's "empty chair" tactic 30 years earlier), under which his ministers vetoed virtually every proposal under consideration – even those the UK itself had put forward. This was in a vain attempt to force the EU to lift its ban on UK beef exports. The UK government abandoned this self-defeating tactic after six weeks, but continued its generally negative attitude until May 1st 1997, when it went down to a heavy electoral defeat. The newly elected Labour government immediately announced a "fresh start" in relations with the EU, and this enabled the inter-governmental conference to complete its work amicably, and its recommendations were duly adopted at the Amsterdam summit in June 1997. The treaty which was signed, however, was a modest document and agreement was postponed on important institutional questions which needed to be resolved before the entry of the new candidate states from central and eastern Europe. These included the weighting of votes in the Council of Ministers, the size of the commission and the extension of qualified majority voting to all but the most important issues. A further IGC was held during 2000, and agreement was eventually reached at a lengthy and notably ill-tempered summit at Nice in December 2000.

Economic and monetary union

Meanwhile, it became increasingly likely that the third stage of economic and monetary union (EMU), leading to a single currency, would start as planned on January 1st 1999, and that a majority of member states would participate. At the Madrid summit, in December 1995, it was agreed that the new currency would be called the euro and that it would be of equal value to the European currency unit (ecu), based on a basket of national currencies and used to calculate payments within the EU's budget. A year later, at the Dublin summit, a stability pact was agreed, designed to ensure that the countries which satisfied the criteria for entry into EMU would continue to do so thereafter. Finally, as described on page 143, the special EU summit, held in Brussels on May

1st–2nd 1998, approved the recommendations of the commission and the European Monetary Institute that 11 of the 15 member states should join the third stage of EMU, and participate in the single currency, from January 1st 1999. Greece was excluded because of its failure to meet the Maastricht criteria, and the UK, Denmark and Sweden declined to join – largely for political reasons. The UK government indicated that it was in principle in favour of joining, but would not do so until after a referendum was held. The summit also appointed Wim Duisenberg as the first president of the European Central Bank, which replaced the European Monetary Institute on June 1st 1998.

On December 31st 1998 the Ecofin council agreed the fixed rates of exchange against the euro for the 11 participating national currencies (see page 143). From January 1st 1999 the euro became operational for banking purposes, and in January 2001 Greece was the twelfth country to join the euro zone. Exceptional care was taken to prepare for the introduction of euro notes and coins in January 2002 and the withdrawal of national currencies in the succeeding month. In the event, the operation was extremely successful, passing off with hardly a hitch (see page 144).

Resignation of Santer Commission

In December 1998 the first shots were fired in a developing row between the European Parliament and the commission, which led to the latter's resignation four months later. The Parliament refused to approve the final accounts of the 1996 budget because of concerns about fraud, mismanagement and cronyism, allegedly involving several commissioners, notably Edith Cresson, the former French prime minister, who was responsible for research and education. To head off a possible vote of censure, Jacques Santer agreed to the appointment of a five-member independent committee to audit the work of the commission. The five "wise men" produced a report within five weeks, as requested by the Parliament. It strongly criticised Mrs Cresson for appointing a dentist friend to a fictitious job and for her lax management of the Leonardo vocational training programme, but made only minor criticisms of other commissioners. Despite having turned up little in the way of active corruption, however, the report contained the stinging phrase "it is becoming difficult to find anybody who has even the slightest sense of responsibility".

Parliament did not have the power to censure individual commissioners, and Mrs Cresson refused to resign or, indeed, offer any sign of contrition nor did Santer take it upon himself to demand her resignation.

Within a day or two of the report's appearance it became clear that the Parliament would be able to muster the necessary two-thirds majority to require the dismissal of the entire commission, and in anticipation of this all 20 members submitted their resignations on March 11th 1999. Two weeks later the EU heads of government, meeting in Berlin, nominated a former Italian prime minister, Romano Prodi, to succeed Santer, but it was only in September that the European Parliament voted to appoint him and a new team of commissioners, which included only four survivors from the Santer Commission, to serve out the remaining four months of Santer's term and then another five years until January 2005.

New budget perspective

The other main business at the Berlin summit was to settle the budget perspectives for the EU for the seven-year period 2000–06. The newly elected German chancellor, Gerhard Schröder, had hoped to secure a major cut in his country's budget contribution to the EU, which largely exceeded that of all the other 14 member states combined. In the end, however, in the interest of getting a general agreement he settled for only marginal relief, and the annual British rebate (strongly criticised by the other member states) remained intact (see page 108) The agreement reached enabled EU activities to expand at a modest rate during the seven years, while providing a package of pre-accession aid to the candidate countries in central and eastern Europe, most of which secured entry to the EU in 2004.

The convention and Constitutional treaty

There had been a great deal of dissatisfaction with the handling of the 2000 Nice summit, where Jacques Chirac, the French president, had been severely criticised for his overbearing and maladroit chairmanship. This had led to the adoption of what many considered to have been botched conclusions, particularly concerning several provisions of the Nice treaty, which were perhaps responsible, at least in part, for its rejection by Irish voters in the June 2001 referendum. There was also concern about increasing evidence of public disenchantment with the EU, which had been manifested by the record low turnout in the European Parliament elections of 1999. Largely at the behest of the German government, it was therefore decided that a further IGC should be held in 2004. This should consider a wide range of possible future reforms, including a constitution which would replace, or supplement, the Treaty of Rome and the subsequent amending treaties, and which would be a simplified document that ordinary citizens could understand.

At the Laeken summit in December 2001, it was decided that the IGC should be preceded by a convention, whose 105 members should include not only national governments, but also MPs and MEPs, as well as representatives of the 12 candidate states currently negotiating membership, as well as Turkey, and of the other EU institutions. Voluntary organisations were given facilities to feed ideas to the convention, which would be presided over by Valéry Giscard d'Estaing, a former French president.

The convention started meeting in February 2002 and was able to produce an agreed text, approved almost unanimously, to present to the Thessalonica summit in June 2003. This took the form of a draft Constitutional treaty, replacing all the previous EU treaties (apart from that of Euratom), but incorporating and consolidating most of their provisions while giving a much clearer definition than in the past of the respective responsibilities of the Union and the member states, and the areas where responsibility is shared. It proposed the appointment of a permanent president to preside over meetings of the European Council, and of an EU foreign minister, who would preside over the Council of Foreign Ministers, but would also be a vice-president of the commission. Probably most importantly, it also proposed the replacement of the ludicrously complicated system of qualified majority voting contained in the Nice treaty with a more simple and transparent formula based on a "double majority" of members states and of the overall population of the Union.

The EU heads of government handed over the draft to an IGC, made up of foreign ministers, which almost succeeded in producing a somewhat watered-down version (though including some 95% of the convention's proposals) for adoption at a summit in Brussels in December 2003. Agreement, however, was thwarted by the resistance of Spain and Poland, two countries whose voting power had been grossly overweighted under the Nice treaty provisions and which refused to give up their privileged position. So the IGC was put back to work, but the defeat in the March 2004 election of the right-wing Spanish government, and its replacement by a Socialist administration which was more cooperative, led to the isolation of Poland, which eventually gave way, and the revised document was finally agreed at the June 2004 summit.

The treaty that emerged did envisage a limited increase in EU competences but was far from being a blueprint for a European super-state, as it had been painted by the Eurosceptic press, particularly in the UK (see

Chapter 38). It was more than the "tidying up exercise" which the British government claimed, but it still meant that the member states kept a firm hold on sensitive policy areas, such as foreign policy, defence, taxation, criminal law, social security and education, where unanimity in decision-making was retained.

The Treaty establishing a Constitution for Europe (summarised in Appendix 9) should have come into force in October 2006, provided that it had been ratified by the European Parliament and by all 25 member states. By June 2005, it had been ratified by ten countries, but negative votes in referendums in France and the Netherlands put a large question-mark against its future.

Enlargement to 25 – and then 27

Meanwhile, in December 2002 accession negotiations with ten candidate states were successfully concluded, and it was agreed at a summit in Copenhagen that Cyprus, the Czech Republic, Estonia, Hungary, Latvia, Lithuania, Malta, Poland, Slovakia and Slovenia should all become member states on May 1st 2004. Target dates in 2007 were set for Bulgaria and Romania, with which negotiations were still continuing. It was also agreed that the question of Turkish membership should be reviewed in December 2004, in the light of Turkish progress in fulfilling the Copenhagen criteria (see page 272), and that a decision should then be taken on whether to open membership negotiations in 2005.

During 2003, accession treaties with the ten new member states were successfully ratified by the parliaments of the existing 15 members, the European Parliament and the ten applicants, nine of which held referendums to approve the entry conditions. The exception was Cyprus, where ratification was approved by the parliament of the Republic of Cyprus. A UN plan for the reunification of the island, which would have enabled both parts to enter as a federalised state, was put to referendums in both the republic and the Turkish controlled north of the island. The Turkish Cypriots approved the plan by a two-to-one majority, but it was rejected by the Greek Cypriots, on the advice of their president, Tassos Papadopoulos – to the fury of the EU – by three to one. Consequently the island remained divided, and only the Greek Cypriot state joined the Union on May 1st 2004, when the number of member states increased to 25.

Negotiations with Bulgaria and Romania were concluded by the end of the year, leading to their entry as the 26th and 27th member states on January 1st 2007. Meanwhile, Croatia and the former Yugoslav Republic of Macedonia applied for membership, negotiations beginning with the former in October 2005 and entry now likely by 2012. With Macedonia, however, progress was stalled, partly because of a dispute with Greece over the country's name, which the Greeks maintain implies a claim to their own province of Macedonia. By the end of 2009 this dispute had not been settled, despite active mediation by the UN, and entry talks had still not begun. Membership negotiations with Turkey also began in October 2005, but have continued only fitfully, partly because of the continuing hostility of several member states, notably France and Austria, as well as the repercussions of the continued division of Cyprus, with Turkish troops still occupying the northern part of the island. Unless the reunification talks between the newly elected president of the Republic of Cyprus, Dimitris Christofias, and his Turkish Cypriot counterpart, Mehmet Ali Talat, which began on March 1st 2008 but have made only slow progress, lead to success, the prospects of Turkish membership appear bleak. Even in the best of circumstances, most observers believe that it will be another ten years before this large and complex country is ready to take its place in the Union (see Chapter 37).

Barroso Commission

In June 2004, the European Council was expected to nominate a president elect of the commission in place of Romano Prodi, whose term of office was due to end on October 31st. In the event, it failed to reach agreement. The hot favourite for the nomination was Guy Verhofstadt, the Belgian prime minister, who was strongly supported by France, Germany and several other member states, but he was blocked by, among others, the British and Italian governments. An attempt by the right-of-centre European People's Party, the largest group in the European Parliament, to push for the nomination of Chris Patten, the commissioner for external relations, a former British Conservative cabinet minister and the last governor of Hong Kong, was also unsuccessful. After a delay of 11 days, a compromise candidate, José Manuel Barroso, the centre-right prime minister of Portugal, was unanimously approved at an emergency meeting of the European Council.

Under the terms of the Nice treaty, the new commission was to consist of 25 members, one from each member state. In consultation with Barroso, the national governments made their own nominations, which were approved by the Council of Ministers, before being submitted for approval by the European Parliament. It had the right to approve or reject the whole commission, but not each commissioner individually.

Nevertheless, it held committee hearings on each commissioner which made recommendations to the Parliament as a whole before it made its decision. In several cases, the committee hearings resulted in negative recommendations, notably on Rocco Buttiglione, a right-wing Italian Catholic who had been allocated the justice and home affairs portfolio by Barroso. Buttiglione upset large numbers of MEPS by making disparaging remarks about gay people and women, and by declaring that homosexuality was a "sin". They demanded that Buttiglione's nomination be withdrawn, or at least that he should be allocated a less sensitive portfolio. Barroso resisted, but when it became apparent that the Parliament would vote the whole commission down, he halted the proceedings at the last moment and asked for a delay in the parliamentary vote. Consequently, the Italian government withdrew Buttiglione's nomination, offering instead that of its foreign minister, Franco Frattini. Barroso then switched the portfolio he had intended for the Hungarian nominee, Lászlo Kovács, replaced the Latvian nominee, who had been implicated in a party funding scandal, and finally secured a positive vote in late November. As a result, the handover to the new commission occurred three weeks later than planned. This chain of events greatly heartened parliamentarians as it was a sign of their growing influence. This had already been demonstrated when the European People's Party, which having won the largest number of seats in the Euro elections in June 2004, insisted that the new president of the commission should reflect the election results, and come from the centre right. The European Council took the hint, and declined to consider the claims of several highly qualified candidates, including former prime ministers, who were socialists.

Towards the Lisbon treaty

The Barroso Commission had been in office for barely seven months when, in late May and early June 2005, the EU was shaken by the defeat of the Treaty establishing a Constitution for Europe (TCE) in referendums in France and the Netherlands. Despite the fact that the treaty had been ratified by the European Parliament and by most member states, and had secured far bigger majorities in referendums in Spain and Luxembourg, it was soon acknowledged that it was dead. After a time, however, member states, led by the German chancellor, Angela Merkel, who led the Council of Ministers during the first half of 2007, resolved to save what they could from the wreckage, by seeking to draft a less ambitious treaty. This would, however, retain most of the institutional reforms contained in the TCE, but would exclude many of the trimmings which could lead people to conclude, however mistakenly, that the object was to convert the EU into a "super-state". Mindful that referendums were likely to be influenced by extraneous factors, notably the perhaps temporary unpopularity of sponsoring governments, the leaders informally agreed that, wherever possible, they would seek to have the treaty approved by parliamentary rather than popular votes. Their lead was eventually followed in all member states, with the exception of Ireland, where the government was advised that it was legally required to hold a referendum by its own constitution. In the UK, however, the opposition Conservative Party, backed by the majority of the predominantly Europhobic popular press, waged a virulent campaign in favour of a referendum, which, they claimed, had been promised by all three main parties for the TCE. The government, asserting that the projected new treaty was not the same as the TCE, successfully saw off the demand and opted instead for parliamentary ratification. In no other member state were there significant demands that referendums be held.

Accordingly, at an informal summit in June 2007, under the German presidency, it was agreed to appoint an inter-governmental conference (IGC), largely composed of the foreign ministers of the 27 member states, to draw up a new draft treaty. This was approved at a subsequent summit, held under the Portuguese presidency, at Lisbon in October 2007, and signed, again in Lisbon, on December 13th 2007. Within four days it had been ratified by the first member state – Hungary – and it was confidently predicted that it would come into effect by the autumn of 2008. Yet on June 12th 2008, Irish voters unexpectedly rejected the treaty, by a vote of 53.4% to 46.6%. The other governments quickly made it clear that this would not signify the demise of the treaty, the UK proceeding to ratify it, by parliamentary vote, six days later. Most of the other states followed suit.

Meanwhile the Irish government held an inquest to discover what had motivated Irish voters to reject the treaty, despite it being backed by all political parties, with the exception of Sinn Fein, and by both sides of industry. A series of opinion polls soon established that voters' opposition to the treaty had little to do with its contents. Rather, many concerns were related to Irish neutrality, taxation, workers' rights and social issues, notably abortion. There was also strong resistance to the probable loss of automatic Irish representation on the commission. These concerns were relayed by the Irish prime minister, Brian Cowen, to successive meetings of the European Council and, in December 2008, a deal was struck. By then many other national governments were having second thoughts about the desirability of restricting the membership of the commission to less than the number of member states, and all of them were prepared to commit themselves to making a unanimous decision, under the Lisbon treaty, which would permit all member states to continue to be represented, at least until 2014. They also agreed, provided the Irish government committed itself to holding a further referendum by October 2009, to provide "binding guarantees" that the treaty would not affect Irish sovereignty in three specific areas: taxation, neutrality, and family-related and "ethical" issues. By then 25 national parliaments had ratified the treaty, but optimism was qualified by serious doubts about whether Irish voters would change their minds the second time round.

Recession

Virtually all the member states of the Union were adversely affected by the worldwide recession sparked by the subprime mortgages crisis in the United States and the collapse of Lehman Brothers on September 15th 2008, though some were shown to be more vulnerable than others. One of the worst affected was Ireland, whose banks were shown to be seriously overcommitted, and it soon became clear that only its membership of the EU had saved it from the fate of neighbouring Iceland, whose banks had been bankrupted and whose currency collapsed. The Icelanders, who had been lukewarm about joining the EU, were quick to draw the consequences of their isolated position. After a general election in April 2009, in which the previously dominant right-of-centre Independence Party was roundly defeated, the Icelandic parliament voted in June 2009 to apply for membership of the EU. The strong probability is now that it will become the 28th or 29th member state, perhaps joining at the same time as Croatia in 2012, or even earlier (see Chapter 37).

Although there was little co-ordination among the EU member states, they generally followed the example of the British government – spelled out by Gordon Brown at a meeting of euro-zone heads of government, to which he had been specially invited – in providing a massive bail-out for their banks and investment funds to stimulate their economies. The various national efforts were pulled together at a summit meeting in December 2008, and presented as a grandly named European Economic Recovery Plan. The national contributions were topped up by the commission with €5 billion resulting from savings in the agricultural budget, and by €30 billion from the European Investment Bank for small and medium-sized enterprises, renewable energy and clean transport projects. The total amount was €200 billion, or roughly 1.5% of the Union's GDP.

The summit came towards the end of a highly eventful French presidency, which had been marked by the hyperactivity of President Nicolas Sarkozy. The highlight had undoubtedly been his decisive intervention in the Russo-Georgian war, in August 2009, when, in lightning visits to Moscow and Tbilisi, he succeeded in negotiating a ceasefire agreement. This did not prevent the virtual Russian annexation of South Ossetia and Abkhazia, and it was not implemented in full by the Russians, but at least it prevented a great deal of bloodshed and saved the bulk of Georgia from being overrun by Russian troops. Sarkozy received a lot of credit for his prompt response and widespread appreciation that – purely by chance – the EU had been led by a major state with an internationally renowned president rather than by one of the smaller countries during this period. Few people believed that if the war had occurred during the previous Slovene or subsequent Czech presidencies such an intervention would have been probable. Sarkozy's performance led many to believe that the projected appointment of a permanent president of the Council of Ministers, under the Lisbon treaty would, however, increase the power of the Union to act decisively in future international crises.

Perhaps this was a factor in swinging support in Ireland for the treaty in the second Irish referendum, which took place on October 2nd 2009. More likely it was the effect of the recession, which brought home to many voters the value of EU support, but the result was a triumphant reversal of the earlier vote, with 67.1% voting in favour and 32.9% against. This opened the way to the treaty coming into effect on December 1st 2009. Two other countries, Poland and the Czech Republic, whose parliaments had endorsed the treaties, had had their ratification held up by stubbornly Eurosceptical presidents. Both of these now threw in their hand and signed the treaty. Even David Cameron, the equally Eurosceptical leader of the British Conservative Party, now recognised that the game was up, and conceded that a future Conservative government would not hold a referendum on the treaty, though he claimed that it would attempt to "repatriate" certain powers now vested in the Union.

New appointments

The way was now clear to proceed with filling the two new important posts created by the treaty: the permanent presidency of the Council of Ministers and the high representative for international relations, who would double up as vice-president of the commission. Only one high-profile candidate was in the running for the first of these. Tony Blair was not a declared candidate but clearly wanted the post, and was strongly backed by the British prime minister, Gordon Brown. His strongest declared rival was Jean-Claude Juncker, the Luxembourg prime minister and the longest-serving member of the European Council. Those who wanted a Sarkozy-style figure, who would be accepted on more or less equal terms by leaders in the United States, China and Russia, were willing to back Blair, but he suffered from two major handicaps. The greater of these was his role as a wholehearted supporter of the invasion of Iraq, which fatally antagonised his fellow socialists, in particular, and failed to rally their support. His other handicap was that he was not from the centre-right, as were the majority of European leaders, who decided that the choice should be from their own ranks. They passed over Juncker in favour of Herman Van Rompuy, a consensually minded figure, who had been prime minister of Belgium for less than a year, but who had greatly impressed by his ability to heal wounds in a deeply divided country. To balance the choice of a centre-right figure as president, and to compensate the UK for losing the presidency, the high representative post went to a socialist, Catherine Ashton, a former leader of the House of Lords, who had replaced Peter Mandelson as trade commissioner a year earlier. Like Van Rompuy, she was seen as a quietly effective figure who was unlikely to make a big splash on the international scene, at least initially. These two will effectively share the burden of representing the EU in the wider world over the next few years, together with José Manuel Barroso, who was appointed to a second five-year term as commission president in September 2009. Only time will tell if the EU heads of government have made wise choices, or if they have lost a great opportunity.

Notes

1 Alfred Grosser, *op. cit.*, page 189.
2 Steps to European Unity, *European Documentation*, 1985.
3 The UK, Denmark and Portugal subsequently left EFTA on joining the EC, but Finland, Iceland and Liechtenstein became EFTA members.
4 The European Agricultural Guidance and Guarantee Fund.

3 Treaties

The Treaty of Rome

The bible of the European Community, which provides the ultimate authority for the greater part of its decisions and responsibilities, is the Treaty of Rome, signed on March 25th 1957 by representatives of Belgium, France, West Germany, Italy, Luxembourg and the Netherlands. It was actually only one of two treaties signed in Rome by the same signatories on the same day; the other established Euratom, the European Atomic Energy Community. Six years earlier on April 18th 1951 the six countries had signed the Treaty of Paris, setting up the European Coal and Steel Community (ECSC).

The Treaty of Rome is a bulky document comprising 248 articles and an additional 160 pages of annexes, protocols and conventions. The first four articles, quoted here in their entirety, define the purposes of the European Economic Community, and the principal institutions to be created to ensure their achievement.

Article 1   By this Treaty, the HIGH CONTRACTING PARTIES establish among themselves a EUROPEAN ECONOMIC COMMUNITY.

Article 2   The Community shall have as its task, by establishing a common market and progressively approximating the economic policies of Member States, to promote throughout the Community a harmonious development of economic activities, a continuous and balanced expansion, an increase in stability, an accelerated raising of the standard of living and closer relations between the States belonging to it.

Article 3   For the purposes set out in Article 2, the activities of the Community shall include, as provided in this Treaty and in accordance with the timetable set out therein:

(a) the elimination, as between Member States, of customs duties and of quantitative restrictions on the import and export of goods, and of all other measures having equivalent effect;

(b) the establishment of a common customs tariff and of a common commercial policy towards third countries;

(c) the abolition, as between Member States, of obstacles to freedom of movement for persons, services and capital;

(d) the adoption of a common policy in the sphere of agriculture;

(e) the adoption of a common policy in the sphere of transport;

(f) the institution of a system ensuring that competition in the common market is not distorted;

(g) the application of procedures by which the economic policies of Member States can be co-ordinated and disequilibria in their balances of payments remedied;

(h) the approximation of the laws of Member States to the extent required for the proper functioning of the common market;

(i) the creation of a European Social Fund in order to improve employment opportunities for workers and to contribute to the raising of their standard of living;

(j) the establishment of a European Investment Bank to facilitate the economic expansion of the Community by opening up fresh resources;

(k) the association of the overseas countries and territories in order to increase trade and to promote jointly economic and social development.

Article 4

1. The tasks entrusted to the Community shall be carried out by the following institutions:

- an ASSEMBLY
- a COUNCIL
- a COMMISSION
- a COURT OF JUSTICE

Each institution shall act within the limits of the powers conferred upon it by this Treaty.

2. The Council and the commission shall be assisted by an Economic and Social Committee acting in an advisory capacity.

Articles 5-248 These articles deal with the following areas:

- 5-8: the setting up of the Community during a transitional period of 12 years.
- 9-11: free movement of goods.
- 12-29: the establishment of a Customs Union.

- 30–37: the elimination of quantitative restrictions.
- 38–47: provisions for agriculture.
- 48–73: the free movement of persons, services and capital.
- 74–84: the requirements for a common transport policy.
- 85–102: competition policy, taxation and the approximation of laws.
- 103–116: economic and trade policy.
- 117–128: social policy.
- 129–130: the establishment of a European Investment Bank.
- 131–136: the association of overseas countries and territories.
- 137–198: the composition and powers of the various Community institutions.
- 199–209: financial provisions.
- 210–248: the legal personality of the Community, the admission of additional members, the setting up of the institutions and various miscellaneous points. Article 240 states that "The Treaty is concluded for an unlimited period". The treaty came into effect on January 1st 1958.

Other treaties

A number of other treaties, protocols and conventions have been signed by the member states over the years, which supplement the original provisions of the Treaty of Rome. The most important of these are as follows:

1 The treaty amalgamating the three European Communities (ECSC, EEC and Euratom), signed in Brussels on April 8th 1965, usually known as the EC treaty.
2 The treaty concerning the admission of Denmark, Ireland, Norway and the UK, signed in Brussels on January 22nd 1972. (Norway subsequently declined to ratify this treaty after a referendum.)
3 Equivalent accession treaties with Greece, signed in 1980, with Spain and Portugal, signed in 1985, and with Austria, Finland, Sweden and Norway, signed in 1994. (Norway again failed to ratify.) Later treaties were signed in 2002 with Cyprus, the Czech Republic, Estonia, Hungary, Latvia, Lithuania, Malta, Poland, Slovakia and Slovenia, and in 2005 with Bulgaria and Romania.
4 The Single European Act, signed in 1986 which, among other provisions, amended several articles of the Treaty of Rome regarding voting procedures in the Council of Ministers, while somewhat enlarging the legislative powers of the European Parliament. The

The three pillars of the European Union 3.1

THE EUROPEAN
UNION

THE EUROPEAN
COMMUNITY

COMMON FOREIGN
AND SECURITY POLICY

JUSTICE AND
HOME AFFAIRS

institutions
and legislative
procedures

agricultural
policy

the internal
market

environment

citizens' rights

economic and
monetary union

regional policy

etc

asylum
policy*

immigration*

the fight
against drugs

police
co-operation

etc

*Transferred to Pillar One under the Amsterdam treaty.

main objective was to facilitate the adoption of the programme of nearly 300 measures to complete the Community's internal market (see Chapter 16). These were the first substantial amendments to the Treaty of Rome in its first 30 years in operation.

5 The Treaty on European Union, otherwise known as the Maastricht treaty, agreed in December 1991 and signed in February 1992. This was a much more thorough-going revision of the Rome treaty, comprising two major sets of provisions: those aiming at the establishment of an economic and monetary union (EMU), at the latest by January 1st 1999; and those defined as steps towards the achievement of a political union, involving common foreign and defence policies. Other provisions extended or defined more precisely the Community's competences in other policy areas and amended the powers of various EC institutions. The treaty established three pillars for the EU. Pillar One embraced the three existing European Communities treaties (the ECSC, EC and Euratom). Pillar Two contained new provisions on a common foreign and security policy (CFSP), and Pillar Three provided for co-operation between the member states

on justice and home affairs. Pillars Two and Three were not subject to the EC institutions and were organised on an inter-governmental basis (see Figure 3.1). This treaty is summarised in Appendix 8.

6 The Treaty of Amsterdam, agreed in June 1997 and signed in October 1997, which came into effect after ratification by all the contracting parties on May 1st 1999. This was largely a tidying-up exercise, transferring much of the decision-making under Pillar Three to Pillar One, improving the arrangements for the Common Foreign and Security Policy, bringing the Protocol on Social Policy and the Schengen Agreement into the EC framework, extending the powers of the European Parliament and the president of the commission, adding Employment and 'Flexibility' clauses, and providing for greater transparency. This treaty, also, is summarised in Appendix 8.

7 The Treaty of Nice, agreed in December 2000 and signed in February 2001, which, however, only came into effect on 1 February 2003. It was rejected by a referendum in Ireland in June 2001, but was ultimately approved in a second referendum in October 2002, by which time it had been ratified by all the other member states. The treaty, which is summarised in Appendix 8, was mainly concerned with revising the membership and voting powers of the EU institutions following the expected large increase in the number of member states during the first decade of the 21st century.

8 The Treaty establishing a Constitution for Europe (TCE), agreed in Brussels on June 18th 2004, and signed in Rome on October 29th 2004, consolidated all previous treaties into a single document. It clarified which decisions shall be taken by the EU, which by member states and which should be shared; gave a greater role in decision-making to national parliaments; revised the system of qualified majority voting in the Council of Ministers; gave more legislative power to the European Parliament; and extended the scope of majority voting, while retaining national vetoes on areas such as the budget, social security, foreign policy and defence. It provided for the appointment of a president of the European Council and an EU foreign minister, who would also be a vice-president of the commission and would head the Union's own diplomatic corps, the External Action Service (EAS). It also incorporated a charter of fundamental rights. The treaty was due to come into force on November 1st 2006, but only after ratification by the European Parliament and all 25 member states. After being rejected by referendums in France and the Netherlands in May and June 2005, the treaty was abandoned.

9 The Treaty of Lisbon, agreed in Lisbon on October 19th 2007, and signed there on December 13th 2007, was finally ratified in November 2009, and came into force on December 1st 2009. A slightly watered-down version of the TCE, it is also an unreadable treaty, as it does not comprise a single coherent document but rather a long series of amendments to the Treaty of Rome and other European treaties. Apart from that, its main substantive difference from the TCE is that it provides for the commission to continue to be made up of one representative from each member state, instead of being more restricted in size. The treaty is summarised in Appendix 9.

2

THE INSTITUTIONS

Under the Treaty of Rome, four main institutions were established to give effect to the provisions of the treaty. The following is a simple definition of their functions:

- ◪ The European Commission initiates policies and implements those already decided upon.
- ◪ The Council of Ministers decides, or legislates, on the basis of proposals brought forward by the commission.
- ◪ The European Parliament had a largely advisory role, but its powers have subsequently been increased and it is now a co-legislator with the Council of Ministers on the bulk of EU business.
- ◪ The European Court of Justice interprets the Community's decisions and the provisions of the treaty in the event of dispute.

The Community institutions continue their functions under the Treaty on European Union (the Maastricht treaty) and the subsequent treaties of Amsterdam, Nice and Lisbon. Since the Maastricht treaty the former European Community (EC) has been known as the European Union (EU) and has acquired additional powers that are not subject to the institutions of the EC, but are dealt with on an inter-governmental basis. These include a common foreign and security policy (see Chapter 36) and certain aspects of co-operation over judicial, police and immigration issues (see Chapter 29). Strictly speaking the EU is now a hybrid organisation consisting of the EC, with its carefully defined division of powers between its constituent institutions, and an additional inter-governmental component. Part 2 of this book describes in some detail the principal EC institutions.

4 The Commission

The European Commission is the executive organ of the Community. It is often seen as the embodiment of the European idea as its members, although appointed by national governments, are under no obligation to them, and their total loyalty is pledged to the interests of the Community as a whole. Each commissioner, on assuming office, makes the following solemn declaration:

> I solemnly undertake:
> To perform my duties in complete independence, in the general interest of the Communities;
> In carrying out my duties, neither to seek nor to take instructions from any Government or body;
> To refrain from any action incompatible with my duties.
> I formally note the undertaking of each Member State to respect this principle and not to seek to influence Members of the commission in the performance of their task.
> I further undertake to respect, both during and after my term of office, the obligations arising therefrom, and in particular the duty to behave with integrity and discretion as regards the acceptance, after I have ceased to hold office, of certain appointments or benefits.

To the extent that the reality falls short of these aspirations, the commissioners will be failing in their allotted role, and the purposes of the Community will be imperfectly realised.

The commissioners

The commission currently consists of 27 members, one from each member state. They are appointed for a five-year term by the Council of Ministers, on the nomination of their own national governments, and the appointment of the commission as a whole is approved by the European Parliament. Before 1995 the term was only four years, and before 2004 the five largest member states were entitled to two members each. The term of office is renewable, and in the past at the end of each four- or five-year period typically about half of the commissioners have been reappointed, the remainder being replaced by new nominees. Most of the commissioners are politicians, usually from the governing party (or parties) in the member states. A minority of commissioners have been senior administrators, trade union leaders or businessmen.

The presidency

The president of the commission was originally appointed for a two-year term, although in practice this was normally extended to four years, virtually automatically. Each commission term is referred to colloquially under the name of its president; for example, the Jenkins Commission, the Thorn Commission, the Delors Commission, the Barroso Commission. Under the Maastricht treaty the arrangements for appointing the commission were changed. From January 1st 1995 the term of office of both the commission and the president was increased to five years. The governments of the member states are now required to consult the European Parliament before nominating the president of the commission. They must also consult the president-elect before nominating the other commissioners. The president and other members of the commission are then subject to approval, as a body, by a vote of the European Parliament. Only if this vote is positive will the president and the commission be formally appointed by the governments of the member states.

When Jacques Santer was nominated by the EU heads of government in July 1994 he narrowly survived an attempt in the European Parliament to reject his nomination. The Parliament went on to vet each of the prospective commissioners and approved the appointment of the whole commission by a substantial majority in January 1995. Following the resignation of the Santer Commission, in March 1999 (see pages 34–5), the EU heads of government nominated Romano Prodi as his successor and subsequently, after consultation with Prodi, 19 other commissioners. They, also, were vetted by the Parliament, which, in September 1999, voted by a three-to-one majority to appoint them to serve out the remaining four months of the term of the Santer Commission, as well as for a full five-year term from January 2000. A similar procedure was followed with the two commissions headed by José Manuel Barroso (see pages 38–9). The first of these served from November 2004 until January 2010, when the second Barroso Commission, which will serve until January 2015, took over.

The president of the commission is often misleadingly compared with a prime minister of a member state in relation to his or her cabinet. In fact the president's dominance over his colleagues is normally much less. He neither selects nor dismisses them, and does not formally determine what portfolios they should hold. His influence on this point is considerable, as he makes a proposal for the distribution of responsibilities at the outset of each term of office, but the actual decision is taken by the commissioners themselves, if necessary by majority vote. The last two presidents have undoubtedly had more clout, partly because of their increased powers under the Amsterdam, Nice and Lisbon treaties, but mostly because of the circumstances of Romano Prodi's nomination. The crisis following the resignation of the Santer Commission enabled him to acquire more authority than any of his predecessors. He was able to insist on the right to allocate portfolios and to change them round, if he chose, at a later stage. He also asked for, and obtained, assurances from each of the nominees that they would resign, at his request, if he felt that this would be in the intererests of the EU. There was no argument when José Manuel Barroso acted in the same way on his appointment in 2004.

Under the Treaty of Nice, the larger member states lost their right to a second commissioner when the next commission was appointed in 2004. The treaty also provided that when the membership of the EU reached 27 or more, member states would no longer have a right to appoint commissioners, who would be allocated on a rotation system in which all states, large or small, would be treated equally. Under the Treaty of Lisbon, the heads of government are permitted – by unanimous agreement – to vary the provisions made by Nice. In the autumn of 2009 they agreed – as part of a deal with the Irish government in advance of the second referendum on Irish ratification – that the system of having one commissioner from each member state would continue at least until 2014. The president would continue to be nominated by the European Council, but in future by qualified majority vote rather than by unanimity.

Responsibilities of commissioners

Commissioners are each allocated an area of responsibility under the treaty, and parts of the administrative machine will report directly to them (see Appendix 3 for the current distribution of responsibilities). They also have the assistance of a small cabinet of half a dozen personal appointees who not only act as advisers but also customarily intervene on the commissioners' behalf at all levels of the commission's bureaucracy.

Responsibilities of the commission

The responsibilities of the commission are listed in Article 155 of the

The Community's decision-making process

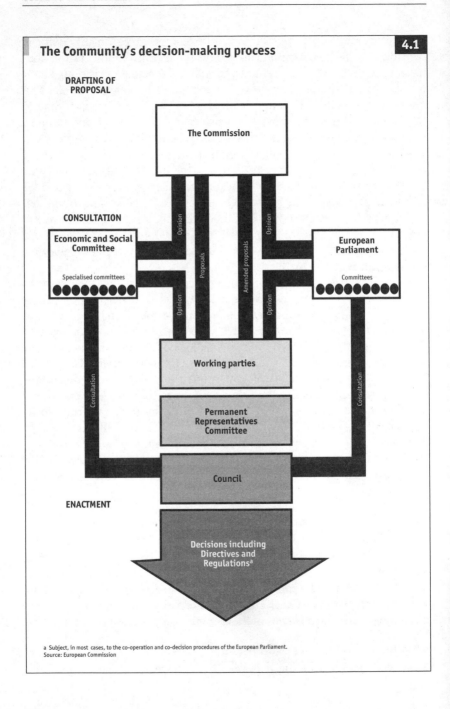

a Subject, in most cases, to the co-operation and co-decision procedures of the European Parliament.
Source: European Commission

Decision-making in the Community

There are five ways in which the institutions of the Community are able to change or influence the law in the member states. The Council of Ministers and/or the commission is able to issue:

- regulations
- directives
- decisions
- recommendations
- opinions.

Legislation, as normally understood, is undertaken through regulations and directives. Both are initiated by the commission and adopted by the Council of Ministers, in most cases after having received an opinion from the European Parliament and, when appropriate, the Economic and Social Committee and the Committee of the Regions. Regulations are of general applicability: they are binding in their entirety and directly applicable in all member states. Directives are binding on the member states to which they are addressed as regards the result to be achieved, but leave the form and methods of achieving it to the discretion of the national authorities (most often this is achieved by passing national legislation, based on the directive).

Decisions by the council or the commission, derived from the authority bestowed by the Rome treaty or through regulations or directives already approved, may be addressed to a government, an enterprise or an individual. They are binding in their entirety on those to whom they are addressed. Recommendations and opinions are not binding. (See also Figure 4.1.)

A sixth way in which national laws are affected is by case law resulting from decisions taken by the Court of Justice, whose role is to interpret the Rome treaties affecting the European Community, and to adjudicate in disputes between the other institutions or between any of them and one or more member states (see Chapter 9).

Rome treaty. They have been summarised as being those of initiative, implementation and supervision.

Initiative
The treaty gives a general responsibility to the commission to ensure that its provisions are carried out, but it also gives it the specific right to put proposals before the Council of Ministers, which in most circumstances is unable to make decisions in the absence of such a proposal.

Implementation
The commission is entrusted with the implementation of the decisions taken by the council. It also has substantial autonomous powers relating to competition policy and the running of the common agricultural policy. The commission administers the various funds established by the Community (the Agricultural Guidance and Guarantee Fund (EAGGF), Social Fund, Regional Fund, Cohesion Fund, and so on). It prepares a draft budget which must be approved by the council and the European Parliament. It also negotiates international agreements on behalf of the Community, though these can only be concluded by the council.

Supervision
The commission supervises the implementation of EU law by the member states. Whenever it concludes that a member state has infringed its treaty obligations it is required to deliver an "opinion" to this effect, and may afterwards bring an action in the Court of Justice against the state concerned.

Location
The commission is based in Brussels, and occupies the Berlaymont building, a purpose-built glass-fronted building constructed in 1969. In early 1992 the Berlaymont was closed down, and was comprehensively reconstructed over a period of 13 years, owing to the risk of infection from the large amounts of asbestos contained in the original structure. In the meantime the commission and its immediate staff were housed in the nearby Breydel building. The reconstruction took almost twice as long as originally estimated, and the Berlaymont did not re-open its doors until September 2004. Only a minority of commission staff can be accommodated in the building, the facilities of which have been greatly improved. The remaining staff are based in a score of other locations.

Staff

The commission employs about 20,000 people, one-third of whom are concerned with interpreting or translating between the 23 official languages of the Community (English, French, German, Italian, Dutch, Danish, Greek, Spanish, Portuguese, Swedish, Finnish, Czech, Slovak, Estonian, Latvian, Lithuanian, Maltese, Polish, Hungarian, Slovene, Romanian, Bulgarian and Irish). A further 10,000 or so commission employees are engaged in scientific research work at Ispra in Italy, Culham in the UK, Geel in Belgium and various other centres, or are working for other EU agencies.

The staff, part of which is based in Luxembourg, is organised in 36 departments and directorates-general, each of which is subject to one or more commissioners (see Appendix 4).

Working practices

The commission meets as a body every Wednesday morning, and if there is a heavy agenda the meeting may be resumed after lunch. Additional meetings are frequently scheduled, occasionally in more relaxed surroundings, to discuss particular topics or long-term perspectives. Decisions within the commission are normally adopted on the basis of a simple majority vote, and subsequently the principle of collective responsibility applies.

Although all official documents are translated and meetings involving national officials are simultaneously interpreted into all 23 languages, most day-to-day business within the commission is conducted in French or, increasingly, English.

5 The Council of Ministers

If the commission is the institution representing the general European interest, the Council of Ministers is certainly that in which the particular interests of each member state are brought to bear. It is unquestionably the most powerful of the Community's organs and, in the words of the Directorate-General for Research of the European Parliament, "It has now evolved into the actual centre of political control in the European Community".[1]

Structure

The council consists of representatives from each of the member states, and its meetings are also attended by at least one commissioner as well as by officials of its own secretariat. The membership, however, is constantly changing. If agriculture is on the agenda agricultural ministers will attend; industry ministers will come for industrial matters; and finance ministers will attend when the budget is being discussed.

The foreign ministers' meeting, held at least once a month except in August, is known as the General Affairs Council. As well as discussing foreign policy matters, foreign ministers are supposed to exercise general co-ordination over the work of the other ministerial councils and to tackle particularly complicated and/or urgent matters which do not readily fall within the scope of their more specialist colleagues. It is also their task to prepare the meetings of the heads of government, known as the European Council (see Chapter 6). These are held regularly every six months – in June and December. Normally, however, there are one or more special or emergency meetings held during each six monthly presidency, so the council effectively meets four or five times per year.

The presidency

The council has a rotating chairmanship or presidency, with ministers from each member state taking turns for a six-month period in the chair. The foreign ministry of the country concerned undertakes, with the help of the council secretariat, the organisation of the council's business during the six months. A period will thus be characterised as that of the French presidency, the Dutch presidency, and so on, according to which nationality is in the chair. Under the Lisbon treaty, which came into effect on December 1st 2009, a permanent president has been appointe to head the Council of Ministers for a renewable term of 2.5 years. His role is to chair meetings of the European Council, to co-ordinate with the different heads of government and to deal on their behalf with the rulers of countries, particularly the United States, China, Russia and India. A second senior appointment is of a high representative for foreign affairs and security policy, who takes the chair at meetings of the Foreign Affairs Council and also acts as vice-president of the commission. She is responsible for recruiting and controlling a new External Action Service, which will provide diplomatic representation throughout the world and staff the manifold aid projects provided by the EU – by far the world's largest aid donor. The high representative is appointed for a term of five years. Other than the Foreign Affairs Council, the different specialist meetings of the council continue to be chaired by whichever member state is currently running the six-monthly presidency.

It is accepted that it is part of the presidency's duty to oil the wheels of the Community and to strive to get agreement on as many issues as possible. The presidency is therefore expected to exert itself to produce compromise proposals whenever there is a deadlock and to cajole its own national representatives as well as those of other member states to modify their demands.

The rota of the presidency was previously determined alphabetically, but from 1996 onwards a new order was determined, primarily to ensure that the larger states were reasonably well spaced out, rather than being bunched together as they had been. The rota until 2020 is shown in Table 5.1.

Holding the presidency places a heavy burden, particularly on smaller states with fewer diplomatic resources, but for the most part they have been able to rise to the occasion by making a special effort. The new arrangements under the Lisbon treaty should somewhat reduce the burden on them, and – in practice – the smaller the member state the more help it gets from the council's secretariat.

Permanent representatives

Few items reach the agenda of council meetings without having been previously discussed, usually exhaustively, at a lower level. Each member state maintains a large delegation in Brussels, known as its Permanent Representation. These are staffed not only by diplomats but also by officials from each of the domestic ministries that is liable to be affected by decisions taken by the EU. They are backed up by further officials in their home capitals who are deputed to liaise with them.

Table 5.1 **Countries holding the presidency, 2010–20**

	January–June	July–December
2010	Spain	Belgium
2011	Hungary	Poland
2012	Denmark	Cyprus
2013	Ireland	Lithuania
2014	Greece	Italy
2015	Latvia	Luxembourg
2016	Netherlands	Slovakia
2017	Malta	United Kingdom
2018	Estonia	Bulgaria
2019	Austria	Romania
2020	Finland	–

Coreper

The heads of delegations, the permanent representatives, who have the rank of senior ambassadors, meet at least once a week in the Committee of Permanent Representatives, known by its French language initials as Coreper. Coreper will work methodically through all the issues which are awaiting ministerial decision. If, on the basis of instructions which they have received from their national governments, the permanent representatives find themselves in complete agreement on a draft proposal it is normally placed on the council agenda as an "A" point. This would then, except in the unusual event of a government having a last minute change of mind, be adopted without discussion at a subsequent council meeting. More often the permanent representatives find that their viewpoints are still fairly wide apart, and the proposals are referred to expert groups, at a lower level, for more detailed discussion. In most cases it is only when no more than one or two governments are in disagreement with the rest that an issue is passed on to the Council of Ministers in the hope of getting a decision.

Other working groups

Even though the permanent representatives are highly versatile, they cannot possibly maintain a uniform level of expertise on all the highly detailed topics which may appear on their agenda. A substantial range of subjects is entrusted to their deputies, who have a parallel weekly meeting, misleadingly known as Coreper I, while the permanent representatives' own meeting is called Coreper II. Agricultural issues are by tradition invariably dealt with by the Special Committee for Agriculture (SCA), consisting of senior officials of national ministries or of the agricultural councillors at the permanent representations. A large number of working groups staffed by less senior officials meet regularly to haggle over the details of virtually every proposal for Community legislation.

Legislative role

Unlike in a nation state, where the parliament is responsible for enacting legislation, the legislative role in the EU is performed by the Council of Ministers. Community legislation, known as directives or regulations (see page 57), can only be initiated by the commission. The opinion of the European Parliament and frequently of the Economic and Social Committee must in most cases be sought, but the proposals are adopted (or not, as the case may be) by the council. Again, contrary to the practice of national parliaments, the legislative function has previously taken place behind closed doors, although hardly in secret as the large Brussels press corps is normally extensively briefed after each meeting of the council by spokesmen for each of the national governments concerned. Under the Lisbon treaty, the council will meet in public when acting in a legislative capacity.

Meetings

In its various forms, the council meets around 80–90 times a year, usually for one day, sometimes for two and occasionally for longer. Often two or three meetings take place simultaneously, with, for example, foreign ministers in one chamber and finance ministers in another.

Making decisions

When a proposal actually reaches a council meeting, except as an "A" point, it is by no means assured of being adopted. The Treaty of Rome laid down precise rules on decision-making within the council, but these have not always been applied in the manner originally intended. Under Article 148 of the treaty, decisions may be taken by a simple majority, by a qualified majority, or unanimously.

Simple majority decisions are restricted to minor matters, often of a purely procedural nature. Under the Rome treaty it was envisaged that most decisions would be reached by a qualified majority, leaving the unanimity rule for a limited number of issues of major importance. During a transitional period, which was intended to end in 1965, unanimity was prescribed for a much wider range of issues, but at the moment that the Community was scheduled to change over to qualified majority voting a major crisis broke out between the French Gaullist government and the other five original members of the EEC (see page 11).

The Luxembourg compromise

As a result of this crisis, the five members reluctantly acquiesced in the so-called "Luxembourg compromise" to ensure continued French membership of the Community. The operative sentence of this was:

> Where, in the case of decisions which may be taken by a majority
> vote on a proposal from the commission, very important
> interests of one or more partners are at stake, the Members of
> the Council will endeavour, within a reasonable time, to reach
> solutions which can be adopted by all the Members of the
> Council while respecting their mutual interests and those of the
> Community, in accordance with Article 2 of the Treaty.

If subsequent practice had accorded with the wording of the "compromise", which referred specifically to "very important interests", it might not have affected the decision-making process very often. In practice, however, the council showed extreme reluctance to bring any issue at all to a vote, and the unanimity rule was effectively extended to a vast range of decisions which could not conceivably be regarded as affecting the "very important interests" of member states. Accordingly, the Luxembourg compromise has seldom been formally invoked. One occasion was in May 1982 when the UK government attempted to block a farm price settlement for purely tactical reasons related to a quite different issue (the UK budget dispute). The other members refused to accept the validity of the UK claim and proceeded to approve each of the 20-odd draft regulations involved in the settlement by qualified majority voting.

Amendments under the Single European Act

After that there was a growing feeling, shared by the French government, that qualified majority voting should be used more often. Although the Luxembourg compromise, which had no legal force, still stands, the Single European Act, which came into force in July 1987, amended the Treaty of Rome to reduce the number of issues on which unanimity was required. In particular, qualified majority voting was authorised for most of the 300 or so measures which had to be adopted if the 1992 programme to complete the EC's internal market was to be ratified. The Maastricht treaty, which came into force in January 1993, also extended the range of issues to which qualified majority voting would apply, including transport and the environment, and the list was further extended by the Amsterdam treaty, which took effect in May 1999, and by the Nice treaty, which came into force in February 2003. Consequently, in the areas concerned it is no longer possible for proposals to be held up for years because one or two member states object to them. Under the Lisbon treaty, qualified majority voting has been extended to a wider range of subject areas, and it is now only in a limited number of sensitive areas such as foreign and defence policy, taxation and institutional changes that the unanimity rule has been maintained.

Decisions are taken

In view of the above it is hard to see how any decisions are made at all, given the difficulty of persuading 27 separate nation states to sink their differences. In fact many decisions are taken on a "log-rolling" basis, with governments giving way on particular points on which they are not convinced in exchange for concessions on often unrelated issues.

Allocation of votes

Under the system of qualified majority voting the member states are allocated votes roughly in proportion to their size. Germany, France, Italy and the UK have 29 votes each, and the other countries' representation, going down to a mere three votes for Malta, is as shown in Table 5.2. Under the Lisbon treaty, a more simplified formula for reaching a qualified majority is specified: a proposal will need the support of at least 55% of the member states, representing at least 65% of the total EU population. This provision, however, will only take effect in 2014.

Other council responsibilities

As well as adopting EU legislation, the council has joint responsibility with the European Parliament to adopt the Community budget. It also has the power of appointment to the other institutions, such as the Economic and Social Committee and the Court of Auditors. The multifarious nature of its activities has been well summarised by a former British permanent representative, Sir Michael Butler, who wrote:[2]

> *In one sense, Coreper and the council together are a forum for a permanent negotiation between member governments on a*

wide range of issues simultaneously. In another, they are the legislature of the Community. In a third, they are the senior board of directors taking many of the day-to-day decisions on its policies.

Table 5.2 **The weighting of votes under the Nice treaty**

Members of the Council	Weighted votes	Members of the Council	Weighted votes
France	29	Austria	10
Germany	29	Bulgaria	10
Italy	29	Sweden	10
United Kingdom	29	Denmark	7
Poland	27	Finland	7
Spain	27	Ireland	7
Romania	14	Lithuania	7
Netherlands	13	Slovakia	7
Belgium	12	Cyprus	4
Czech Republic	12	Estonia	4
Greece	12	Latvia	4
Hungary	12	Luxembourg	4
Portugal	12	Slovenia	4
		Malta	3
Total EU-27	**345**		

Acts of the council shall require for their adoption at least 258 votes in favour, cast by a majority of members, where this treaty requires them to be adopted on a proposal from the commission. In other cases, for their adoption acts of the council shall require at least 258 votes in favour cast by at least two-thirds of the members. When a decision is to be adopted by the council by a qualified majority, a member of the council may request verification that the member states constituting the qualified majority represent at least 62% of the total population of the Union. If that condition is shown not to have been met, the decision in question shall not be adopted.

Location

The council and its secretariat are based in the Justus Lipsius building in Brussels, a vast, tasteless mausoleum facing the Berlaymont across the road. This was opened in 1995, the Council previously occupying the Charlemagne Building, next door to the Berlaymont. During three months of the year (April, June and October), however, its meetings are held in Luxembourg, a legacy from the merger of the three Communities which took place in 1965, the former ECSC having been based in Luxembourg.

Notes

1 Fact Sheet 1/B/2, European Parliament, Directorate-General for Research, 1987.
2 Michael Butler, *Europe: More than a Continent*, Heinemann, London, 1986, page 30.

6 The European Council

The Treaty of Rome made no provision for meetings of the heads of government of the member states, and during the first ten years of the EEC they met on only three occasions. Yet it gradually became clear that a more regular exchange of views was necessary to give a sense of strategic direction to the Community and to resolve problems to which the Council of Ministers and the European Commission had not been able to find solutions through the EC's normal processes.

Inauguration

In December 1974 it was formally decided at a summit meeting in Paris that the heads of government should meet three times each year under the title of the European Council. Starting in Dublin in March 1975, the European Council duly met on this basis until December 1985, when it was agreed that only two meetings a year would henceforward be held. However, since 1990, when two additional "emergency" summits were held, it has been accepted that there may, in fact, be three, four or even five meetings of the European Council each year. These meetings took place in the member state currently holding the presidency of the Council of Ministers, with its prime minister (or, in the case of France, its president) taking the chair and being responsible for the organisation of the meetings. Under the Treaty of Nice, all normal meetings of the European Council have been held in Brussels since 2004.

Status

The Single European Act, adopted in December 1985, gave legal recognition to the European Council without, however, defining its powers. In fact it has had the same status as an ordinary meeting of the Council of Ministers, although it has usually avoided giving formal effect to the decisions it has taken, leaving it to a subsequent meeting of foreign ministers to adopt them on a "rubber stamp" basis. Indeed, a major purpose of the European Council is that its deliberations are informal. They take place without the presence of national officials, the heads of government sitting round the table, accompanied only by their foreign ministers, while the president of the commission is supported only by one vice-president. The more sensitive discussions normally take place in the intervals between the actual sessions (which are spread over two days), particularly during and after dinner on the evening of the first day when most if not all of the heads of government speak in English and simultaneous interpretation is dispensed with.

Increasing influence

The European Council has, to a large extent, replaced the commission as the motor of the Community. This was especially notable during the period 1974–81, when President Valéry Giscard d'Estaing and Chancellor Helmut Schmidt co-operated closely to play a leadership role. Their joint departure within a few months heralded the beginning of a period of 2–3 years in which few significant decisions were taken by the European Council. The deadlock was broken at Fontainebleau in June 1984 when, largely owing to the initiative of President François Mitterrand, a solution was finally found to the UK budget problem (see pages 18–20) which had plagued the Community for several years, and the way was cleared for the admission to membership of Spain and Portugal.

Since then the go-ahead for other major new Community initiatives, like the launch of the 1992 programme, the acceptance of a united Germany within the EC, the convening of inter-governmental conferences on economic and monetary union and on political union, the offer of economic aid to the former Soviet Republics and the decision in principle to negotiate membership with the countries of central and eastern Europe, has been given at meetings of the European Council. The European Council also agreed the Single European Act at Luxembourg in December 1985, the Treaty on European Union at Maastricht in December 1991, the Treaty of Amsterdam in June 1997, the Treaty of Nice in December 2000, and the Treaty establishing a Constitution for Europe at Thessalonica in June 2004. The Lisbon treaty itself was similarly agreed at a meeting in the Portuguese capital in October 2007.

Such major and difficult issues can only be resolved at a summit, as only the heads of government have the authority and political clout not only to impose unwelcome decisions but also to reconcile them with political forces and pressure groups in their home countries.

Decision-making on minor issues held up

On the debit side, however, is the undoubted fact that the existence of regular summit meetings actually retards decision-making on many less far-reaching issues which would otherwise be resolved at a lower level. Time and again the heads of government have been called upon to discuss technical matters on which their subordinates have failed to agree because they were unwilling to take the responsibility. The European Council ought not to have to act as a final court of appeal, except on issues of the first importance, but it seems condemned to do so.

Under the Lisbon treaty, the European Council now has a permanent president, elected by its members for a renewable term of two and a half years, to preside over its meetings and co-ordinate its work. It was implicitly assumed that the candidate would be a current or former prime minister, and the person chosen to be the first occupant of the post, at a special meeting of the European Council on November 19th 2009, was the Belgian prime minister, Herman Van Rompuy.

7 The European Parliament

The European Parliament is intended to bring a measure of democratic control and accountability to the other institutions of the EC. Its powers, however, are restricted; it is not the primary legislative authority of the Community, and its status compares badly with that of the national parliaments in the different member states. The European Parliament is the successor to the Assembly of the ECSC, which was established in Strasbourg as a purely advisory body in September 1952. It had 78 members, all of them members of national parliaments who had been deputed to attend the Assembly as an ancillary duty to their main functions. The Assembly was expanded to 142 members in 1958, when its competences were extended to the EEC and Euratom, which merged with the ECSC seven years later. Its membership was increased to 198 in 1973, with the accession of Denmark, Ireland and the UK, and its powers (particularly in the budgetary field) were modestly increased under treaties signed in Luxembourg in April 1970 and in Brussels in July 1975.

Direct elections instituted in 1979

Much more significant was the institution of direct elections to the Parliament in June 1979 when 410 members were elected, during a four-day period from nine member states, to a greatly enlarged Parliament. In the second direct elections in June 1984, 434 members (or Euro-MPs) were elected from ten member states, comprising 81 each from France, West Germany, Italy and the UK, 25 from the Netherlands, 24 from Belgium and Greece, 16 from Denmark, 15 from Ireland and 6 from Luxembourg. They were later joined by 60 Spanish and 24 Portuguese members, making a total of 518. Yet this much larger Parliament of 518 full-time members directly elected by over 100m voters was given no greater formal power than had been enjoyed by the previous appointed Assembly of part-timers. Later the total membership was increased to 626, including 59 members from Austria, Finland and Sweden. In 2004 the membership rose to 732, with the adhesion of a further ten member states, and it went up again in 2007 when Bulgaria and Romania joined the EU and an additional 54 MEPs were elected. In June 2009, a new Parliament was elected, in anticipation of the coming into force of the Lisbon treaty, with a total of 736 members.

Euro-MPs

Euro-MPs are elected for fixed five-year terms, and the next election is due in June 2014. Under Article 138 of the Rome treaty there should be a common electoral system in all member states, and the Parliament itself proposed such a system in 1982 and again in 1993. However, the Council of Ministers was unable to agree to this, largely because of the reluctance of the then UK government to abandon its first-past-the-post system in favour of proportional representation (PR). Thus the first four direct elections were held with different systems operating in all the member states, although all except the UK have used variations of PR. The Labour government elected in the UK in May 1997 agreed that the UK, too, would adopt PR for the next Euro-elections in June 1999. Thus, although these elections were held under 15 different systems, all the Euro-MPs for the first time were chosen by proportional representation. This was again the case in 2004 and in 2009, when the elections were held under 27 different national systems, all of them by proportional representation, mostly based on the d'Hondt system.

Salaries

Euro-MPs were previously paid the same salary as MPs in their own countries which means that there was a wide variation. Since July 2009, however, all MEPs have been eligible to receive the same salary, of €7,665.31 per month, or €5,963.33 after tax. The basic salary was set at 38.5% of the salary of a judge at the European Court of Justice. MEPs who were elected before 2009 have the option of being paid under the previous system, but few have chosen to do so. There are also generous travel, attendance, research and secretarial allowances which are paid on the same basis to all members.

Political groups

Euro-MPs do not sit in national delegations but in cross-national political groups. After the 2009 election there were seven of these, with 27 members choosing to remain non-affiliated, as shown in Table 7.1.

The two largest groups combined can command over 60% of the membership of the Parliament, and when they work together can dominate its proceedings. The European People's Party comprises Christian Democrat and Centre Right parties from all but one of the 27 member states. The British Conservatives used to belong to the group, but in a highly controversial move split off in 2009 to form their own Eurosceptic group (see below). The Socialists & Democrats group, comprising Labour, Socialist

Table 7.1 **Political groups in the European Parliament**

European People's Party (Christian Democrats) (EPP)	265
Socialists & Democrats (S&D)	184
Alliance of Liberals and Democrats for Europe (ALDE)	84
Greens/European Free Alliance (EFA)	55
European Conservatives and Reformists (ECR)	54
European United Left/Nordic Green Left Group (EUL/NGL)	35
Europe of Freedom and Democracy (EFD)	32
Independents (non-affiliated) (NI)	27
Total	**736**

and Social Democratic parties, is the only group with members from all 27 countries. The Alliance of Liberals and Democrats for Europe Group, which includes 11 British Liberal Democrats, is now clearly the third largest grouping in the Parliament, with members from 19 member states.

The strong Green representation in the Parliament is split between two groups: the Green/European Free Alliance Group, with 55 members, who are allied with small home rule or separatist groups, including the Scottish National Party and Plaid Cymru; and the Confederal Group of the United European Left/Nordic Green Left, a more avowedly left-wing group, with 35 members, many of them formerly communists. The fifth largest group is the European Conservative and Reformists' group, dominated by the British Tories and containing only two other significant parties – the Law and Justice Party of Poland and the Civic Democratic Party of the Czech Republic. In order to qualify for recognition as a parliamentary group, for which a minimum of 25 members from at least seven member states is required, a single MEP was recruited from five other countries. The Tories were widely criticised for their lack of discrimination in their choice of parliamentarians, several of whom were accused of being homophobic, anti-semitic or otherwise having extreme right-wing views. Even more Europhobic is the Europe of Freedom and Democracy group, dominated by the United Kingdom Independence Party (UKIP), which has 32 members from nine member states. The 27 unaffiliated, or non-inscribed, members are a mixed bunch of independents and representatives of fringe parties. (For a more detailed breakdown of group membership see Appendix 6.)

Voting in the European Parliament is less disciplined than in most national parliaments and ad hoc coalitions are often formed on issues

Table 7.2 **European Parliament election, 2009**

Country	Seats	Voting method
Austria	17	PR, national lists
Belgium	22	PR, regional lists
Bulgaria	17	PR, national lists
Cyprus	6	PR, national lists
Czech Republic	22	PR, national lists
Denmark	13	PR, national lists
Estonia	6	PR, national lists
Finland	13	PR, national lists
France	72	PR, national lists
Germany	99	PR, regional lists
Greece	22	PR, national lists
Hungary	22	PR, national lists
Ireland	12	PR, single transferable vote
Italy	72	PR, regional lists
Latvia	8	PR, national lists
Lithuania	12	PR, national lists
Luxembourg	6	PR, national lists
Malta	5	PR, national lists
Netherlands	25	PR, national lists
Poland	50	PR, regional lists
Portugal	22	PR, national lists
Romania	33	PR, national lists
Slovakia	13	PR, national lists
Slovenia	7	PR, national lists
Spain	50	PR, regional lists
Sweden	18	PR, national lists
United Kingdom	72	PR, regional lists
of which:		
Northern Ireland	3	PR, single transferable vote

that cross normal ideological and national barriers. There is, accordingly, often some uncertainty about how the Parliament may vote.

Elections to the European Parliament

Since 1979 the European Parliament has been elected simultaneously in all the member states. The term of office is five years, with no provision for early dissolution. There should be a common electoral system but, as mentioned above, agreement on this has not yet been reached. Consequently each member state has used its own system, which, in most cases, resembles that used for the election of its own national parliament.

The following elections have been held:

- ◪ The 1979 election was held in nine member states on June 7th–10th 1979. Greece, which joined the Community on January 1st 1981, subsequently elected 24 members on October 18th 1981.
- ◪ The 1981 election was held in ten member states, on June 14th–17th 1984. Spain and Portugal, both of which joined the EC on January 1st 1986, subsequently elected 60 and 24 members respectively, on June 10th and July 19th 1987.
- ◪ The third election, when all the states polled simultaneously, was held on June 15th–18th 1989.
- ◪ The fourth election, for an enlarged house comprising 567 members, took place on June 9th–12th 1994.
- ◪ Separate elections were held during 1995 and 1996 to elect a further 59 members from the new member states of Austria, Finland and Sweden, making a total membership of 626.
- ◪ The fifth election, for a house of 626 members, was held in all member states on June 10th–13th 1999.
- ◪ The sixth election, for a house of 732 members, was held in all member states on June 10–13th 2005.
- ◪ The seventh election, for a house of 736 members, was held in all member states on June 4–7th 2009. An additional 18 "observers" were elected who were only eligible to take their seats after the coming into force of the Lisbon treaty. Their addition takes the total membership of the Parliament to 754.

The electoral systems used in 2009, and the number of members for each country, are shown in Table 7.2.

Powers of the European Parliament

The European Parliament has supervisory powers over the commission and the council, the right of participation in the legislative process and budgetary powers.

Supervisory powers

These are defined by the Treaty of Rome as including the right to put questions, written or oral, to the commission, to discuss its Annual General Report, to discharge the annual budget and to adopt a motion of censure which would lead to the resignation of the commission as a body. Thus in 2008 some 6,570 written and 752 oral questions were put to the commission, and a further 547 written and 463 oral questions to the Council of Ministers. These were answered by ministers from the country currently holding the presidency, who attend each plenary session of the Parliament for this purpose. Since December 1981 the practice has grown up that the prime minister of this country makes a personal report to the Parliament after each meeting of the European Council. The Parliament is able to exercise more intensive supervision over the commission than the treaty envisages, as members and senior officials of the commission attend meetings of its committees and the commission submits its annual programme of work in advance to the Parliament, as well as its annual report, which can only be used as the basis for retrospective checks.

The power of the Parliament to dismiss the commission remained for many years largely a theoretical threat. The motion of censure may be carried only by a two-thirds majority of the votes cast, representing a majority of the Euro-MPs. It is not possible to censure a particular commissioner, which might prove a more effective sanction. In practice Euro-MPs had regarded the power as analogous to possession of a nuclear weapon, the consequences of actually using it being regarded as too horrible to contemplate. Yet in March 1999 it became clear that, as the Parliament was frustrated by its inability to secure the dismissal of Edith Cresson, a French commissioner accused of nepotism and other shortcomings, a large majority of its members were prepared to vote to dismiss the whole commission. In anticipation of this, the entire Santer Commission submitted its resignation, prompting a major crisis in EU affairs (see pages 34–5). One effect of this was undoubtedly to raise the profile of the Parliament and make the Council of Ministers and the commission more wary of coming into conflict with it. Similarly, in November 2004, the imminent threat of the Parliament refusing to endorse the appointment of the Barroso Commission was sufficient to secure a postponement of the vote, and the subsequent replacement of two potential commissioners to whom the Parliament objected (see pages 38–9).

Under the Maastricht Treaty, the Parliament was authorised to appoint a European ombudsman to consider complaints of maladministration by the EC institutions (other than the Court of Justice). The first ombudsman, Jacob Söderman, was appointed in July 1995. He is empowered to receive complaints from any citizen of the Union or any natural person residing in a member state or legal person (that is, a company or organisation) having its registered office there. Initially, he received about 1,000 complaints each year, but only about one-quarter of these were admissible as the others did not fall within the jurisdiction of EU institutions. The number of complaints has since increased by around 10% a year. Söderman's successor, Nikiforos Diamandouros, was elected in January 2003; his appointment was renewed for a further five years in January 2005 and again in January 2010. He has set up a network of national and local ombudsmen and other bodies to whom complaints that fall outside his remit are transferred.

Legislative role

The legislative role of the Parliament began as essentially an advisory one. The treaties designate a large number of areas in which the Council of Ministers cannot enact legislation without first consulting the European Parliament. In practice, in addition to this mandatory consultation the Parliament is normally invited to submit an opinion on any other draft directives or regulations tabled by the commission. Amendments proposed by the Parliament may be incorporated by the commission when it presents a revised draft to the council, and it has undertaken to explain to the Parliament the reasons why an amendment has not been adopted.

The legislative role of the Parliament was significantly strengthened by the Single European Act, which came into effect in July 1987, and by the Maastricht treaty, which took effect in November 1993. This provides for processes of consultation and co-decision by the Parliament which strengthen its ability to amend legislation and, through a "negative assent" procedure, gives it the right to veto certain legislation by a vote of a majority of its members. The Maastricht treaty gave the Parliament a new right of initiative, whereby it may by a majority vote require the commission to propose action in any area. The treaty also gave the right to any EU citizen to petition the Parliament if the matter is of direct and individual concern, and it authorised the Parliament to appoint an ombudsman to receive complaints about deficiencies in the administration of EU institutions. The Parliament may, at the request of a quarter of its members, set up a temporary committee to examine allegations of infringement or bad administration of Community law, unless the matter is *sub judice*. Under the Amsterdam treaty, which came into force in May 1999, the co-decision procedure, enabling the Parliament to veto proposed legislation, was extended to a majority of the policy areas where the EU has competence. The Parliament's legislative role was further strengthened in both the Nice treaty, which came into force in February 2003, and the Lisbon treaty, which became operative on December 1st 2009. Despite these changes the Parliament still falls somewhat short of being an equal partner of the Council of Ministers in the legislative process.

Budgetary powers

The budgetary powers of the Parliament are more substantial. It is officially designated as jointly forming the budgetary authority with the Council of Ministers, and no budget may be adopted without its agreement. Even so, its influence, although considerable, is clearly less than that of the council, as a brief description of the process will make clear.

There are five stages in the budgetary process:

1 The tabling of the preliminary draft budget, which is the responsibility of the commission. This is laid before the Council of Ministers by September 1st of the previous year.
2 The council amends the preliminary draft, invariably reducing the expenditure proposed, and establishes the draft budget, which is submitted to the Parliament by October 5th.
3 The Parliament has 45 days to state its position, during which it may propose amendments or modifications. Before the Lisbon treaty came into effect it was precluded from amending the so-called compulsory part of the budget, notably including agriculture. This restriction is now removed and Parliament may seek to amend all parts of the budget – a major increase in its powers.
4 The council takes a decision on the Parliament's proposed modifications and amendments. If the Parliament insists on them, a compromise has to be reached between the two institutions by means of a "conciliation procedure".
5 The Parliament may amend these modifications and it then adopts the budget. It may decline to do so by a two-thirds majority of the votes cast, representing a majority of all members.

The Parliament has refused to adopt the budget on three occasions, which resulted in the Community entering a new calendar year without a budget being approved. When this happens, total expenditure is restricted during each month to one-twelfth of the total budgeted for the previous year. On each of these occasions the Parliament subsequently adopted a revised draft which differed only marginally from the budget it had originally rejected. On the whole, it has enjoyed more success when it has used the established conciliation procedures and has played off one member state against another in the Council of Ministers than when it has gone for outright rejection. Every year, however, there is a struggle of wills between the council and Parliament, with the latter invariably wanting a larger budget and one less heavily committed to agriculture. Euro-MPs were intensely dissatisfied with their inability to amend compulsory expenditure, but they have won this right under the Lisbon treaty.

Location

The member states have not yet fulfilled their obligation under the treaties to establish a single seat for the Parliament, and its effectiveness is undermined by the geographical fragmentation of its work. The monthly plenary sessions are held in Strasbourg (with additional meetings in Brussels), most committees meet in Brussels and the bulk of the secretariat is based in Luxembourg. This, plus the fact that it needs to conduct its business in 23 different languages with simultaneous interpretation, and the requirement that all documents shall be translated into each of the 23 languages, greatly increases the cost of running the institution, whose budget for 2009 amounted to €1.53 billion, or just over €3 per EU resident.

Most Euro-MPs would undoubtedly prefer that the Parliament's activities should be concentrated in Brussels, but the Luxembourg and French governments are vehemently opposed to this and they have prevented a decision on a permanent seat from being taken. Under the treaties this would need to be unanimous. A protocol to the Amsterdam treaty, adopted in June 1997, confirmed that 12 plenary sessions per year, including the budget session, will continue to be held in Strasbourg, that additional plenary sessions and committee meetings will be in Brussels and the secretariat will remain in Luxembourg.

Sessions

The Parliament normally meets in plenary session for one week in each calendar month except August, with additional part sessions in March and October to consider its opinions on agricultural prices and the annual budget. Much of its work, however, takes place in committees, of which there are currently 21, and a rather larger number of subcommittees. These usually meet during two other weeks each month, leaving at least one week free for party or constituency activities.

8 The Economic and Social Committee and the Committee of the Regions

A purely advisory body, the Economic and Social Committee (ESC) must nevertheless be consulted by the European Commission and the Council of Ministers over a wide range of issues. The Treaty of Rome specifies a number of areas where consultation is mandatory before directives and regulations may be approved, but the council and the commission customarily consult with the ESC over many other issues. In general, there is little hindrance to the ESC offering opinions on any subject on which its members may wish to pronounce.

Membership

The membership of the ESC is made up of interest groups throughout the Community, and it provides a useful sounding board for their representatives whenever legislation that concerns them is envisaged. The members are divided into three groups:

- Group I representing employers;
- Group II representing workers;
- Group III representing various interests such as consumers, farmers, the self-employed, academics, and so on.

Members are appointed by the Council of Ministers on the nomination of their governments, which normally consult with the interest groups most concerned (particularly the trade unions and employers' organisations) before choosing their nominees.

The current membership is 344, consisting of 24 each from France, Germany, Italy and the UK, 21 each from Spain and Poland, 15 from Romania, 12 each from Austria, Belgium, Bulgaria, the Czech Republic, Greece, Hungary, the Netherlands, Portugal and Sweden, 9 each from Denmark, Finland, Ireland, Lithuania and Slovakia, 7 each from Estonia, Latvia and Slovenia, 6 each from Cyprus and Luxembourg, and 5 from Malta. The members are appointed for a renewable term of four years; the current term of office ends in September 2010. The ESC elects its own chairman, who serves for two years, and it is customary to rotate the chairmanship between the three groups. ESC members are part-timers, who are allowed time off from their normal jobs.

Location and working practices

The headquarters of the ESC is in Brussels and it meets there every month. Its detailed work is, however, undertaken in specialist sections (currently six), which draft opinions for approval by the ESC meeting in plenary session. The sections are as follows:

- Agriculture, Rural Development and the Environment
- Transport, Energy, Infrastructure and Information Society
- Economic and Monetary Union and Economic and Social Cohesion
- Employment, Social Affairs and Citizenship
- External Relations
- Single Market, Production and Consumption

On issues such as workers' rights to be consulted or to participate in management, the ESC normally splits on left–right lines, with the members of Groups I and II on opposing sides. In these circumstances the members of Group III are left with the casting votes, and more often than not they have come down predominantly on the trade union rather than the employers' side. On most questions considered by the ESC, however, divisions occur within each group rather than between them. The influence of the ESC, which by 2009 had given well over 3,600 opinions, is in any event seldom significant on controversial political matters. Where it can, and does, influence the content of Community legislation is on more technical issues, where the expertise of its members is often brought to bear.

Committee of the Regions

A similar body, known as the Committee of the Regions, was appointed under the Maastricht treaty provisions, and met for the first time in March 1994. This committee is asked to give its opinion on proposed EC legislation likely to have an impact on the various regions of the member states. In particular, it must be consulted on five policy areas:

- education, vocational training and youth;
- culture;
- public health;

- ◢ trans-European networks for transport, telecommunications and energy;
- ◢ economic and social cohesion.

Like the ESC, it has 344 members appointed for a four-year renewable term. The national membership quotas are the same as for the ESC. The committee is based in Brussels and at the beginning shared premises and secretariat with the ESC. Since 1997, however, it has had its own establishment.

9 The Court of Justice

The task of ensuring that the law is applied throughout the Community in accordance with the provisions of the treaties is devolved upon the European Court of Justice,[1] based in Luxembourg.

Composition
The court currently comprises 27 judges (one from each member state) and eight advocates-general.

The judges are chosen by the Council of Ministers, on the nomination of member states, "from persons whose independence is beyond doubt and who possess the qualifications required for appointment to the highest judicial offices in their respective countries or who are juriconsultants of recognised competence" (Article 167 of the Treaty of Rome). They are appointed for a renewable term of six years, half the court being renewed every three years. The advocates-general are appointed on the same basis.

The judges select one of their number to be president of the court for a renewable term of three years. For more important cases, and invariably in cases brought by a member state or a Community institution, the court sits as a single body. Other cases are assigned to chambers set up within the court: there are currently six such chambers. At any stage a chamber may refer a case to the full court if it considers that it raises points of law requiring definitive rulings.

Jurisdiction
In general six types of cases come before the court or its chambers:

- Disputes between member states.
- Disputes between the EU and member states.
- Disputes between the institutions.
- Disputes between individuals, or corporate bodies, and the EU (including staff cases).
- Opinions on international agreements.
- Preliminary rulings on cases referred by national courts.

The last type of case is of crucial importance for ensuring that Community law is uniformly applied throughout the EU. It illustrates an essential difference between the Court of Justice and the US Supreme Court, with which it is often compared. Both courts are supreme in the sense that there is no appeal against their decisions. But the US court is at the apex of a structure of federal, state and district courts, all of whose rulings may be appealed upwards to it. The Court of Justice is, by contrast, the only EU court within the Community, and has no hierarchical relationship to the lower courts, all of which form part of one of 27 different legal systems. When a case comes before a national court involving Community law, which takes precedence over national laws, if there is any question as to the effect of the Community law with regard to that case it should be referred to the Court of Justice for a preliminary ruling, which the judges in the national court must then apply in giving their own judgments. In the application and interpretation of purely national laws, which make up the great bulk of cases in other courts, the Court of Justice has no jurisdiction whatever.

Court procedure

Proceedings before the court may be initiated by a member state, a Community institution (most often the commission) or by a corporate body or individual (providing he or she has a direct personal interest in the subject of the case). The court procedure involves two separate stages, one written and one oral.

In the first stage, on receipt of a written application from a plaintiff, the court establishes that it falls within its jurisdiction and that it has been lodged within the time limitations determined by the treaties. The application is then served on the opposing party, which normally has one month in which to lodge a statement of defence. The applicant has a further month to table a reply, and the defendant one more month for a rejoinder.

Each case is supervised by a judge-rapporteur, who is appointed by the president. On receipt of all the documents the judge-rapporteur presents a preliminary report to the court, which decides whether a preparatory enquiry (involving the appearance of the parties, requests for further documents, oral testimony, and so on) is necessary, and whether the case shall appear before the full court or be assigned to one of the chambers. The president then sets the date for the public hearing, at which the two sides appear before the judges, present their arguments and call evidence if they so wish. The judges and the advocate-general (whose role is somewhat similar to that of the public prosecutor in French courts) put to the parties any questions they think fit. The advocate-general gives his opinion some weeks later, at a further hearing, analysing the facts and the legal aspects in detail and proposing a solution to the dispute.

The advocate-general's opinion often gives a clear indication of which way the judgment will go, but this is not invariably the case. The judges consider their ruling in private, on the basis of a draft prepared by the judge-rapporteur. If, during their deliberations, they require additional information they may reopen the procedure and ask the parties for further explanation, oral or written, or order further enquiries.

The judgments of the court are reached by majority vote; where the court is equally divided the vote of the most junior judge is disregarded, although in most cases it is arranged that an uneven number of judges will be sitting (the quorum for the full court is seven). The judgment is given at a public hearing, which, on average, occurs some 18 months after the receipt of an application.

Case load

The case load of the court has built up steadily since its foundation in 1953. Judgments had been delivered in more than 7,000 cases by the end of 2009. Table 9.1 gives a detailed breakdown by subject matter of the cases heard in 2008. For many years, given the importance and complexity of the common agricultural policy, agricultural cases easily headed the list of cases coming before the court. But following significant reforms and simplification of the CAP there has been a dramatic fall in such cases, and issues concerning the environment, taxation, freedom of movement, intellectual property and the area of freedom, security and justice now predominate.

In earlier years a large number of cases had concerned complaints brought by employees of the different EU institutions on such matters as recruitment, salaries, promotion, disciplinary procedures, and so on, which under national administrations would go to employment tribunals. It was an anomaly that the Court of Justice, whose primary function should be to rule on significant issues of Community law, should have its timetable clogged up with a mass of petty cases, most of which could be adequately dealt with at a far lower level.

Court of First Instance (General Court)

The Single European Act (see page 46), which took effect in July 1987, provided for the establishment of a Court of First Instance, which would hear certain classes of cases brought by individuals, including actions brought by EU officials. This court, which now consists of 27 judges,

Table 9.1 **Court of Justice: 2008 cases analysed by subject matter**

Subject matter of the action	Direct actions	References for a preliminary ruling	Appeals	Appeals concerning interim measures and interventions	Total	Special forms of procedure
Agriculture	4	11	–	–	15	–
Approximation of laws	15	10	–	–	25	–
Area of freedom, security and justice	12	26	–	–	38	–
Commercial policy	–	3	2	–	5	–
Common Customs Tariff	–	12	–	–	12	–
Common foreign and security policy	–	1	1	–	2	–
Community own resources	3	–	–	–	3	–
Company law	9	9	1	–	19	–
Competition	–	3	7	–	10	–
Customs union	–	8	1	–	9	–
Economic and monetary policy	1	–	–	–	1	–
Energy	4	–	–	–	4	–
Environment and consumers	49	34	5	6	94	–
European citizenship	–	6	–	–	6	–
External relations	2	7	–	–	9	1
Fisheries policy	2	1	–	–	3	–
Free movement of capital	3	9	–	–	12	–
Free movement of goods	2	8	–	–	10	–
Freedom of establishment	26	7	–	–	33	–
Freedom of movement for persons	28	14	–	–	42	–
Freedom to provide services	12	20	–	–	32	–
Industrial policy	3	5	–	–	8	–
Intellectual property	1	12	23	–	36	–
Law governing the institutions	3	1	21	2	27	1
Principles of Community law	–	3	1	–	4	–
Regional policy	–	–	2	–	2	–
Rome Convention	–	1	–	–	1	–
Social policy	5	26	–	–	31	–
Social security for migrant workers	–	2	–	–	2	–
State aid	1	6	4	–	11	–
Taxation	14	35	–	–	49	–
Transport	12	4	–	–	16	–
EC Treaty	209	284	68	8	569	2
EU Treaty	1	4	–	–	5	–
Procedure	–	–	–	–	–	7
Staff regulations	–	–	9	–	9	–
Others	–	–	9	–	9	–
Overall total	210	288	77	8	583	9

Note: Totals may not add up due to rounding.
Source: Court of Justice

began work in September 1989. The removal of staff cases from the work of the main court should have shortened the delay in arriving at judgments in other cases. From its creation in 1989 until December 1st 2009, when it was renamed the General Court under the terms of the Lisbon treaty, the Court of First Instance decided some 5,000 cases. Since 2005, staff cases have been heard by the new European Union Civil Service Tribunal, with a right of appeal, on points of law only, to the Court of First Instance.

Who brings the cases

Cases involving member states, normally alleging failure to carry out their obligations under the treaties, are often initiated by the commission. Occasionally, one member state is brought to court by another. As Figure 9.1 shows, Italy has historically been the major culprit. The Italian Parliament is notoriously slow in passing laws, and a large number of these actions have been for failure to apply directives, adopted by the Council of Ministers, within the appointed time. Other countries with a poor record of meeting their obligations include Greece and Luxembourg. The new member states which joined in 2004 and 2007 are still going through a transitional period, and the figure probably does not accurately reflect their comparative performance, but it is notable that the Czech Republic and Malta are doing worse than the others. Of the more established member states, Denmark has the best record. The commission heads the lists both of complainants and defendants. It is its responsibility to take action, against individuals and companies as well as member states, to ensure that the treaties are being applied, for example in competition cases. However, it is also the commission that is the defendant in virtually all actions alleging loss or damage caused by the carrying out of EU policies.

Sometimes cases have involved one institution lodging a complaint against another. The Council of Ministers has more than once initiated action against the Parliament for allegedly exceeding its budgetary powers, while the Parliament took the council to court for failure to implement a common transport policy within the period foreseen by the Rome treaty.

Beneficial effect of judgments

The judgments of the court have helped to consolidate the Union, ensuring that its citizens as well as national governments are both protected by, and subject to, the provisions of EU law. It has been effective in many of its judgments in preventing governments from backsliding from the

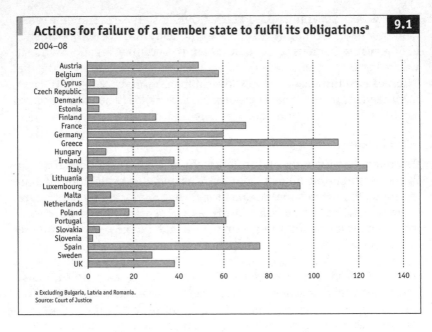

9.1

Actions for failure of a member state to fulfil its obligations[a]

2004–08

a Excluding Bulgaria, Latvia and Romania.
Source: Court of Justice

obligations that they (or their predecessors) assumed in signing the treaties. Also, although it has few sanctions against member states – being unable, for example, to send erring ministers to prison – its judgments have nearly always been complied with, occasionally after some delay, and sometimes following a further ruling by the court. The Maastricht treaty gave the court the power to impose fines on member states failing to comply with its judgments within a time-limit set by the commission.

One particular judgment provided a useful stimulus to the removal of non-tariff barriers to intra-Community trade. In 1979 and 1980 the court ruled in the "Cassis de Dijon" case that where a product (in this case a category of alcoholic drink, but it has subsequently been applied to particular foodstuffs) is legally retailed in one member state, its sale cannot be prohibited in another member state except on the grounds of risk to public health.

Note

1 Not to be confused with the European Court of Human Rights, based in Strasbourg, which was set up by the Council of Europe, under the European Convention of Human Rights, signed in 1950. All the member states of the EU recognise the jurisdiction of this court in human rights cases.

10 The Court of Auditors

The least known of the EU's institutions is the Court of Auditors, based in Luxembourg. It was established in 1977, when it replaced an earlier Audit Board which had less sweeping authority.

Membership

There are 27 members, one from each member state, who are chosen from persons who belong or have belonged to external audit departments in their own countries, or who are otherwise specially qualified. They are appointed for a renewable six-year term by the Council of Ministers, and appoint their own chairman from among their number for a renewable term of three years.

Responsibilities

The court's task is to examine all accounts of revenue and expenditure of Community institutions, and of any other bodies set up by the EU, to ensure that all revenue has been received and all expenditure incurred in a legal manner. It also has the responsibility of ensuring that the financial management has been sound. Its function is similar to that of bodies like the Comptroller and Auditor General's department in the UK.

An influential role

The court produces an annual report, as well as periodic specific reports undertaken at the request of any of the Union's other institutions or on its own initiative. It has frequently thrown up evidence of wasteful expenditure, especially on support to agriculture, and occasionally of financial misconduct. Its role is highly influential, and its reports have led to a considerable tightening up of EU procedures.

11 The European Investment Bank

The European Investment Bank (EIB) is both an EU institution and a bank. Established in 1958, under Article 130 of the Rome treaty, it is the EU's bank for financing capital investment promoting the balanced development of the Community. It raises the bulk of its financial resources on capital markets (where it has a AAA rating), and on-lends the proceeds, on a non-profit-making basis, for capital investment meeting priority EU objectives. The major part of its lending activity is focused on the Union's less prosperous regions. It also contributes towards deploying EC development aid programmes, notably under the co-operation or association agreements which the EU has concluded with 12 countries in the Mediterranean region and with 79 African, Caribbean and Pacific countries under the fourth Lomé Convention (see Chapter 35). It also lent considerable amounts, under the EU's Phare and TACIS programmes, to countries in central and eastern Europe and the former Soviet Union, as well as, on a smaller scale, to a number of Asian and Latin American countries and, since 1995, to South Africa.

Members and financial resources

The members of the EIB are the 27 member states of the EU. They have collectively subscribed the bank's capital of €164 billion (of which €7.5 billion is paid up). During 2008 it borrowed €59.5 billion and lent €57.7 billion. It is now, by a wide margin, the largest borrower and lender on international financial markets.

Activities in the EU

Loans are made to each of the member states. Table 11.1 shows the amount which each received in 2008, and over the five-year period from 2004. Italy has long been one of the greatest beneficiaries of the EIB, together with Spain and Portugal, with France and the UK also receiving significant amounts. Germany has also become a major borrower since unification, mainly to finance investments in eastern Germany, and in recent years has been among the largest recipients. The new member states which joined the EU in 2005 and 2007 are increasingly benefiting from the bank's activities, with Poland to the fore.

EIB loans within the Community during 2008 and 2009 were principally for regional development, energy, industry, advanced technology,

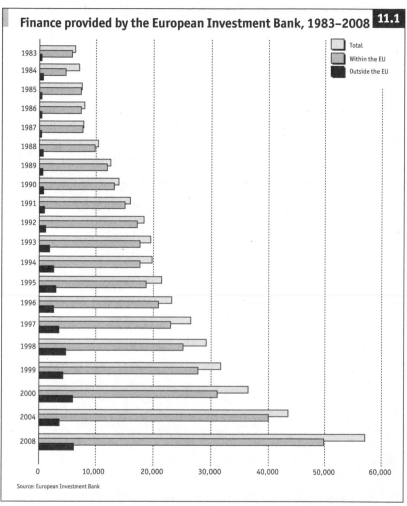

Finance provided by the European Investment Bank, 1983–2008 **11.1**

Legend:
- Total
- Within the EU
- Outside the EU

Years (vertical axis): 1983, 1984, 1985, 1986, 1987, 1988, 1989, 1990, 1991, 1992, 1993, 1994, 1995, 1996, 1997, 1998, 1999, 2000, 2004, 2008

Horizontal axis: 0, 10,000, 20,000, 30,000, 40,000, 50,000, 60,000

Source: European Investment Bank

modernisation and conversion of enterprises, transport, telecommunications and other infrastructure development, and environmental protection. In 2008, the latest year for which figures are available, loans signed by the EIB totalled €51.5 billion, compared with €39.6 billion in 2002. In the closing months of 2008, the lending activity of the bank sharply increased as it responded to the challenge of the recession sparked off by the subprime mortgage crisis in the United States and the collapse of Lehman Brothers. The extra investment was focused largely on helping to provide finance for small and medium-sized enterprises,

Table 11.1 **Geographical breakdown of finance contracts signed (€m)**

| | 2008 | | 2004–08 | |
	Amount	%	Amount	%
Austria	1,318	2.6	5,655	2.6
Belgium	1,418	2.8	4,389	2.0
Bulgaria	455	0.9	1,693	0.8
Cyprus	30	0.1	645	0.3
Czech Republic	1,111	2.2	5,467	2.5
Denmark	379	0.7	1,881	0.9
Estonia	87	0.2	207	0.1
Finland	710	1.4	3,636	1.7
France	4,651	9.0	21,615	10.0
Germany	6,919	13.4	33,758	15.6
Greece	1,165	2.3	5,382	2.5
Hungary	1,525	3.0	6,195	2.9
Ireland	450	0.9	2,319	1.1
Italy	8,280	16.1	31,457	14.5
Latvia	610	1.2	934	0.4
Lithuania	10	0.0	128	0.1
Luxembourg	40	0.1	453	0.2
Malta	150	0.3	203	0.1
Netherlands	1,578	3.1	3,976	1.8
Poland	2,837	5.5	11,002	5.1
Portugal	2,644	5.1	8,817	4.1
Romania	1,112	2.2	2,994	1.4
Slovenia	159	0.3	1,652	0.8
Slovakia	161	0.3	799	0.4
Spain	8,573	16.7	37,725	17.4
Sweden	1,311	2.5	3,901	1.8
United Kingdom	3,796	7.4	18,883	8.7
EFTA[a]	–	–	802	0.4
European Union	**51,480**	**100.0**	**216,569**	**100.0**

Note: Totals may not add up due to rounding.
a Financing operations in the members of EFTA equivalent to operations in the EU.
Source: European Investment Bank

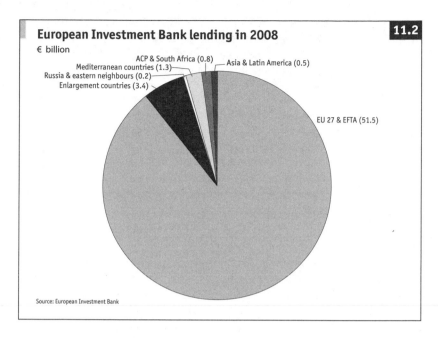

European Investment Bank lending in 2008 `11.2`
€ billion

ACP & South Africa (0.8)
Mediterranean countries (1.3)
Russia & eastern neighbours (0.2)
Enlargement countries (3.4)
Asia & Latin America (0.5)
EU 27 & EFTA (51.5)

Source: European Investment Bank

for energy, climate change, infrastructure and clean transport projects, and for convergence lending to poorer regions. The bank also committed itself to increasing its lending within the Union by 30% in both 2009 and 2010. About 10% of ESB lending is beyond the EU's borders. The geographical distribution for 2008 is shown in Figure 11.2.

Location and structure

The EIB is based in Luxembourg. Its Board of Governors consists of the finance ministers of the member states who meet once a year. It also has a part-time Board of Directors (27 members nominated by the member states and one member nominated by the European Commission), and a full-time Management Committee of the bank's president and seven vice-presidents. They are appointed by the Board of Governors, on the nomination of the Board of Directors, for a renewable six-year term.

European Bank for Reconstruction and Development

Since 1990 the EIB has been lending money to countries in eastern Europe to help towards their transition to market economies. It also contributed to the establishment in April 1991 of the European Bank for Reconstruction and Development (EBRD), which has its headquarters in

London, whose specific function is to lend money for this purpose, including to all the successor states of the Soviet Union. Although 40 countries participated in its establishment, more than half of the EBRD's capital of $10 billion was contributed by the EU and its member states. The EIB's share in the bank's capital is 3%.

12 Other EU bodies

As well as the main European institutions described on the preceding pages, there are a number of specialised agencies, foundations and centres set up by a decision of the European Commission or the European Council. Most of these were established in 1994 or 1995, following decisions made at the Brussels summit in December 1993, although two of them were established 20 years earlier. In a different category was the **European Monetary Institute**, set up under the Maastricht Treaty as a forerunner to the **European Central Bank**, which replaced it in June 1998. The bank is based in Frankfurt, and its functions are described on page 141.

European Agency for the Evaluation of Medicinal Products (EMEA)

With its base in London, the EMEA became operational on January 1st 1995. Its purpose is to ensure that in the EU's single market pharmaceutical products are marketed with identical conditions of usage and should benefit from an independent, scientifically based evaluation to protect both the consumer and the industry.

European Environment Agency (EEA)

The EEA and its wider network, EIONET, were set up in Copenhagen in 1994 to deliver high-quality environmental information to the member states of the EU, as well as to the general public. The main aims of the agency are to describe the present and foreseeable state of the environment and to provide relevant information for the implementation of the Community's environment policy.

European Training Foundation

The European Training Foundation was inaugurated in Turin in January 1995. It was set up to co-ordinate and support all EU activities in the field of post-compulsory education. This was part of the overall Phare and TACIS programmes for economic restructuring in the partner states of central and eastern Europe and Central Asia.

European Centre for the Development of Vocational Training (CEDEFOP)

CEDEFOP was established in Berlin in 1975, but recently moved to Salonica. The centre is contributing to the development of vocational training in Europe through its academic and technical activities.

European Centre for Drugs and Drug Addiction (EMCDDA)

EMCDDA was established in 1994 and located in Lisbon. The centre's aim is to provide "objective, reliable and comparable information at European level concerning drugs, drug addiction and their consequences". As the drugs phenomenon comprises many complex and closely interwoven aspects, the centre has the task of providing an overall statistical, documentary and technical picture of the drugs problem to the member states and the Community institutions as they embark on combat measures.

European Foundation for the Improvement of Living and Working Conditions

Established in Dublin in 1975, the foundation's aim is "to contribute to the planning and establishment of better working and living conditions through action designed to increase and disseminate knowledge likely to assist this development". Effectively an advisory body, its main task is to supply the commission and other EU institutions with scientific information and technical data.

Office for Harmonisation in the Internal Market (OHIM)

OHIM (Trade Marks and Designs) began its work on September 1st 1994 in Alicante. The office is responsible for the registration and subsequent administration of Community trade marks, and in the future Community designs, which have effect throughout the EU. The aim of the OHIM is to contribute to harmonisation in the internal market in the domain of intellectual property, in particular trademarks and designs.

Community Plant Variety Rights Office

This office became operational on April 27th 1995, and is temporarily located in Brussels. It is independent of the EU's institutions and is exclusively responsible for the implementation of the new regime of Community plant variety rights, like patents and copyrights. Plant breeders may ask for protection throughout the EU by a single application to the Community Plant Variety Rights Office.

European Agency for Safety and Health at Work

Located in Bilbao, the agency began work on October 27th 1995. Its first priority is to create a network linking up national information networks and to facilitate the provision of information in the field of safety and health at work.

Translation Centre for Bodies in the European Union

The Translation Centre for Bodies in the European Union was set up in 1994 in Luxembourg. It carries out translations for most of the bodies and agencies mentioned above.

Other agencies

Since 2001 a number of other agencies have been created, many of which came into operation much later than intended because of a repeated failure by the European Council to agree on their location. Two of the more important of these, the European Food Safety Authority (EFSA) and Eurojust (the European judicial co-operation unit), had to start work in temporary locations but are now firmly established respectively in Parma and the Hague (see Appendix 5).

13 The bureaucracy: facts, figures and costs

Number of employees

Despite frequent suggestions that the EU has a vast bureaucracy, its payroll is modest compared with that of the national civil services of the member states. The European Commission has fewer than 20,000 permanent employees, excluding some 5,700 working in scientific research institutes and other units; the remaining institutions together employ about half that number. The total number of employees at the end of 2008 is shown in Table 13.1.

Table 13.1 **EU employees, end-2008**

	Permanent	Temporary
Commission	19,796	366
Research institutions, etc	5,741	177
Specialised agencies	4,163	326
Council of Ministers	3,461	36
Parliament	5,004	127
Court of Justice	1,455	438
Court of Auditors[a]	600	100
ESC and Committee of the Regions[a]	1,100	50
Total	41,320	1,620

a Estimated.
Source: European Commission

Recruitment

Recruitment to the commission's staff, apart from a limited number of senior posts to which national governments make nominations, are filled by open competition, the competitions being advertised periodically in the *Official Journal* of the Community, and in leading newspapers in the member states. Normally there is an upper age limit for new recruits, which effectively means that most Eurocrats join early in their careers, in their 20s or early 30s. Appointments are made without regard to race, creed or sex and, in principle, no posts are reserved for nationals of any specific state. In practice, there are unofficial national quotas designed to ensure that each member state gets a reasonable share of posts at each level of the administration. Otherwise the general qualifications are as set out in Article 28 of the Community's Staff Regulations.

An official may be appointed only on condition that:

(a) he is a national of one of the Member States of the Communities, unless an exception is authorised by the appointing authority, and enjoys his full rights as a citizen;
(b) he has fulfilled any obligations imposed on him by the laws concerning military service;
(c) he produces the appropriate character references as to his suitability for the performance of his duties;
(d) he has ... passed a competition based on either qualifications or tests, or both qualifications and tests;
(e) he is physically fit to perform his duties; and
(f) he produces evidence of a thorough knowledge of one of the languages of the Communities and of a satisfactory knowledge of another language of the Communities to the extent necessary for the performance of his duties.

Candidates for posts as interpreters or translators must have a good knowledge of two Community languages other than their own.

Training

In addition to its permanent staff, the commission makes provision for the in-service training of about 200 stagiaires each year. The training lasts for 3–5 months, and the posts are open, also on a competition basis, primarily to recently graduated students. There is no guarantee of future employment, but the "stages" provide excellent experience for those interested in future careers at a European level, either with the Community or otherwise.

Salaries

The salary scales for employees of the commission and the other European institutions are based on 16 career grades, as defined in the Staff Regulations. The highest grade (16) applies to directors-general and a very small number of other very senior officials. The lowest grade (1) includes junior filing clerks and attendants. The remuneration of members of the commission is linked to the maximum of the 16th grade. The president of the commission receives 138% of this (€293,073), vice-presidents 125% (€265,465) and commissioners 112.5% (€236,640). They all also qualify for the various allowances paid to employees, notably the expatriation allowance, which adds 14% to the above figures for all except the Belgian commissioner.

EU employees pay income tax to the Community (currently at a standard rate of 25%) rather than to the country in which they are employed, and the rates of pay are set rather higher than for national civil servants in order to compensate for living and working in a different country. In addition to basic salaries, there are family allowances and expatriation allowances, and a number of other "perks", such as free education for children at one of the European schools maintained by the commission. The salary scales are published from time to time in the *Official Journal*, where they are expressed monthly in euros (€). The most recent scales, which came into force on July 1st 2008, are shown in Table 13.2. Apart from the top grade, which has three incremental steps, there are five yearly increments.

Table 13.2 **Basic monthly salaries in each category, 2008 (€)**

Grade	1	2	3	4	5
16	16,299.08	16,983.99	17,697.68	–	–
15	14,405.66	15,011.01	15,641.79	16,076.97	16,299.08
14	12,732.20	13,267.22	13,824.73	14,209.36	14,405.66
13	11,253.14	11,726.01	12,218.75	12,558.70	12,732.20
12	9,945.89	10,363.83	10,799.33	11,099.79	11,253.14
11	8,790.51	9,159.90	9,544.81	9,810.36	9,945.89
10	7,769.34	8,095.83	8,436.01	8,670.72	8,790.51
9	6,866.80	7,155.35	7,456.03	7,663.46	7,769.34
8	6,069.10	6,324.13	6,589.88	6,773.22	6,866.80
7	5,364.07	5,589.48	5,824.35	5,986.40	6,069.10
6	4,740.94	4,940.16	5,147.76	5,290.97	5,364.07
5	4,190.20	4,366.28	4,549.76	4,676.34	4,740.94
4	3,703.44	3,859.06	4,021.22	4,133.10	4,190.20
3	3,273.22	3,410.76	3,554.09	3,652.97	3,703.44
2	2,892.98	3,014.55	3,141.22	3,228.61	3,273.22
1	2,556.91	2,664.34	2,776.31	2,853.56	2,892.98

Note: On December 1st 2009 the euro was worth £0.91 and $1.50.
Source: *Official Journal of the European Union*

3
THE COMPETENCES

The EU is still a long way from becoming the political union to which its founders aspired, and which has several times been reaffirmed by the heads of government as their eventual aim. It is far from being a European government, and its progress has been markedly lopsided. The removal of customs duties between member states and the development of a common agricultural policy long remained the most concrete achievements of the Community, but there are many other areas of economic activity where it has a competence, which is often shared, to a varying extent, with that of the member states. The Maastricht treaty enshrined the principle of "subsidiarity" by asserting that decisions should be "taken as closely as possible to the citizens", but nevertheless extended the competences of the EC institutions in several directions, as did the subsequent Amsterdam and Nice treaties. Part 3 surveys the principal fields of action of the Community without, however, purporting to provide a comprehensive account of all of its activities.

14 Financing the Union

The EU's budget is modest compared with that of the member states, no more than around 2.5% of the sum of the national budgets – and about one-sixteenth the size of the US federal budget. In 2009 each EU citizen would have paid an average of €268 to the Union, and perhaps 50 times that amount to their own country. Despite this disparity, the EU's budget has been a source of periodic dispute between the member states and between them, the commission and the Parliament.

Revenue

Sources

The EU's sources of revenue have changed over the years. The ECSC, which had its own operational budget, was always financed by a levy on the production of coal and steel firms. The general Community budget was originally financed by a system of national contributions based mainly on the GDP of the member states. In 1970 it was decided progressively to replace these contributions by the Community's "own resources". These consist of sources of revenue which, although collected mainly in the member states, belong to the Community as a right. At present they consist of four separate elements:

1 Contributions from member states based on national income (65.4% of the total in 2009). A simple multiplier is applied to the calculated gross national income (GNI) for the country concerned. This is the last recourse for raising funding for a budget year, so the actual figure is adjusted within predetermined limits to obtain the budget total required. Revenue is currently capped at 1.24% of GNI for the EU as a whole.
2 Traditional "own resources" such as customs duties, agricultural duties and sugar levies (16.5%).
3 A proportion of value-added tax. VAT rates and exemptions vary in different countries, so a formula is used to create the "harmonised tax base" upon which the EU charge is levied (16.9% of the total in 2009).
4 Other revenue, such as unspent amounts from the previous year (1.2%).

Table 14.1 **Budget revenue, 2008–09 (€m)**

	2008	%	2009	%
Agricultural duties and sugar levies	1,990.60	1.7	1,550.30	1.3
Customs duties	14,945.70	12.9	17,655.80	15.2
VAT-based resource	18,096.76	15.6	19,616.10	16.9
GNI-based resource	73,290.31	63.3	75,914.12	65.4
Other revenue	7,447.91	6.4	1,359.72	1.2
Total	**115,771.28**	**100.0**	**116,096.04**	**100.0**

Source: European Commission

Expenditure

Figure 14.1 shows the expenditure provided for in the EU's general budget of 2009, and compares it with 1973, the first year in which the UK was a member. Table 14.2 provides a detailed breakdown of the expenditure estimates. The principal elements in the budget are as follows.

Agriculture and fisheries
In the 2007–13 financial package, this is listed as "Preservation and management of natural resources", but it is essentially the EU's farm and fish policies. It represented some 40% of estimated expenditure in 2009, a sharp reduction on previous years. The main reason agriculture absorbs such a high proportion of the budget is that it is the one area of major expenditure where a substantial amount of publicly financed support passes through the EU's budget. It threatens to crowd out programmes in other areas, for example, technological research, where the Union ought to be making a far larger contribution. Efforts have been made in recent years to curtail agricultural spending, and at least to ensure that it rises at a slower rate than EU expenditure as a whole (see pages 159–61).

Regional policy
Regional policy accounts for most of what is currently entitled "Sustainable growth" in the budget – some 35.5% of estimated expenditure in 2009. In 1973 there was no regional spending in the budget. The European Regional Development Fund was established in 1975, following the accession in 1973 of the UK, Denmark and Ireland. It helps to finance development programmes, infrastructural investment and industrial

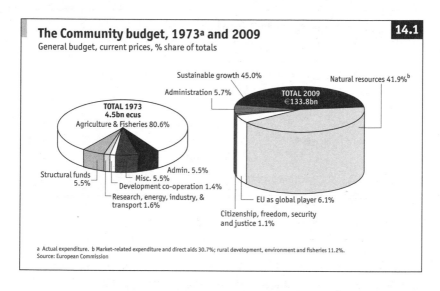

The Community budget, 1973ª and 2009 14.1
General budget, current prices, % share of totals

Sustainable growth 45.0%

Administration 5.7%

Natural resources 41.9%ᵇ

TOTAL 2009
€133.8bn

TOTAL 1973
4.5bn ecus
Agriculture & Fisheries 80.6%

Structural funds 5.5%

Admin. 5.5%
Misc. 5.5%
Development co-operation 1.4%
Research, energy, industry, & transport 1.6%

EU as global player 6.1%

Citizenship, freedom, security and justice 1.1%

a Actual expenditure. b Market-related expenditure and direct aids 30.7%; rural development, environment and fisheries 11.2%.
Source: European Commission

and service projects in poorer regions and areas particularly hit by recession. The fund normally operates on the basis of matching contributions from the member state concerned. Under the Maastricht treaty, a new Cohesion Fund was established to provide assistance for infrastructure investment in the poorest member states. This covers all member states with a GNI of less than 90% of the EU average, which currently means all the new members who joined in the 2004 and 2007 enlargements as well as Greece and Portugal. Regional policy also covers social policy, which was a separate entity until 2007.

Social policy
Also part of the "Sustainable growth" chapter in the 2007–13 package, it is 8.4% of the 2009 budget. Most of this expenditure is through the European Social Fund, which co-finances training and retraining schemes and aid for recruitment.

Energy, research, industry, transport and the environment
Another part of the "Sustainable growth" chapter in the 2007–13 package (covered by the broad heading, "Competitiveness for growth and employment"), it is 8.4% of the 2009 budget. It is evidently only a tiny fraction of the amount spent by member states in these fields. The largest proportion went on research, which was widely seen as being a totally inadequate response to the research efforts of the United States

Table 14.2 **EU budget 2009 in figures: expenditure estimates for EU policies**

	Budget 2009 (€bn)	% change on 2008
Sustainable growth	**60.2**	**3.2**
Competitiveness, incl:	11.8	6.2
Education & training	1.1	6.5
Research	6.8	10.9
Competitiveness & innovation	0.5	22.2
Transport & energy networks	1.9	−4.6
Social policy agenda	0.2	5.5
Cohesion, incl:	48.4	2.5
Convergence	39.0	4.4
Regional competitiveness & employment	8.1	−5.6[a]
Territorial co-operation	1.2	−1.3
Natural resources	**56.1**	**1.0**
Environment	0.3	18.8
Agricultural expenditure & direct aids	41.4	0.3
Rural development	13.7	2.6
Fisheries	0.9	0.3
Citizenship, freedom, security & justice	**1.5**	**12.3**
Freedom, security & justice[b]	0.9	18.1
Citizenship[c]	0.6	−5.4[d]
EU as a global player	**8.1[e]**	**7.3**
Pre-accession	1.5	5.6
European neighbourhood	1.6	3.8
Development co-operation	2.4	5.5
Humanitarian aid	0.8	3.4
Democracy & human rights	0.2	6.9
Common foreign & security policy	0.2	−14.8
Instrument for Stability	0.2	4.1
Administration	**7.7**	**5.7**
European Commission	3.6	4.5
Other institutions	2.8	6.5
Compensation to new EU countries[f]	**0.2**	**1.2**
Total	**133.8**	**2.5**

Note: Totals may not add up due to rounding.
a Decrease due to reduction in allocation to the so-called "phasing-in regions", which were eligible under Objective 1 between 2000 and 2006. b Including fundamental rights and justice, security and liberties, migration flows.
c Including culture, media, public health and consumer protection. d Excluding the amounts allocated in 2008 from the Solidarity Fund. e Including emergency aid reserve. f Amounts fixed by the accession treaties.
Source: European Commission

and Japan. Attempts by the commission to persuade the member states sharply to increase the appropriations for research have so far met with only partial success.

External activities
The EU is the world's largest aid donor, if you include donations by individual member states. Within the member states, spending is mostly focused on the countries along the EU borders. This money, around 5.5% of the 2009 budget, funds cross-border projects to foster good relations with neighbouring countries, which may also receive direct funds for other projects. Money is also given to candidate countries, such as Turkey and Croatia. Development aid goes to reduce poverty and boost economic development in Latin America, Asia, Central Asia, the Middle East and South Africa. The Lomé (now Cotonou) Convention provides for financial and technical aid to African, Caribbean and Pacific countries, which is in practice financed separately from the EU budget through national contributions and loans from the European Investment Bank (see Chapter 35).

Administration
The administration budget, around 5.75%, covers salaries, pensions, buildings and equipment. As much of the EU's work takes place in Belgium and Luxembourg, almost three-quarters of the spending is allocated to these two countries. The European Commission accounts for about half of the total spending on EU administration, employing around 33,600 people in 2009.

Crime and border control
Listed as "Citizenship, freedom, security and justice", this is a new heading for the 2007–13 package, and represents only 1.1% of the budget. In 2008, the EU received almost 240,000 asylum applications and many thousands more people were smuggled illegally across the EU's land borders and through its ports. Most EU expenditure on asylum and immigration is spent on developing a co-ordinated approach to border control, through the European external borders fund, and assisting refugees.

Appropriations and expenditure
The 2009 budget will amount to €133.8 billion in commitment appropriations, a slight increase of 2.5% compared with 2008. This corresponds to

Table 14.3 **Appropriations for commitments, 2007–13 (€m, current prices)**

	2007	2008	2008	2009	2010	2011	2012	Total
Sustainable growth	53,979	57,653	59,700	61,782	63,638	66,628	69,621	433,001
Competitiveness for growth & employment	8,918	10,386	11,272	12,388	12,987	14,203	15,433	85,587
Cohesion for growth & employment	45,061	47,267	48,428	49,394	50,651	52,425	54,188	347,414
Preservation & management of natural resources	55,143	59,193	59,639	60,113	60,338	60,810	61,289	416,525
of which: market-related expenditure & direct payment	45,759	46,217	46,679	47,146	47,617	48,093	48,574	330,085
Citizenship, freedom, security & justice	1,273	1,362	1,523	1,693	1,889	2,105	2,376	12,221
Freedom, security & justice	637	747	872	1,025	1,206	1,406	1,661	7,554
Citizenship	636	615	651	668	683	699	715	4,667
EU as a global player	6,578	7,002	7,440	7,893	8,430	8,997	9,595	55,935
Administration[a]	7,039	7,380	7,699	8,008	8,334	8,670	9,095	56,225
Compensation	445	208	210	–	–	–	–	862
Total commitments appropriations	124,457	132,797	136,211	139,489	142,629	147,210	151,976	974,769
% of GNI	1.04	1.06	1.04	1.02	1.00	0.99	0.98	1.02
Total payments appropriations	122,190	129,681	123,858	133,505	133,452	140,200	142,408	925,294
% of GNI	1.02	1.03	0.94	0.97	0.93	0.94	0.91	0.96
Margin available (%)	0.22	0.21	0.30	0.27	0.31	0.30	0.33	0.28
Own resources ceiling, % of GNI	1.24	1.24	1.24	1.24	1.24	1.24	1.24	1.24

a Expenditure on pensions included under the ceiling for this heading is calculated net of staff contributions to the relevant scheme, within the limit of €500m at 2004 prices for the period 2007–13.
Source: European Commission

1.03% of EU gross national income (GNI). Payment appropriations will reach €116.1 billion, a slight increase of 0.3% compared with 2008, representing 0.89% of EU-27 GNI.

Financial frameworks

Like any government institution, the EU operates on an annual basis. But in 1988, after a succession of budget crises, the institutions agreed their first financial perspective, which lays down maximum amounts ("ceilings") by broad category of expenditure ("headings") for the period in question.

The current framework covers the period 2007–13. The financial framework table is enshrined in an Inter-institutional Agreement between the European Parliament, the Council and the European Commission which also sets out the rules and procedures for managing the framework on a year-to-year basis (procedures for revision, technical adjustment, and so on) and for improving the annual budgetary procedure. The 2007–13 budget places limits on spending in each of the EU's policy areas for each of the seven years – but a detailed annual budget still has to be agreed every year.

After the final agreement, the annual average ceiling on payment appropriations for the financial framework amounts to 1.03 % of EU-27 GNI. The total expenditure commitment for the seven-year period is €974.8 billion, or an average of €139.3 billion a year.

Who gains, who loses?

For many years there was no precise information about the net contributors and net beneficiaries of the EU budget. Everybody knew that Germany was, by far, the biggest contributor, that the UK's contribution was substantially reduced by the annual rebates it had received since 1984 and that Ireland – in relation to its size – was the biggest beneficiary. When the UK won the rebate in 1984 it was one of the poorest countries in the EU, but by 2005 it was one of the richest, and was under fierce pressure to scrap the rebate. The main reason for granting the rebate to the UK was that it received only a small share of CAP funds. That was still the case, but it was also true that the amount of the budget spent on agriculture had declined from 70% to 40%. By then, all other member states had to contribute towards the rebate, even the poorest – a situation that many saw as unfair. Other major net contributor countries, such as Germany, the Netherlands and Sweden, asked why the UK should get a rebate when they did not. So at a summit in December 2005, the UK sacrificed part of its rebate, accepting it had to do this in order to pay its fair share of the costs of enlargement. The UK rebate in the 2007 budget was around €5.2 billion.

In absolute terms, thanks mainly to farm subsidies, France is largest

Table 14.4 **Financial perspective, 2007 (€m)**

	Administration	Total expenditure	Operating expenditure[a]	National contribution[b]	Share of EU national contribution (%)	Adjusted national contribution[c]	Operating budgetary balance[d]
Austria	20.0	1,598.4	1,578.4	2,017.0	2.16	2,142.2	−563.8
Belgium	3,694.1	5,678.8	1,984.7	2,686.8	2.87	2,853.6	−868.9
Bulgaria	12.2	591.5	579.3	230.0	0.25	244.3	335.0
Czech Republic	15.1	1,721.0	1,705.9	988.2	1.06	1,049.5	656.4
Cyprus	5.7	126.8	121.1	123.9	0.13	131.6	−10.5
Denmark	47.6	1,449.2	1,401.6	1,889.2	2.02	2,006.5	−604.9
Estonia	8.6	376.9	368.3	133.8	0.14	142.1	226.2
Finland	23.1	1,423.4	1,400.3	1,480.5	1.59	1,572.4	−172.1
France	270.6	13,897.2	13,626.6	15,656.4	16.76	16,628.2	−3,001.6
Germany	167.2	12,483.6	12,316.4	18,583.2	19.89	19,736.7	−7,420.3
Greece	29.2	8,429.1	8,399.9	2,790.3	2.99	2,963.5	5,436.4
Hungary	15.4	2,427.6	2,412.2	759.4	0.81	806.5	1,605.7
Ireland	41.7	2,166.7	2125	1,368.3	1.46	1,453.2	671.8
Italy	229.4	11,315.3	11,085.9	12,336.9	13.20	13,102.6	−2,016.7
Latvia	7.7	675.0	667.3	168.1	0.18	178.5	488.8
Lithuania	11.1	1,043.8	1,032.7	225.5	0.24	239.5	793.2
Luxembourg	1,102.1	1,280.9	178.8	276.6	0.29	293.8	−115.0
Malta	13.2	89.3	76.1	45.2	0.05	48.0	28.1
Netherlands	77.7	1,916.4	1,838.7	4,429.3	4.74	4,704.2	−2,865.5
Poland	27.2	7,786.4	7,759.2	2,470.1	2.64	2,623.4	5,135.8
Portugal	24.8	3,904.4	3,879.6	1,323.3	1.42	1,405.4	2,474.2
Romania	18.8	1,602.4	1,583.6	930.3	0.99	988.0	595.6
Slovakia	9.6	1,082.6	1073	428.7	0.46	455.3	617.7
Slovenia	7.5	390.1	382.6	276.8	0.29	294.0	88.6
Spain	67.8	12,795.9	12,728.1	8,548.0	9.15	9,078.6	3,649.5
Sweden	24.0	1,659.0	1635	2,476.7	2.65	2,630.4	−995.4
United Kingdom	140.5	7,412.9	7,272.4	10,771.9	11.53	11,440.5	−4,168.1
EU-27	6,111.8	105,324.5	99,212.7	93,414.5	100	9,9212.7	0

a Total expenditure minus administration. b Does not include traditional own resources (TOR). c Established by multiplying the member state's share of EU national contribution by the EU operating expenditure (€99,212.7m). d Established by subtracting the operating expenditure from the adjusted national contribution.
Source: European Commission

recipient of EU expenditure. European Commission figures show that in 2007 as in 2006, it was ahead of Spain, which was first in 2003, 2004 and 2005. Germany was in third position, followed by Italy, Greece and Poland.

Fraud

It is estimated that fraud perpetrated against the EU budget runs to around €500m each year, covering issues ranging from unpaid VAT to tax evasion to elaborate mafia scams, which cream off the profits of legitimate businesses.

The European Anti-Fraud Office (OLAF) in was set up 1999 to investigate fraud that harms the EU budget. It is an independent investigative body, but it has no judicial or disciplinary powers and it cannot oblige national prosecutors to act. OLAF has 400 staff, of which 160 are investigators. The Lisbon treaty also provides for the post of a European Public Prosecutor to investigate and prepare for court cases concerning EU fraud which cut across state boundaries.

The European Court of Auditors (ECA) has consistently refused to sign off the EU's financial accounts. The ECA's annual report usually criticises nearly every major area of the EU's expenditure, saying there are weaknesses across the board, and complains of neglect and presumed attempts at fraud. For example, the ECA found that in 2007, at least 11% of the €42 billion spent on cohesion should not have been paid out because the EU's rules were not complied with. The European Commission's usual response is that the ECA criticisms of irregularities are more about procedure than fraud; but it still blames member states for most audit failings.

15 Trade

Removal of tariff barriers

The Treaty of Rome provided for the removal of all tariff barriers inside the Community within 12 years, and in fact the original six member states completed the process 18 months early, in 1968. The consequence was an enormous and sustained growth in intra-EU trade. Later entrants proceeded in stages: the UK, Ireland and Denmark by 1977; and Greece by 1986. Spain and Portugal, which joined the Community in 1986, removed all their tariffs against other EC members by the end of 1992. Austria, Finland and Sweden had already removed theirs long before joining the EU in 1995. As internal tariffs were removed, a common external tariff was introduced against the goods of other countries. Originally set at an average of around 10%, this was gradually reduced, following successive rounds of negotiations in the General Agreement on Tariffs and Trade (GATT), and the weighted average of EU customs duties fell to just under 5%, a little lower than in the United States but higher than in Japan. Under the GATT Uruguay round agreement reached in December 1993, this weighted average has fallen to around 3%, and it should be further reduced under continuing negotiations in the World Trade Organisation (WTO), which replaced the GATT in 1995.

Soon after the Uruguay round, the EU announced plans for another set of global trade talks and tried to rustle up support from the rest of the WTO. But negotiating fatigue, lingering suspicion about who was benefiting from the WTO, weak public support and organisational incompetence all led to the fiasco of the WTO's Seattle meeting in late 1999. Besieged by rioting activists, the Seattle talks broke down in mutual recrimination between rich and poor nations about how to take the agenda forward.

The EU was better prepared in November 2001, at the WTO ministerial meeting in Doha, Qatar. After spending much of the previous two years alliance building with poorer nations, Pascal Lamy, the EU trade commissioner, helped usher in the so-called Doha Development Agenda, a wide-ranging negotiating plan which was scheduled to end in 2005. One of the main sticking points in Doha was, unsurprisingly, agriculture. The delegates eventually accepted a text with the commitment to phasing out agriculture subsidies, but it was preceded by the words "without prejudging the outcome of the negotiations", meaning that there was no need actually to achieve that aim. Everything then seemed to fit into place: the environmental plans pushed by the EU were cleared, as were new issues of investment, competition and procurement. But a ministerial meeting in Cancun, Mexico, in September 2003 collapsed in disarray as ministers failed to reach agreement on their targets for the Doha round. After that, the Doha round seemed to stumble from one crisis to another. At a ministerial meeting in Hong Kong, in December 2005, only meagre progress was made. Negotiations were suspended for six months in 2006, and resumed in 2007, but at a meeting in Geneva in July 2008 they collapsed, mainly as a result of farming disputes involving the United States, India and China. Since then, there have been intermittent calls to renew negotiations, and the G20 summit of world leaders in London in 2009 included a pledge to complete the Doha round.

Member states represented by EU

The treaty stipulated that the European Commission should represent its members in matters of external trade, and the member states formally transferred some of their sovereign powers to the Community. As a result some 165 countries established diplomatic relations with the EC. Most of these have embassies or missions in Brussels which often double up with embassies accredited to Belgium, although the EU role is in most cases by far the more important. The EU, normally represented by the commission, speaks for the member states in the WTO and the North Atlantic Fisheries Organisation.

The EU has signed agreements with most countries in the world as well as some 30 multilateral agreements. Most of them concern EU trade, and their effect has been to profoundly modify its pattern. The trading arrangements fall into four main categories: European Economic Area; other developed countries; former communist countries; developing countries.

EFTA

EU's largest trading partner

In 1973 the EC formed an industrial free-trade area with the then seven countries of the European Free Trade Association (EFTA): Austria, Finland, Iceland, Liechtenstein, Norway, Sweden and Switzerland. Customs duties and restrictions on trade in manufactured goods were abolished, and some reciprocal concessions were made for agricultural produce. This effectively extended the size of the common market for manufactures to 370m people. EFTA was the EU's largest trading partner.

European Economic Area

Following the launch of the EC's single market programme, the EFTA countries expressed a desire for closer association with the Community. Negotiations began in December 1989 to establish a European Economic Area (EEA) in which the EFTA states would assume many of the obligations and disciplines of EC membership, including the acceptance of the free movement of capital, persons and services, in return for sharing in most of the expected benefits of the single market programme. The EEA should have started on January 1st 1993, but the agreement was turned down in a referendum in Switzerland in December 1992. Following further negotiations with the remaining countries it only came into effect in January 1994, with Switzerland left out and Liechtenstein's membership deferred to a later date (1995). For three of the countries concerned, however, the EEA acted as no more than a staging post on the way to full EU membership. Austria, Finland and Sweden became members of the EU in January 1995. Norway also negotiated full membership, but its voters rejected the move in a referendum in December 1994, so it remains in the EEA, along with Iceland and Liechtenstein. The Swiss government negotiated a series of bilateral agreements with the EU, its membership application being indefinitely suspended. (See also pages 270–71.) Switzerland is now the EU's second largest trading partner, after the United States.

Other developed countries

North America

Trade relations with the United States are largely governed by agreements in the GATT and the WTO. Both sides profess free-trade principles, but each often accuses the other of protectionist tendencies and/or of giving unfair advantages to its own exporters through state subsidies. Disputes concerning agriculture and steel, in particular, became increasingly frequent during the 1980s, leading on occasion to the introduction of counter-measures which were usually withdrawn when the other side belatedly offered concessions. Similar disputes concerning such topics as EU restrictions on the importation of hormone-treated meat and discrimination against banana imports by US companies in Latin America have more recently been resolved by the disputes procedure of the WTO, whose judgments on both these issues favoured the US position. A full-scale trade war, which would be as deeply damaging to both sides as to world trade as a whole, has several times seemed a distinct possibility, but so far at least cooler counsels have prevailed when tension has mounted.

Perhaps the most damaging recent dispute erupted in October 2004, when the United States announced it would challenge the EU's subsidies to Airbus at the WTO and the EU countered that it would seek action against US aid to rival Boeing. While both sides say they want to contain the dispute, it has remained a source of tension, particularly as Airbus has gradually caught up with Boeing in aircraft sales, and in 2003 overtook it. The United States claims Airbus has received more than $15 billion in loans since 1967. The EU's counter claim is that Boeing has benefited since 1992 from $23 billion in indirect aid through state-level tax breaks, military research and Japanese aid to suppliers. A 1992 EU–US bilateral agreement permits repayable EU government loans to Airbus to develop new aircraft, covering up to 33% of the contract value. It also set guidelines for indirect subsidies at 3% of turnover.

Canada is in a similar position to the United States, although in 1976 a framework agreement was concluded which established mechanisms for commercial and economic co-operation. In November 1990 a transatlantic declaration was signed between the EC, the United States and Canada, providing for closer co-operation in areas of common interest and a more permanent dialogue to resolve or contain the trade disputes that would inevitably continue to occur.

Japan

The EU's trading relations with Japan have been difficult, largely owing to the substantial trade deficit. Japan imports half as much from the Union than it exports to it. This imbalance is particularly painful because Japanese exports are focused on a fairly small number of sectors – cars, electronics, audio-visual equipment, computers and telecommunications – where European firms have been struggling to maintain or achieve a viable share in the world market. Although Japanese tariffs are, on average, lower than the EU's, the Union has repeatedly called for the removal of non-tariff barriers and for more decisive action by the Japanese authorities to open up their domestic market to foreign imports.

High-level meetings with Japanese ministers and officials take place regularly, as well as quadrilateral meetings that include the United States and Canada. The pressure applied at these meetings has resulted in Japanese initiatives to encourage importers and to ease or remove impediments in their domestic markets. The EU's trade deficit with Japan has shrunk over the years, however. In 2008, it was €32.4 billion – down from €46.6 billion in 2000 – with imports of €74.8 billion and exports of €42.4 billion.

Australasia

Australia and New Zealand are important trading partners, supplying food and raw materials and taking mainly manufactured goods from the Union. Australian and New Zealand food exports to the UK were adversely affected when the UK joined the EC. New Zealand was partially compensated by the award of temporary export quotas for cheese and butter. The cheese quota expired after five years, but the arrangements for importing a limited amount of butter have been extended, despite the EU's own excess production.

In 2008, the EU and Australia signed a partnership agreement that includes trade. It aims to boost trade in industrial products by reducing technical barriers, including assessment procedures. This covers mutual recognition of conformity assessment procedures, with the objective of reducing the costs of testing and certification of products exported to and imported from Australia. Since 1999 the EU and New Zealand have been bound by a similar bilateral agreement that aims to facilitate merchandise trade.

Former communist countries

Trade with the countries of central and eastern Europe before the collapse of communist rule in 1988–90 was hampered by the lack of normal trading relations and by the inherent inefficiencies of command economies. After the collapse of the Soviet Union in 1991, trade and co-operation agreements were signed with Poland, Hungary, Czechoslovakia, Bulgaria and Romania. At the same time considerable economic and technical aid was made available and humanitarian aid was given to Bulgaria, Romania and the former states of the Soviet Union.

Association agreements
Negotiations began in 1990–91 with a view to concluding far-

reaching association agreements (known as Europe Agreements) with the new democracies of central and eastern Europe. These would provide tariff-free access for most of their manufacturing goods while maintaining restrictions on their free export of textiles and agricultural products. The first three agreements were concluded with Czechoslovakia, Hungary and Poland in December 1991. Less comprehensive agreements were signed with other former communist countries, from the Balkans to the Baltic, the Caucasus and even Central Asia. Some of these were effective stepping stones for eventual EU membership. For the western Balkans, all countries have been offered Stabilisation and Association Agreements (SAAs) and autonomous trade preferences and have a clear EU perspective. The south Caucasus countries of Armenia, Azerbaijan and Georgia have seen trade with the EU intensify since their inclusion in the European Neighbourhood Policy in 2004, and the Eastern Partnership initiative in May 2009 could boost it further. Partnership and Cooperation Agreements (PCAs) have been signed with Central Asian countries, but they are non-preferential.

Developing countries

The Mediterranean

The EU has signed association agreements with all Mediterranean countries excluding Syria. These give duty-free access to all, or most, of their industrial products, specific concessions for some of their agricultural produce and a certain amount of financial aid in the form of grants and loans. A similar agreement has been concluded with the countries belonging to the Gulf Co-operation Council.

In 1987 Turkey applied for full membership (see page 268–9), and entered into a customs union with the EU on December 31st 1995. An earlier two-stage agreement for a customs union, including agricultural produce, came fully into force during 1997.

The ACP

EU relations with the 78 African, Caribbean and Pacific countries (ACP) are governed by the 20-year Partnership Agreement, signed in Cotonou, Benin, on June 23rd 2000 (see pages 249–50 and Appendix 7). All the ACP countries, except Cuba, are signatories to the Cotonou Agreement: 48 African countries, covering all sub-Saharan Africa, 15 countries in the Caribbean and 14 states in the Pacific. Of the 49 least developed countries covered by the EU's "Everything But Arms" initiative, 40 are ACP. South Africa is a signatory of the Cotonou Agreement but its membership of the ACP group is qualified. The new trade regime envisaged by the Cotonou Agreement represents a radically different perspective for ACP partners. To promote sustainable development and the eradication of poverty, ACP and the EU agreed to conclude WTO-compatible Economic Partnership Agreements (EPAs) that will progressively remove barriers to trade between them and enhance co-operation in all areas relevant to trade. Negotiations on EPAs began in 2002, but in 2007 many ACP nations balked at the pace of liberalisation in the deal, and by 2009 it was still incomplete.

In 2007, EU trade with the ACP countries totalled €80 billion, with the EU importing some €40.2 billion and exporting some €39.7 billion. For most of the ACP countries – and for virtually all African ACP countries – the EU is the main trading partner, representing about one-third of both imports and exports. ACP countries already export about 93% of their goods, in value terms, duty free into the EU. Imports and exports are both roughly 2.75% of the EU total. This continues a longer-term gradual decline since 2000, strongly linked to commodity prices.

Asia

Countries such as India, Bangladesh, Pakistan and Sri Lanka benefit from the EU's generalised system of preferences (GSP), which gives developing countries duty-free access for finished and semi-finished goods. The EU also has separate economic and development agreements with India and Pakistan, and a co-operation agreement with the ten-nation Association of South-East Asian Nations (ASEAN). The first Asia-Europe (ASEM) summit meeting, in Bangkok in March 1996, which included Japan, China and South Korea as well as the seven ASEAN countries, established a framework for continuing consultation at heads of government level every two years. ASEM now includes meetings of economic ministers, finance ministers and the Asia-Europe Business Forum (AEBF). ASEM leaders have also agreed a Trade Facilitation Action Plan (TFAP), aimed at the reduction and removal of non-tariff barriers to trade between the two regions, and an Investment Promotion Action Plan (IPAP), aimed at promoting two-way investment flows between Asia and Europe.

Latin America

There are economic and trade co-operation agreements with most of the principal countries, including the Mercosur association, the five members

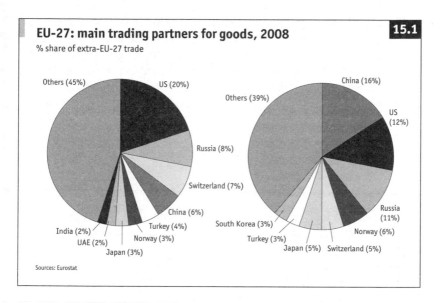

EU-27: main trading partners for goods, 2008
% share of extra-EU-27 trade

Others (45%) US (20%) China (16%)
Others (39%) US (12%)
Russia (8%)
Switzerland (7%)
Russia (11%)
China (6%)
South Korea (3%) Norway (6%)
India (2%) Turkey (4%)
UAE (2%) Norway (3%) Turkey (3%)
Japan (3%) Japan (5%) Switzerland (5%)

Sources: Eurostat

15.1

of the Andean Pact and the six countries of the Central American isthmus. All Latin American countries benefit from generalised preferences.

The EU is Latin America's second most important trading partner – and the most important trading partner for Mercosur, Chile and the Andean Group. The EU has gradually strengthened its economic and trade links with Latin America, resulting in trade figures that quadrupled between 1990 and 2007.

Trade policy

Industrial products

The external trading policy of the EU is based on free trade, or the aspiration to achieve it, so far as industrial products are concerned, although this attitude has been greatly modified in relation to Japan. Notable exceptions are shipbuilding, steel and textiles. Textile imports into the EU were regulated by the Multi-Fibre Arrangement (MFA), a deal conceived in 1973 to open up markets to developing country suppliers while the ailing textile industries of the industrialised world were slowly run down. Under the Uruguay round agreement the MFA was gradually dismantled over a period of ten years until 2005 and the EU market progressively opened up to textile imports.

In the mid-1990s, the EU also began negotiating Mutual Recognition Agreements (MRAS) with its main trading partners. These were designed to cut red tape in safety and testing standards by setting single certification procedures for various products. For example, with the United States, it meant companies were able to test their products in the EU according to American rules of certification to gain access to the American market, and vice versa. The EU has MRAS with the United States in a number of sectors such as chemicals, medical devices, foodstuffs, pharmaceuticals, automobiles and tyres, and cosmetics. The EU also entered into similar agreements with Australia, Canada, Japan and New Zealand.

Agriculture

Agricultural trade is governed by protectionism. Apart from special arrangements to buy quotas of sugar from India and the ACP countries at guaranteed prices, virtually no temperate agricultural products are imported into the EU since the agricultural levies (see Chapter 20) effectively make them uncompetitive. This will be less true in the future as a result of the Uruguay round. The EU remains, however, the world's largest food importer. It still has a substantial deficit in its agricultural trade because of its purchases of tropical products and animal feed.

In 2001, the EU opened up its market to exports from the world's poorest 48 countries under the "Everything But Arms" (EBA) initiative.

Trade defence

The EU maintains a number of its own instruments to combat what it might see as unfair trade, most importantly anti-dumping and anti-subsidy measures. Anti-dumping measures are used against predatory pricing, when a manufacturer in one country exports a product at a price which is either below the price it charges in its home market or is below its costs of production. Countervailing measures are used when government subsidies are determined as the factor behind the dumping. They are applied only after a commission investigation – using complex calculations – into whether dumping is taking place and whether the dumped imports are causing material injury to the EU producers, importers, users and consumers.

EU the world's leading trader

The result of these arrangements is that the EU is the world's leading trader. It needs to trade to this extent because of its paucity of energy and raw materials. Nearly 45% of the EU's energy needs are met by imports, as well as three-quarters of other vital raw materials. In order to pay for these it needs to export mainly finished products to the rest of the world. Although internal trade between member states has expanded enormously since the establishment of the Community in 1958, its share of world trade has somewhat declined in the face of much stronger competition from Japan and from newly industrialised countries such as South Korea, Brazil and Singapore.

16 The single market

"Common market" proved elusive

The creation of a single European economic area based on a common market was a fundamental objective of the Treaty of Rome. But by the 1980s, there was growing concern that the Community was still far from being the "common market" that it was usually called: there were still too many frontier controls, businesses and individuals faced obstacles in other member states, and different taxes distorted trade.

- Frontier formalities delayed and added to the cost of transporting goods from one member state to another.
- It was still impossible for many EC citizens to pursue their professional duties in another member state, despite the provisions of the Rome treaty concerning free movement.
- Service industries such as insurance were prevented from operating on a Community-wide basis.
- Differential indirect tax rates distorted intra-Community trade.
- Public procurement contracts in each member state were effectively reserved for national suppliers rather than being put out to open tender.

The European Council takes action

In 1985, it was decided to instruct the commission to draw up a detailed programme with a specific timetable for completing the single market by 1992. At the same time, the Community's leaders summoned an inter-governmental conference to consider amending the Rome treaty to enable qualified majority voting to be applied to most of the internal market issues which had previously required unanimity; this eventually led to the Single European Act, which came into force on July 1st 1987 (see pages 64–5).

White paper on single market drawn up

Lord Cockfield, the commissioner responsible for the internal market, produced a document listing some 300 actions which would need to be taken if the single market was to be achieved. These were divided into three categories:

- ▪ **Physical barriers.** The white paper set as its target the total abolition, not simply the alleviation, of frontier controls by 1992.
- ▪ **Technical barriers.** These were barriers created by different national regulations and standards. The commission proposed that its laborious programme to harmonise national standards for thousands of different manufacturing processes should be replaced by a system of mutual recognition of national standards, pending the adoption of European standards. Other proposals included:
  - – the liberalisation of public procurement;
  - – the establishment of a common market for services such as transport, banking, insurance and information marketing;
  - – the free movement of capital throughout the Community;
  - – the removal of legal restraints on the formation of EC-wide companies;
  - – the adoption of a Community trademark system.
- ▪ **Fiscal barriers.** These mainly concerned the approximation of VAT and excise-duty rates. The commission did not consider that total harmonisation was necessary and was content to see rates varying by +/–2.5% of whatever target rate or norm was chosen.

The 300 measures were later consolidated into 282 proposed directives or regulations. By the target date of December 31st 1992 no fewer than 258 of these (over 90%) had been adopted by the Council of Ministers, and 79% were already being implemented by the member states.

The Schengen Agreement

The biggest failure was that, although all customs controls on goods were abolished at internal EU frontiers on January 1st 1993, systematic passport checks continued to be made at many frontier crossings, particularly at seaports and airports. Already several years earlier some governments, notably that of the UK, had argued that to abolish border checks would cause problems relating to the control of terrorism, illegal immigrants and drug-trafficking, and the containment of animal-borne diseases. It was in order to bypass this opposition that, in June 1990, five member states decided to go ahead on their own with an agreement to do away with all their internal EC frontiers, while strengthening controls at external borders. Thus the Schengen Agreement, named after the Luxembourg village where it was signed, was concluded by Belgium,

France, Germany, Luxembourg and the Netherlands. Two important areas covered by the agreement are as follows:

◪ **External borders.** The free movement of people is guaranteed under the agreement, which removes checks at most of the EU's internal frontiers and strengthens controls at the EU's external borders. There are no border controls when travelling by land between the Schengen members. But passport and visa requirements continue to apply at the external Schengen borders for non-EU member nationals.

◪ **Judicial matters.** To prevent criminals of all sorts turning the system to their advantage, the EU responded by creating a system of frontier-free police and criminal justice co-operation. Europol, the European police force, is part of that response. So is the Schengen Information System (sis), whereby national police exchange information on wanted or suspected wrongdoers. Under the Eurojust project, member states second senior prosecutors, policemen and lawyers to a central team working to fight organised crime. Schengen has also simplified extradition procedures, and makes it possible for people convicted in one country to serve their sentences in another.

The agreement got under way towards the end of 1994. By 2009, 22 of the 27 member states had agreed to join, together with Switzerland, Norway and Iceland from outside the EU (Bulgaria, Cyprus and Romania still had to implement the agreement). The only member state that will not give up its border controls is the UK, but Ireland also stayed out of the Schengen Agreement because it wished to maintain existing arrangements whereby Irish citizens do not face passport checks when entering the UK and vice versa.

After 1992

The 1992 programme was launched in the belief that it would bring substantial economic benefits to the countries and people of the Community. In October 1996 the commission issued a progress report, which showed that in the first three and a half years, GDP had risen by between 1.1% and 1.5%, investment was 2.7% higher and up to 900,000 extra jobs had been created. Inflation had also markedly been reduced, but there were several black spots largely owing to the failure of some member states adequately to enforce the single market legislation. This was especially true with regard to public procurement. The failure to agree on a common collection system for VAT meant that suppliers still had to face a mass of burdensome paperwork, and the lack of progress on tax harmonisation has undoubtedly acted as a restriction on trade.

The Lisbon strategy

By 2000, it was clear there was much unfinished business left from the supposed completion of the single market in 1992, with the European Commission launching a staggering 1,500 lawsuits against EU governments for failing to respect single-market rules.

At the Lisbon summit in March 2000, EU leaders agreed an agenda that aimed to tackle financial barriers, streamline labour markets and transform the EU into the most competitive region in the world. The Lisbon strategy set the target of making the EU the most competitive economic area in the world by the year 2010. The leaders agreed to create at least 20m jobs in a decade, matching America's job-creation and technology-harnessing record with practical steps. Chief among these is dismantling local telephone monopolies – opening the "local loop" to competition, to use the jargon – so that rival phone and cable operators can provide high-speed services directly to homes and install their equipment in the incumbent's local exchanges. The summit also called for EU-wide legislation establishing a legal framework for e-commerce, copyright, e-money and the distance-selling of financial services.

The leaders also agreed to flank the measures with the European Social Policy Agenda, which aims to both liberalise labour markets and provide crucial guarantees for workers (see page 177). The legislation pushed through afterwards included a consultation directive that gives unions a say in management decisions, including lay-offs and company restructuring, full rights to temporary workers, and gender and race laws. Lisbon also launched the idea of a regular spring summit on economic and social affairs to establish a strategy for the year's economic and social policy, give a mandate to EU ministers in the various Council formations and ensure that decisions are effectively implemented.

One of the key decisions at Lisbon was to endorse the Financial Services Action Plan (FSAP). This includes some 42 measures, from binding regulations to voluntary codes of conduct, covering the entire financial services field from securities and banking to insurance, and from financial institutions to retail customers. The results include the Money Laundering Directive, an agreement on cross-border payments regulation and adoption of the European Company Statute.

For capital markets, a specific blueprint emerged in February 2001 from Baron Alexandre Lamfalussy, a former Belgian central banker and president of the European Monetary Institute. The two new committees on securities – the ESC and a Committee of European Securities Regulators (CESR) – were key demands of the Lamfalussy report.

However, despite the heady language of the Lisbon strategy, it was soon clear that it would not meet its objective. In 2005, the strategy was refocused on actions that promote growth and jobs in a manner that is fully consistent with the objective of sustainable development.

At the same time, the commission launched a major review of the single market to assess how it had evolved since 1992 and identify remaining gaps. It found delays had affected financial services and transport, where separate national markets still existed. The fragmented nature of national tax systems also put a brake on market integration and efficiency. The commission also said it had "witnessed the proliferation of a range of practices at the retail end of the market which seem to be distorting consumer choice and behaviour and might even act as barriers to effective competition".

Services Directive

In 2005, the European Parliament approved a law boosting competition in services, widely seen as one of the most important EU directives for a decade. The Services Directive aims to make it easier for caterers, software companies, plumbers and other service providers to do business across European borders. It is designed to create a free market in services – the fourth "basic freedom" of the EU, after free movement of persons, goods and capital. The law was at first opposed by some EU member states, afraid of being undercut by countries with lower labour costs. However, they and MEPs eventually backed it, but excluded a range of services. The directive will not affect local labour law or collective agreements in member states, and does not include health care, social services, public transport, financial services and some other areas. MEPs also removed the controversial "country of origin" principle, which would have allowed businesses to operate in another member state under the rules of their home country. The agreed version is scheduled to take effect from the end of 2009.

The single market and the economic crisis

When the financial and economic crisis hit at the end of 2008, the single market found itself facing intense political pressures from certain member states seeking the return of protectionist policies. In February 2009, the French president, Nicolas Sarkozy, said he wanted French car-makers to build factories at home rather than abroad, which prompted an emergency summit aimed at re-establishing the EU's commitment to the single market (Sarkozy later denied that his comments were protectionist). The single market also faced criticism: some said the crisis was exacerbated by the liberalisation of various financial service rules, allowing rapacious speculators to lose far more money than they should have. But others said the single market was a valuable shield, preventing beggar-thy-neighbour policies in which countries try to pass problems on to neighbours instead of tackling them themselves.

The commission insisted that the single market was more valuable than ever during the downturn, but it also took the opportunity to propose new rules that would complete the Financial Services Action Plan and strengthen regulatory oversight. Former IMF managing director Jacques de Larosière was called on to chair an expert group to look into financial sector reforms. His proposals, which were broadly agreed by EU leaders in 2009, call for:

- a European Systemic Risk Board, whose job would be to spot any threats to financial stability across the EU;
- a European System of Financial Supervisors, whose job would be to monitor individual financial firms.

17 Competition policy

There was little point in creating a customs union, the EC's founding fathers thought, if free competition between firms from different member states could be thwarted by cartels and restrictive agreements. Thus Articles 85 and 86 were inserted into the Treaty of Rome. The first outlaws deals between companies to fix prices, share out markets, limit production, technical development and investment, and other restrictive practices. The second bans "abuses of dominant position" by firms or groups of firms. Furthermore, Articles 92–94 forbid government subsidies that distort or threaten to distort competition.

The commission has wide powers

The power to prevent such abuses is in the hands of the commission, which can act without reference to the Council of Ministers, although its decisions may be, and often are, challenged before the Court of Justice by the companies concerned. The commission acts either on its own initiative or following complaints by member states, companies or individuals. Several hundred cases are dealt with each year involving firms with household names as well as more obscure ones – some in both categories having their headquarters outside the EU – and covering a range of industries and products.

In many instances cases are resolved by voluntary policy changes by the countries or companies concerned. A famous early example was when IBM was accused, in 1980, of abusing a dominant position in the computer market by withholding information on new products and "bundling" its products (that is, selling several of them together in a package, so that customers must either take all of them or none). After spending a small fortune in lawyers' fees, IBM eventually backed down in 1984 and came to a voluntary agreement with the commission to modify its trading practices.

In other cases the commission finds in favour of the accused or it finds the case proved, and orders policy changes or imposes fines, sometimes running to millions of euros (there is no limit to such fines, although they may not amount to more than 10% of the actual sales affected by the abuse with which a company is charged). The most serious intervention so far took place in March 2004, when the commission ruled that Microsoft had abused its dominant position on the software market. It ordered Microsoft to sell a version of its main Windows software without the movie and music playing Windows Media Player, and to disclose more information to rivals about how its server software works. The commission also set a then-record fine of €497.2m, to which it later added €1.18 billion for not complying with the ruling.

The commission has wide powers of investigation. Its staff can visit companies without warning to demand access to documents and to take away photocopies as evidence. It then holds hearings with the companies concerned to discuss the case before giving its verdict. Convicted firms may appeal to the Court of Justice against both the conviction and the size of the fine, which has sometimes been reduced on appeal. The court has built up a large body of case law. EU competition law takes precedence over national law and is directly applicable in member states. Businesses and individuals believing themselves to be victims of infringements of EU competition rules can bring direct actions before national courts.

Any agreements that may fall foul of treaty provisions must be notified in advance to the commission. Companies may apply for a "negative clearance", which means that free competition is not threatened, or for an "exemption", which spares a restrictive agreement from the overall ban if substantial public benefits (as defined in the treaty) can be demonstrated. The commission is empowered to declare illegal and order the termination of an agreement or other unacceptable practices at any time.

The commission has banned the following types of agreements:

- **Market-sharing agreements.** For example, the quinine cartel, which led the commission to impose its first fines (1969); the car glass producers' cartel, where Asahi, Pilkington, Saint-Gobain and Soliver were fined over €1.3 billion for illegal market sharing (2008); and the 1975 deal between German energy giant E.On and Gaz de France (GDF) Suez to carve up gas markets between them, which cost them €553m in fines (2009).
- **Price-fixing agreements.** For example, in 1998 British Sugar and three other firms, controlling 90% of the UK market, were fined €50.2m for concluding price-fixing agreements for white granulated sugar. In 2001, eight firms were fined €855.2m for fixing prices and sales quotas of vitamins. And in 2007, the Otis, KONE, Schindler and ThyssenKrupp groups were fined over €990m for a lifts and escalators cartel.

- **Exclusive purchase agreements.** These have been banned for a wide variety of products ranging from gramophone records to heating equipment. Computer chipmaker Intel was fined a record €1.06 billion in 2009 for squeezing out competition by paying PC-makers and retailers not to use rival chips.
- **Agreements on industrial and commercial property rights.** The exclusive use of patents, trademarks or works of art is not necessarily exempt from competition rules. In a 1982 case, involving maize seed, the Court of Justice ruled against the total territorial protection granted by a patent licensing contract.
- **Exclusive or selective distribution agreements.** For example, those, such as in the motor car trade, which seek to restrict parallel imports. Among companies which have been heavily fined, or otherwise penalised, for applying such agreements have been Ford, AEG-Telefunken and the Moët-Hennessy group. In 1998 Volkswagen, for example, was fined €102m for prohibiting its Italian dealers selling cars to foreign buyers.

Enforcement has become more rigorous

The commission was somewhat lax in applying the competition policy until 1977, since when there has been a substantial increase in its activity. This is largely because the individual commissioners holding the competition portfolio since that year have been far keener on exercising their powers than their predecessors. The commission has, however, continued to use its power to give industrial exemptions or en bloc waivers, where it judged that the threat to competition was small or non-existent and was outweighed by the likely public benefits. It has been particularly concerned not to hamper co-operation between small and medium-sized enterprises, and it has identified a number of types of agreement which it feels should escape the general ban. These are as follows:

- Exclusive representation contracts given to trade representatives.
- Small-scale agreements, based on turnover (not more than 50m ecus) and market share (not more than 5%).
- Subcontracting agreements.
- Information exchanges between companies, joint studies and joint use of plant.

The commission also takes account of the economic climate facing companies seeking individual exemptions. If there is a long-term down-turn in demand for a product, it has been known to authorise firms to co-ordinate a run-down in overcapacity. This occurred, for example, in the synthetic fibre sector in 1984.

Jurisdiction over mergers

Until 1990 the commission had no specific power to prevent mergers, although it intervened on several occasions, using the general authority given to it under Articles 85 and 86 of the Rome treaty, when it believed that they posed a threat to effective competition in the Community. As long ago as 1973 it sought agreement on a regulation which would give it powers to vet cross-border mergers in advance, while leaving member states to police mergers within their own territories. The proposal was revived in 1987, and finally came into effect on September 21st 1990. It gave the commission jurisdiction over larger-scale company mergers and takeovers affecting more than one member state and exceeding certain thresholds. The main thresholds concerned are:

- €5 billion for the worldwide turnover of the companies concerned;
- €250m for the individual turnover within the EU of at least two of the companies concerned, while no more than two-thirds of this turnover should be concentrated within a single member state.

Projected mergers which meet these criteria must be reported in advance to the commission, which will decide within one month whether there is a possibility that they would breach the competition rules. If no such possibility is discerned, the merger may go ahead; otherwise an investigation will be launched which must be completed within a further four months.

Subsequently, the number of notifications of mergers substantially increased. In 1997 the number of notifications rose to 172, and 135 final decisions were adopted. One of these was Boeing's acquisition of the McDonnell Douglas Corporation, which came under the commission's jurisdiction because of the extensive European operations of the two aircraft companies. The merger was eventually approved, but only after Boeing had greatly modified its original proposal and had given commitments concerning several specific elements.

The numbers kept rising, and by 2001, the commission had received

335 notifications and adopted 322 final decisions. The most controversial decision of the year – like McDonnell Douglas/Boeing – concerned two American companies and the avionics sector: General Electric's (GE) planned takeover of Honeywell. The case also exposed a difference in cultures, with the EU's competition policy geared towards preventing dominant positions and the far more laissez-faire American antitrust rules. The €47 billion merger was cleared easily enough in the United States, and Jack Welch, GE's ebullient chairman, assumed the EU decision would be a mere formality. But the commission thought otherwise, saying the bid would create an unhealthily dominant aerospace giant, giving it the leverage to eliminate competition. It was the first time the commission had killed off a merger between two American companies that had already been approved in the United States.

The merger between music groups Sony and Bertelsmann in 2004 created different problems. It would reduce the music sector's five "majors" to four, and – according to critics such as independent labels – would further cement an effective cartel. The commission's own statement of objections (SO) on the deal said it would strengthen a collective dominant position in the market for recorded music and in the wholesale market for licences for online music. Nonetheless, its final verdict was that there was no "smoking gun" to prove such a cartel, and the deal was cleared.

The commission has been notified of 4,129 mergers between September 1990, when the merger regulation first came into force, and July 2009. The number of annual notifications fluctuates, from 335 in 2001, down to 211 in 2003 and up to 402 in 2007. From 1990 to July 2009, the commission cleared a total of 3,574 cases after only a routine one month/six weeks' review: more than 95% of mergers examined by the commission are cleared in the first-phase examination. Only 20 mergers have been blocked since 1990, representing less than 0.5% of the total notified concentrations.

Government subsidies

Government subsidies to either publicly owned or private firms are normally banned if they distort or threaten to distort competition. Some types of aid are exempt from control, including: special help at times of natural disasters; aid to depressed regions; and aid to promote new economic activities.

Member states are supposed to notify the commission of all aid planned, and it decides whether the aid can be exempted from the treaty rules. It has the power to order the repayment of unauthorised aid and may impose fines on member states that break the rules. Two examples occurred during 1988, when Sir Leon Brittan, the competition commissioner, required both the French and the UK governments to secure repayment of illegal state aids that they had provided. The French government reluctantly agreed to reclaim FFr6 billion (about £600m) paid to Renault, which had then failed to fulfil the conditions the commission had attached to the project. The UK government was also forced to seek repayment of the secret "sweeteners", worth £44m, that it had paid to British Aerospace as an inducement to buy the Rover car company.

During the 1970s and early 1980s the commission approved guidelines for state aid to industries that were especially hard hit by the recession. It insisted that such aid must be exceptional, limited in duration and geared directly to the objective of restoring long-term viability by reducing capacity in struggling sectors. In four industries most severely affected – shipbuilding, textiles, synthetic fibres and steel (see Chapter 25) – special provisions were made.

In principle, the commission believes that all categories of state aid should be kept to a minimum, and as it seeks to enforce the rules more rigorously they are increasingly coming into conflict with national governments under political pressure to maintain employment opportunities for their own citizens.

This was the case in late 2008 and early 2009, when many EU governments sought clearance for subsidy schemes to support their ailing car industries. The French president, Nicolas Sarkozy, controversially suggested that in order to secure French government aid, French companies like Renault and Peugeot-Citroën should move production out of their east European factories and back to France; he eventually backed down.

New challenges

In 2002, the commission's antitrust actions came under serious attack from the EU courts, which overturned three of its rulings blocking mergers. In one case involving French electrical goods makers Schneider and Legrand, the court called into question the commission's economic reasoning, saying there were "several obvious errors, omissions and contradictions".

This prompted radical new reforms to competition policy and law, which came into force on May 1st 2004. The reforms made the merger control mechanism more like that in the United States, with more oversight, economic and consumer assessments, and stricter deadlines. Under the new rules, the first-phase investigation takes 25 working days, and a second-phase in-depth probe takes 90 working days, but both timetables can be extended. The reforms also returned many powers to national authorities: companies no longer need to notify the commission about certain arrangements with other companies, and the onus is on businesses to decide if they are acting within the law.

In December 2003, the European Parliament also ended almost 15 years of gridlock on cross-border takeovers when it approved the Takeover Directive, which lays down rules aligning Europe more closely with US corporate practices. The rules say boards of directors of firms can take key decisions on hostile takeover bids without shareholders' backing. However, Frits Bolkestein, then internal market commissioner, maintained that the compromise eventually agreed watered down most of the key proposals, saying it was "not really worth the paper it is written on".

18 Economic and financial policy

Lack of co-ordination in economic policy

Although Article 103 of the Rome treaty requires member states to determine their economic policies in consultation with each other, as yet little co-ordination has been achieved. In so far as most governments followed rather similar policies in the 1970s and 1980s, it was because they were reacting to worldwide economic pressures rather than a result of joint planning of their overall strategies. Thus despite regular discussions between ministers, there was no common European policy on pooling energy supplies, containing inflation or reducing unemployment. The annual economic reports produced by the commission gave advice to national governments, but were by no means binding upon them.

Broad discussions do take place between the heads of government at meetings of the European Council, when "the economic and social situation in the world and in the Community" is invariably an item on the agenda. More detailed exchanges take place between economic and finance ministers, who meet approximately every two months in Ecofin[1] councils, and sometimes more frequently in the Monetary and Economic Policy committees. The governors of the central banks of the member states also meet regularly in their own consultative committee. National leaders are thus well informed about each other's views and policies, and no doubt take them into account to some extent, but each government remains firmly in charge of its own economic policy. That was the case even in late 2008 and early 2009, when the economic downturn began to hit and many EU member states arranged stimulus packages and bail-out plans for banks and other vulnerable sectors: there were token gestures, but no systematic efforts aimed at co-ordinating the different national measures.

EU element is ancillary

Nor is the EU's budget sufficiently large to have a significant macroeconomic effect on the west European economy in a manner comparable with the way in which national budgets point their economies in an expansionist or deflationary direction. In so far as there is an EU element in the economic policy of member states, it is undoubtedly an ancillary one, and seems likely to remain so for the foreseeable future.

Loans made by EU institutions

There are two areas, however, where the EU undoubtedly plays a significant part. One is in raising loans on behalf of member states, the other in regulating fluctuations in exchange rates. During 1996, for example, the institutions made well over 23 billion ecus available, principally through the following channels:

- The European Investment Bank (see Chapter 11) lent some 21 billion ecus within the Union. Nearly three-quarters went towards developing the economy of the less prosperous regions.
- The European Coal and Steel Community lent approximately 280 million ecus, mainly for productive investment in the coal and steel industries.
- Euratom, which has a loan facility of 4 billion ecus mainly for investments in the nuclear energy and nuclear fuels sectors, has made no new loans since 1992 because of the unfavourable situation in the industry.
- The Edinburgh Growth Initiative, agreed at the December 1992 Edinburgh summit, under which a new temporary lending facility of 5 billion ecus was established within the EIB, while a European Investment Fund (EIF) was created with a capital of 2 billion ecus, which it was hoped would cover guarantees between 10 billion and 16 billion ecus. By the end of 1996 projects totalling 2.3 billion ecus had been approved.

There is also a facility available for short-term loans to member states in temporary balance of payments difficulties. In 1993, 8 billion ecus was lent, all to Italy. Since then no country has used this facility, and by 1998 the EIB was responsible for no less than 98.6% of the total of €29.95 billion lent by EU institutions.

The European Monetary System

The European Monetary System (EMS) was devised primarily as a means of stabilising currency fluctuations, following the breakdown in the early 1970s of the fixed-rate exchange system established by the 1944 Bretton Woods agreement. Originally proposed by Roy Jenkins in October 1977 (see pages 16–17), it included an exchange rate mechanism (ERM), bolstered by various financial solidarity mechanisms and a common currency unit (the ecu).

Under the ERM each participating currency had a central rate against the ecu. Only eight currencies participated initially, the UK "temporarily" staying out when the system was inaugurated in March 1979. The three later entrants to the EC – Greece, Spain and Portugal – felt that they were not yet ready to join. Spain eventually joined in June 1989 and the UK followed suit in October 1990. Portugal joined in April 1992, leaving Greece as the odd man out. The central rate for each currency could be "realigned" if necessary by mutual agreement of the participating countries. From the ecu central rate, bilateral central rates were calculated for each currency against each of the other participants. Each currency was allowed to fluctuate by +/-2.25% around these central rates, or by +/-6% in the case of the pound and the peseta.

If a currency reached its "floor" or "ceiling" rate, the central banks were obliged to intervene in the foreign-exchange markets to maintain it within the agreed limits. In practice, this meant selling the currency which reached its ceiling rate and buying the one at its floor. If a currency stayed at its floor or ceiling over a lengthy period, or appeared likely to do so, it was a clear sign that it should be realigned. When this happened the finance ministers of the EU met, normally over a weekend in Brussels, to approve a realignment. The consequence was that the sudden, often competitive devaluations of the past were avoided, and the currencies within the system fluctuated much less violently than others (including the pound) which were not included.

The EMS helped to bring about a greater convergence in the economies of the member states, and the disciplines built into the system were credited with playing a part in the marked reduction in inflation in the early 1980s in all the participating states. On average, inflation fell from 12% in 1980 to 5% in 1985, and the average divergence between countries went down from 6.2% to 2.8%. Other countries outside the EC recognised the value of the ERM in providing tighter guidelines for their own economic policies. Three Nordic countries – Finland, Norway and Sweden – each tied their own currencies to the ecu in 1990 or early 1991.

In 1992 the ERM came under great strain, partly because of the recession and partly because the removal of financial controls meant that vast amounts of currency changed hands each day, opening the system to manipulation by speculators. The situation was exacerbated by the fact that the pound had been brought into the ERM at an unrealistically high exchange rate and the UK government stubbornly resisted pressure to agree to an orderly devaluation. Consequently, in September 1992 massive speculative movements led to the forced devaluation of several currencies, and the pound and the lira were withdrawn from the ERM altogether and allowed to float. A similar speculative attack in July 1993 was fended off by a decision to widen temporarily the fluctuation margin within the ERM to 15% either side of the bilateral central rates. In practice, the currencies did not fluctuate much beyond the previous more narrow limits, which suggests that, unlike the previous year, none of the currencies were seriously over- or under-valued. The mechanism remained in operation, but without the participation of the UK, Italy and Greece. Italy rejoined the ERM in November 1996, and Greece in March 1998, leaving the UK and Sweden outside. The ERM lost much of its significance on December 31st 1998, when the exchange rates of the 11 countries joining the euro were irrevocably fixed (see page 144), leaving only the Greek drachma and the Danish krona to fluctuate within agreed bands.

The ecu

The ecu (European currency unit)[2] had several other functions besides acting as a marker for the national currencies of the EC. It took the place of the former EUA (European Unit of Account), which was a purely book-keeping measurement for establishing the relative value of payments into and out of the EC accounts. But the ecu (which had the advantage of euphony, and of having the same name as a famous pre-revolutionary French coin) had the backing of a large reserve fund, the European Monetary Co-operation Fund (EMCF), into which the member states were required to pay 20% of their gold reserves and 20% of their dollar reserves.

Consequently, there was a great deal of international confidence in the ecu, which was used for many dealings quite unrelated to the funds of the EU (by 1986 it was already the third most common currency used for international bond issues, after the dollar and the Deutschemark). More and more companies and individuals used the ecu for denominating their bank deposits and travellers' cheques, or for commercial invoices and payments. This was quite an achievement for a currency which did not exist, in so far as neither coins nor banknotes were normally issued in ecus. Its utility for private and commercial financial transactions lay in the fact that its value was unlikely to fluctuate by as much as any individual national currency.

Economic and monetary union

Although anything approaching total convergence (or "cohesion" as it is now known in Eurojargon) between the national economies is unlikely to come about for many years – in the absence of massive financial transfers from north to south within the Union – the institution of the EMS proved to be at least a step on the way. It was undoubtedly the most significant move towards the long-term objective of an economic and monetary union (EMU) that the EC had made until 1989, when a committee of European central bankers and some independent monetary experts, under the chairmanship of Jacques Delors, the commission's president, proposed a three-stage process towards EMU, but without attaching any timetable:

- ◪ **Stage one.** Co-operation and co-ordination in the economic and monetary fields were to be improved. This would lead, among other things, to a strengthening of the EMS, the role of the ecu and the terms of reference of the Committee of Central Bank Governors. The introduction of a multilateral surveillance procedure would pave the way for more effective co-ordination and for closer convergence of national economic policies and performances.
- ◪ **Stage two.** This could not begin until a new treaty (or amendments to the Rome treaty) had been agreed, laying down the basic institutional and operational rules necessary for the realisation of EMU. The most important feature of stage two could be the creation of a federal-type European System of Central Banks (ESCB or EuroFed) which, in the light of experience, would become increasingly independent as regards monetary policies and policies on exchange-market intervention. However, the national central banks would still retain ultimate responsibility for decision-making.
- ◪ **Stage three.** Commencing with the move to irrevocably locked exchange rates and the transfer of responsibilities provided for in the new treaty, this stage would eventually lead to the adoption of a single currency.

The general approach of the Delors committee was acceptable to 11 of the then 12 member states, but the UK government reacted coolly to the concept of a single currency: although it was agreeable to stage one of the process beginning on July 1st 1990, it emphatically reserved its position regarding stages two and three.

Despite British objections, the EC heads of government decided at the

Strasbourg summit in December 1989 that the requisite majority existed to convene an inter-governmental conference (IGC) to decide on the treaty changes which stages two and three would necessitate. It was subsequently agreed that two IGCs, one on EMU and one on political union, should be held, both convening in Rome in December 1990 and completing their work in time to report to the Maastricht summit, scheduled for December 1991.

Before then, the first Rome summit of October 1990 agreed that stage two of EMU, with the creation of the EuroFed, would begin on January 1st 1994. Within the IGC on EMU, the UK put forward a plan for a 13th currency, or "hard ecu", which would take the place of the single currency advocated by the Delors report. Although aspects of this proposal were sympathetically received by some other member states the prevailing view was that a single currency was necessary if the main benefits of EMU were to be obtained.

Treaty on European Union

This is effectively what was decided at the Maastricht summit in December 1991, when the Treaty on European Union was agreed. The treaty included four chapters relevant to the creation of EMU: those on economic policy, monetary policy, institutions and trans-national provisions. The chapter on economic policy requires member states to conduct their economic policy in such a way as to achieve the objectives of EMU and "in accordance with the principle of an open market economy with free competition". Member states are to regard their economic policies as a matter of common concern and are to co-ordinate them through the Ecofin Council. The broad guidelines of economic policy are to be defined by the European Council (that is, by EU summit meetings) and are then to be adopted within the Ecofin Council by qualified majority vote.

A multilateral surveillance procedure had already been instituted under which, to ensure closer co-ordination and sustained convergence in the economic performance of member states, the Ecofin Council, on the basis of reports submitted by the commission, monitors economic developments in each member state. Where it considers that economic policies are not consistent with the broad guidelines agreed, the council is entitled, by qualified majority vote, to make policy recommendations to a member state which it may choose to make public. If, in the future, a member state persists in applying policies inconsistent with the guidelines, and in particular if it persists in incurring excessive budget deficits, it may lay itself open to a range of sanctions culminating in a freeze on lending from EC institutions, a requirement to make non-interest bearing deposits and, ultimately, the imposition of "fines of an appropriate size". The treaty makes clear that there is no question of the EC "bailing out" a member state that gets into financial difficulties, although financial assistance may be available in the event of "natural disasters" or other problems not caused by the improvidence of the member state concerned.

On monetary policy, it laid down that the primary objective "shall be to maintain price stability", that is, a minimal level of inflation. For this purpose a European System of Central Banks (ESCB) was to be created, made up of the national central banks (NCBS) of the member states, all of which should become independent of their national governments, and a new European Central Bank (ECB), to be established at the beginning of the third stage of EMU.

The treaty confirmed that the second stage of EMU would commence on January 1st 1994, by which date all member states were expected to have implemented measures to provide for the free movement of capital, and to have adopted multi-annual programmes to ensure lasting convergence necessary for EMU, in particular with regard to price stability and sound public finances. At the beginning of stage two, the European Monetary Institute (EMI) was set up as the forerunner of the ECB. Its members were the various national banks, and it replaced the Committee of Governors and the European Monetary Co-operation Fund, which ceased to exist. Its task was to prepare the way for stage three.

The EMI, together with the commission, reported to the Ecofin Council on the progress of member states in making their national legislation compatible with EMU. The council was then to assess which member states fulfilled the four conditions for adoption of a single currency, which were defined in a protocol to the treaty:

- Its inflation should, over the previous year, not have exceeded by more than 1.5% that achieved by an average of the three best performing states.
- Its currency had been within the narrow band of the ERM for at least the preceding two years and had not been devalued during that period.
- Its long-term interest rates had not exceeded by more than 2% over the preceding year the average of the three best-performing states so far as price stability is concerned.

◾ It was not subject to a decision of the council that it was running an excessive budget deficit.

An excessive deficit was defined in the protocol as one exceeding 3% of GDP in the annual budget, or an accumulated government debt exceeding 60% of GDP. Yet these criteria were hedged with qualifications in the Maastricht treaty itself, which provided for exceptions for countries which had "reached a level that comes close" to the 3% annual deficit level or if the excess was a result of "only exceptional and temporary" factors. Similarly, with regard to the accumulated deficit, which for several member states, notably Belgium and Italy, was far above the 60% level, the treaty referred only to the necessity for the deficit to be "sufficiently diminishing and approaching the reference value at a satisfactory pace". The inference was that countries whose economies were generally in a good shape and were over-performing on the other criteria would not be excluded from EMU if they failed to meet the deficit targets exactly.

A special protocol to the treaty gave the UK the right to opt out, even if it fulfilled these conditions. It stipulated that the UK should not be obliged to enter the third stage without a separate decision to do so by its government and Parliament. A similar dispensation was subsequently granted to Denmark.

The Madrid summit in December 1995 decided that the new monetary unit should be called the euro, and that it should be exchangeable on a one-to-one basis with the ecu. It would be subdivided into 100 cents. A competition was launched in February 1996 for the design of banknotes denominated in euros, and the winning entries were displayed at the Dublin summit in December 1996. There would be notes for 5, 10, 20, 50, 100, 200 and 500 euros, and coins for 1, 2, 5, 10 and 50 cents and for 1 and 2 euros. Although many banking transactions were to be conducted in euros from 1999 onwards, the coins and notes would not go into circulation until the end of 2001 or the beginning of 2002. This was because the printing and minting of the currency is an enormous operation: replacements would be needed for some 12 billion banknotes and 70 billion coins currently circulating in the Union. There would be a period of no more than two months during which both the old and new currencies would be circulating before the old currency ceased to be legal tender.

The final launch of EMU

In 1997, with Germany worrying about whether sloppy fiscal and budget policies among euro-zone countries could destabilise the currency, the Stability and Growth Pact was agreed. It not only requires members of the euro zone to keep their annual budgetary deficits below 3% of GDP, but also sets up measures to fine countries that breach such limits. In the spring of 1998 the commission and the EMI examined the record of the 15 member states and reported that 11 of them had succeeded in meeting the criteria set out in the Maastricht treaty and were thus eligible to join stage three of EMU on the opening date of January 1st 1999. They were Austria, Belgium, Finland, France, Germany, Ireland, Italy, Luxembourg, the Netherlands, Portugal and Spain. Two other states – the UK and Denmark – had also met the criteria, but were exercising their right to opt out, at least at the outset of stage three. Sweden had met the economic criteria but had not taken steps to ensure the independence of its central bank, which was also a requirement for EMU membership. Greece had failed to meet the criteria, although it had made progress in this direction.

These recommendations were accepted at a special meeting of the European Council held in Brussels on May 1st–2nd 1998. So 11 countries adopted a common currency on January 1st 1999. Greece was able to join two years later, on January 1st 2001. The UK government took a more cautious stance, reiterating that it was in principle in favour of joining, but that it was unlikely to hold the referendum to which it was committed until after the next general election, which took place in May 2001. By May 2005, when a further election was held, there was still no sign of the promised referendum taking place.

The May 1998 summit also appointed the first president, and five vice-presidents, of the ECB. The president was Wim Duisenberg, a former Dutch finance minister and central bank governor, who had been head of the EMI since 1996. On December 31st 1998 the Ecofin Council met and agreed the irrevocably fixed rates of the participating currencies against the euro (see Table 18.1).

Euro launch

The three years between EMU and the launch of the physical currency were remarkably uneventful. The value of the new currency fell steadily against the dollar in the initial weeks, but then stabilised at around 85 cents. The euro was used in company accounts and traded in financial markets and on foreign exchanges, although many firms, retailers and

Table 18.1 **Conversion rates for the euro**

€1 =		
	13.7603	Austrian schillings
	40.3399	Belgian francs
	40.3399	Luxembourg francs
	1.95583	German marks
	166.386	Spanish pesetas
	5.94573	Finnish markkaa
	6.55957	French francs
	0.787564	Irish pounds
	1,936.27	Italian lire
	2.20371	Dutch guilders
	200.482	Portuguese escudos
	340.750	Greek drachma

consumers continued to do business in national currencies. There were regular calls on Duisenberg to cut interest rates to revive the EU's economy, but he usually ignored them. The finance ministers of the euro zone met regularly as the Eurogroup, one day before the Ecofin Council.

The run-up to the euro's launch – an unprecedented logistical and administrative task – was meticulously planned. On December 15th 2001, banks and post offices in the euro zone were given "starter packs" of euro coins of every denomination to sell to the curious public. On December 31st, most banks had replaced national notes with euros in their cash machines. Around 56 billion coins and 13 billion notes had been produced by then. By January 4th, 99% of cash machines had been switched over to euros. Doomsday scenarios of robberies, a flood of counterfeit notes and chaos as shops and customers struggled to adapt to the new currency failed to materialise, as a range of information campaigns stirred retailers and the general public into awareness. By January 15th, more than 90% of cash payments were being made in euros. All euro-zone countries had a transitional period where both the euro and the national currencies were legal tender, with dual pricing, although change was always given in euros. This period varied in length, with the Netherlands, Ireland and France having earlier cut-off points, but by March 1st 2002 all national currencies were no longer legal tender in the euro zone.

The notes were the same throughout the euro zone, but the eight different coins had national faces on one side. As well as the 12 euro-zone countries, Monaco, San Marino and the Vatican had "national" coins.

Many non-EU countries, such as Macedonia, announced that they would adopt the euro, although they were, naturally, not part of the decision-making process for the new currency.

However, since EMU, the Stability and Growth Pact has come under severe strain. When Portugal overstepped the deficit mark in 2002 it was warned, and the government immediately moved to bring the budget into line. But then France and Germany, the two biggest euro economies, repeatedly failed to stay below the ceiling, blaming the difficult economic climate for higher budget deficits. The commission recommended action against both countries – including orders forcing the French and German governments to cut spending and raise taxes by specific amounts – but economic and finance ministers voted not to take the process any further. In October 2002, the commission's president, Romano Prodi, described the Stability and Growth Pact as "stupid", but the commission continued to pursue both Germany and France. In November 2003, the Council of Ministers decided to suspend excessive deficit measures against France and Germany, effectively putting the stability pact on ice indefinitely. The commission took the whole council to the Court of Justice for violation of the pact, and in July 2004 the court ruled that ministers were wrong to suspend the pact, but added that euro-zone governments were not obliged to follow the commission's recommendations when it came to reining in their deficits. At the same time, the commission also proposed weakening the definition of the Stability and Growth Pact by including sustained economic slow-down as an "exceptional circumstance" which could ease the rules.

Meanwhile, Jean-Claude Juncker, Luxembourg's prime minister, became the first semi-permanent chairman of the euro-zone finance ministers in 2005. He speaks for the 16 euro nations at meetings of the IMF and the World Bank and attends ECB governing council meetings.

Perhaps the biggest challenge came at the end of 2008, just before the single currency's tenth anniversary. As the global financial crisis battered European markets, the euro was credited for preventing a currency crisis in addition to the credit crunch. At the same time, a string of countries lined up to dump their national currencies and join the euro zone: eight central and eastern European countries set target dates to join, while even the opt-out countries – Denmark and the UK – were warming to the euro.

By the start of 2009, the euro zone had 16 members and a combined population of around 320 million. However, many more people were directly affected by the euro, from would-be members whose currencies are already pegged to it, to countries like Montenegro and Kosovo whose effective national currency is the euro. France's former African colonies also peg their common currency to Europe's. That means around 500m people rely on the euro or euro-pegged currencies. But the euro is still some way from dethroning the dollar as a global currency – for example, just 27% of global foreign-exchange reserves are held in euros compared with 62% in dollars.

Notes

1 The accepted abbreviation for Economic and Financial Affairs Council.
2 The value of the ecu was determined by a weighted "basket" of currencies of the member states. The basket ceased to exist in 1999, when the ecu was replaced – on a one-to-one basis – by the new single currency, the euro.

19 Taxation

Taxation has been regarded from the outset as a subject reserved to the sovereignty of the member states, except in so far as its incidence may distort competition within the Union or discriminate against nationals of other EU countries. Accordingly, except on such matters as the avoidance of double taxation, decisions on tax matters have been concerned almost exclusively with indirect taxation: customs duties on the one hand, and VAT and excise duties on the other. Virtually every decision relating to taxation requires unanimous agreement in the Council of Ministers, and this requirement was not relaxed in the Single European Act, which substantially widened the range of decisions subject to qualified majority vote. The incidence and range of taxation varies enormously within the Union, with Sweden and Denmark being the highest taxed countries and Romania and Slovakia the lowest (see Table 19.1).

General application of VAT

The main taxation change which has occurred has been the general application of value-added tax (VAT), replacing a variety of different indirect taxes in the member states. Two directives adopted in 1967 provided for those countries not already applying VAT to introduce it within a specific timetable. VAT commended itself to the Community because of its economic neutrality. At each stage in the making or marketing of a product, the tax paid at the preceding stage is deducted from that paid by the vendor. In this way the tax remains proportionate to the value of the goods and services, no matter how many transactions they have been through.

The member states reached agreement in 1977 on a common basis for assessing VAT, although it was subject to many exceptions. It was, however, enough to enable the EC to collect on this basis part of its "own resources", subject to a maximum rate of 1%, raised in 1986 to 1.4%. The member states continued to differ in the level at which VAT was charged, the number of different rates and the goods and services that were excluded or subject to a zero rate.

Excise duty

The other form of indirect taxation which member states have continued to levy is excise duty on certain specific products, such as alcoholic

Table 19.1 **Tax revenue and implict tax rates by type of economic activity**

	Tax revenue, % of GDP			Implicit tax rate[a] on... Labour			Consumption			Capital		
	2000	2006	2007	2000	2006	2007	2000	2006	2007	2000	2006	2007
EU-27[b]	40.6	39.7	39.8	35.9	34.4	34.4	20.9	22.0	22.2	25.5	25.7	28.7
EA-16[b]	41.2	40.3	40.4	34.6	34.2	34.3	20.5	21.4	21.5	27.3	26.9	29.8
Austria	43.2	41.7	42.1	40.1	40.8	41.0	22.1	21.2	21.6	27.3	24.4	26.1
Belgium	45.2	44.5	44.0	43.9	42.7	42.3	21.8	22.3	22.0	29.3	32.0	31.1
Bulgaria	32.5	33.2	34.2	38.7	30.6	29.9	19.7	25.5	25.4	...	...	...
Cyprus	30.0	36.5	41.6	21.5	24.1	24.0	12.7	20.4	21.4	23.8	30.6	50.5
Czech Republic	33.8	36.7	36.9	40.7	41.1	41.4	19.4	21.1	21.4	20.9	25.9	25.6
Denmark	49.4	49.6	48.7	41.0	37.1	37.0	33.4	34.0	33.7	36.0	44.8	44.9
Estonia	31.3	31.3	33.1	37.8	33.9	33.8	19.8	23.4	24.4	6.0	8.3	10.3
Finland	47.2	43.5	43.0	44.1	41.6	41.4	28.6	27.2	26.5	36.0	24.0	26.7
France	44.1	43.9	43.3	42.1	41.9	41.3	20.9	19.9	19.5	38.1	40.8	40.7
Germany	41.9	39.2	39.5	40.7	39.0	39.0	18.9	18.3	19.8	28.9	23.9	24.4
Greece	34.6	31.3	32.1	34.5	35.1	35.5	16.5	15.2	15.4	19.9	15.9	...
Hungary	38.5	37.2	39.8	41.4	38.8	41.2	27.5	25.8	27.1	15.9	16.3	...
Ireland	31.6	32.1	31.2	28.5	25.4	25.7	25.9	26.5	25.6	...	21.1	18.5
Italy	41.8	42.1	43.3	43.7	42.5	44.0	17.9	17.4	17.1	29.6	34.2	36.2
Latvia	29.5	30.4	30.5	36.7	33.1	31.0	18.7	20.1	19.6	11.2	11.0	14.6
Lithuania	30.1	29.4	29.9	41.2	33.6	32.3	18.0	16.7	17.9	7.2	11.6	12.1
Luxembourg	39.1	35.8	36.7	29.9	30.7	31.2	23.1	26.3	26.9	...	...	...
Malta	28.2	33.7	34.7	20.6	21.3	20.1	15.9	19.9	20.3	...	...	...
Netherlands	39.9	39.1	38.9	34.5	34.6	34.3	23.7	26.5	26.8	20.8	17.2	16.4
Norway	42.6	44.0	43.6	...	37.9	37.8	...	29.9	30.3	...	43.2	41.8
Poland	32.6	33.8	34.8	33.6	34.2	35.0	17.8	20.2	21.4	20.5	22.8	...
Portugal	34.3	35.9	36.8	27.0	28.6	30.0	19.2	21.0	20.3	32.7	30.8	34.0
Romania	30.4	28.6	29.4	32.2	30.4	30.1	16.8	17.7	18.1	...	...	...
Slovakia	34.1	29.4	29.4	36.3	30.5	30.9	21.7	20.2	20.6	22.9	18.2	17.5
Slovenia	37.5	38.4	38.2	37.7	37.4	36.9	23.5	23.8	24.1	15.7	22.0	23.1
Spain	33.9	36.5	37.1	28.7	30.8	31.6	15.7	16.4	15.9	29.7	40.9	42.4
Sweden	51.8	49.0	48.3	47.2	44.5	43.1	26.3	27.4	27.8	43.4	29.1	35.9
UK	36.7	36.9	36.3	25.3	25.8	26.1	19.4	18.6	18.4	44.7	44.4	42.7

a Implicit tax rates (ITR) express aggregate tax revenues as a percentage of the potential tax base for each field.
b EU-27 and EA-16 overall tax ratios are calculated as GDP-weighted average of the member states. For ITRs the aggregates are calculated as arithmetic averages of the member states for which the respective annual data are available.
Source: European Commission

drinks, manufactured tobacco and fuels. Despite numerous proposals by the commission, the only common regulations adopted before July 1991 related to the structure of duty on cigarettes. Acting on complaints from the commission, however, the Court of Justice has delivered judgments aimed at preventing member states favouring home-produced beers, wines or spirits to the detriment of imported products, which have led to several of them modifying their range of duties.

The commission also established a common basis for duty-free allowances for travellers between member states. In principle, duty-free allowances should have been abolished from January 1st 1993 when the EU's internal market was completed. It was decided, however, that until June 30th 1999 duty-free sales could continue at airports, on planes and on ferries travelling from one member state to another. Despite intense lobbying by the duty-free industry, largely financed by tobacco and alcoholic drinks manufacturers, the Council of Ministers refused to reverse this decision in June 1999, and duty-free sales for travellers within the EU came to an end on the due date.

Harmonisation of indirect tax rates

A strong impetus to harmonising indirect tax rates was given by the adoption in 1985 of a specific target for completing the Community's internal market. The commission argued strongly (see pages 122–3) that these rates would have to be "approximated" if the objective of removing all internal frontier controls was to be achieved. Approximation meant bringing them so closely together that no significant distortion of trade was likely to be produced. The model was the United States, where the different states levy varying rates of sales tax, but the difference between them is seldom great enough to attract much cross-border trade merely for the benefit of paying a lower rate of tax. In July 1987 the commission produced its proposals, which it said should be implemented by member states no later than December 31st 1992.

VAT

Two rate bands were proposed: a standard rate of 14–20%, and a reduced rate "for items of basic necessity" of 4–9%. The items suggested for this reduced rate were foodstuffs, energy for heating and lighting, water, pharmaceuticals, books, newspapers and periodicals, and passenger transport. Member states were free to fix their national rates at any point between these 5–6 percentage point margins.

Excise duty

The commission proposed a complete harmonisation, and specified a precise amount of duty for all products attracting excise duty.

Agreement took time

It took four years, and a great deal of horse-trading, for the member states to reach any sort of agreement on the proposals. In June 1991 a political agreement was reached, although in a greatly amended and watered-down form.

The amended proposals stipulated that, from January 1st 1993, the standard rate of VAT should be set at a minimum of 15% in all member states; no maximum was suggested. In addition, for a list of 20 or so goods and services, regarded as essential and not extensively traded across national borders (including food, domestic heating and lighting, passenger transport, and books and newspapers), one or more reduced rates of at least 5% could be applied. In a major concession to the UK it was agreed that zero and other rates less than 5% could continue if they were already in effect on January 1st 1991.

The amended proposals were finally approved in July 1992, in a directive which stipulated a minimum standard VAT rate of 15% for a four-year period. All the arrangements were linked to a transitional period, due to end no later than January 1st 1997, during which VAT on goods exported within the EU would be taxed in the country of destination rather than of origin. After that date all goods should be taxed on the same basis, irrespective of where they were sold. The commission was told to come up with proposals for a permanent system, which would make this possible by the end of 1994. Although the commission met this deadline, the member states were unable to agree on a permanent system of collection, and the transitional arrangements continue, with little prospect of an early changeover, despite the desire of both business and consumer groups for a unified system. Nonetheless, there was a considerable convergence of VAT rates between 1987 and 1997, partly owing to market forces but also as a consequence of the adoption of the 1992 directive. The range of maximum rates between member states was reduced from 26% to 10% and all rates above the standard rate were eliminated. By the time that ten new member states joined the Union in May 2004, the convergence had increased. The VAT rates in all member states in early 2009 were as shown in Table 19.2.

Table 19.2 **VAT rates in member states, 2009**

Country	Standard rate, %	Reduced rate, %
Austria	20	12 or 10
Belgium	21	12 or 6
Bulgaria	20	0 or 7
Cyprus	15	5
Czech Republic	19	9
Denmark	25	none
Estonia	20	5
Finland	22	17 or 8
France	19.6	5.5 or 2.1
Germany	19	7
Greece	19	9 or 4.5
Greek islands	13	6 or 3
Hungary	25	5
Ireland	21.5	13.5, 4.8 or 0
Italy	20	10, 6 or 4
Latvia	21	10
Lithuania	19	9 or 5
Luxembourg	15	12, 9, 6 or 3
Malta	18	5
Netherlands	19	6
Poland	22	7, 3 or 0
Portugal	20	12 or 5
Madeira and Azores	15	8 or 4
Romania	19	9
Slovakia	19	10
Slovenia	20	8.5
Spain	16	7 or 4
Canary Islands	5	0 or 2
Sweden	25	12 or 6
United Kingdom	15[a]	5 or 0

a 17.5% from January 1st 2010.

Excise duty proposals virtually abandoned

If the approximation proposals on VAT were severely modified, those on excise duties were virtually abandoned. In place of the complete harmonisation proposed, the Council of Ministers agreed in June 1991 that minimum duties, for the most part well below those actually paid in most member states, should be agreed. It had been impossible to reach agreement between the northern member states, which applied high duties on both revenue and health grounds for alcohol and tobacco, and the Mediterranean countries, large producers of wine and tobacco, which traditionally applied nil or low duties.

Other forms of taxation

The commission had been concerned that certain other taxes have a bearing on the competitive position of companies based in different member states, and it seems likely that it will at some stage produce proposals for harmonising company taxation, although probably not income tax, at least for the foreseeable future. In 1990, the commission succeeded, after a lengthy delay, in persuading the Council of Ministers to adopt three directives which would provide for a common system of taxation applicable to mergers, and to subsidiary or associated companies when these were based in different member states. In 1998, the commission proposed a minimum rate of 20% on interest earned by EU residents on their investments made in another member state. After long delays, the withholding tax was eventually agreed as part of the EU savings directive, which came into effect on July 1st 2005. The aim of the tax is to ensure that citizens of one member state do not evade tax by depositing undeclared funds outside the jurisdiction of residence. The tax is withheld at source and passed on to the EU country of residence. Only Austria, Belgium and Luxembourg refused to disclose the recipient of the interest concerned, although they committed to do so in 2009 as global leaders began targeting tax havens.

There has, however, been little movement on any EU energy taxes. Harmonised energy taxes were first suggested in 1993 by Mario Monti, then internal market commissioner, and have been debated since 1997, mainly as an environmental measure that would help meet the EU's obligations under the Kyoto Protocols. Nonetheless, some member states describe their car taxes as eco-taxes. Because of the lack of EU harmonisation, both the taxation level and schemes differ significantly. In Denmark, for example, the total taxation can easily reach levels well over 100%, meaning the price of the car more than doubles. Luxembourg, however, only applies a VAT rate of 15%. Despite this diversity, there is clearly a shared trend to link car taxation more and more to CO_2 emissions, instead of to mass, power or engine capacity as in the past. Vehicle taxation measures can also give EU member states opportunities to promote or protect their domestic industry. French incentives, for example, tend to progressively penalise high CO_2 emitters, protecting the typically smaller cars produced by French manufacturers. By contrast, German incentives generally lack such an approach and bigger engines are not penalised too much.

20 Agriculture

CAP was the first common policy implemented

The common agricultural policy (CAP) of the EC was, together with the customs union, the objective spelled out in the greatest detail in the Treaty of Rome. It was, indeed, for a long time virtually the only common policy that the Community was able to implement. From the point of view of European farmers it has been a spectacular success, but that success has created enormous problems. On the one hand the CAP has absorbed such a high proportion of the budget that the development of other policies has been aborted. On the other hand the subsidised export of a number of products in which substantial surpluses have built up has distorted world trade, bringing the EU into conflict with the United States and other traditional food exporters, as well as with developing countries whose agricultural economies risk being undermined by those exports.

Effect on EU agriculture

The aims of the CAP, as set out in Article 39 of the treaty, are as follows:

1 To increase agricultural productivity.
2 To ensure a fair standard of living for the agricultural population.
3 To stabilise markets.
4 To guarantee regular supplies.
5 To ensure reasonable prices in supplies to consumers.

The CAP has greatly contributed to the transformation of the structure of the Union's agriculture. Generous price support has combined with technological innovation to generate massive increases in production and productivity. The EU is virtually self-sufficient in all but tropical foods and a number of vegetable proteins and starches for animal feed. Owing to a two-thirds reduction since 1958 in the number of people living off the land, the average standard of living of those remaining has risen sharply. Although the policy has helped to realise the first four objectives listed above, this has generally been at the expense of the fifth. EU farm support prices are almost invariably higher than world prices, often substantially so. The EU consumer has therefore had to pay for the success of the farming sector not only through higher prices but also through taxes, which have contributed to an EU budget predominantly devoted to farm support.

The CAP is based on three main principles:

- A single market for farm goods (free movement throughout the EU and common prices).
- Community preference (a common tariff barrier against imports from outside the EU).
- Common financial responsibility (costs are paid from a common fund to which all members contribute).

How it works

The CAP has an integrated system of measures which works by maintaining commodity price levels within the EU and by subsidising production. There are a number of mechanisms:

- **Price supports.** Prices for major commodities such as some grains (barley, bread wheat and corn), oilseeds, dairy products, beef and veal, and sugar still depend on the intervention price as a guaranteed floor price. An internal intervention price is set; if it falls below the intervention level, the EU will buy up goods to raise the price to the intervention level. The intervention price is set lower than the target price. The internal market price can only vary in the range between the intervention price and target price. Domestic price supports were the historical backbone of CAP farm support, but they have been largely replaced by direct payments (market support now represents less than 10% of CAP spending on "farm support" and about 90 % is paid directly to farmers – see below). Other mechanisms, such as subsidies to assist with surplus storage also support domestic prices.
- **Direct payments to farmers.** These were originally intended to encourage farmers to grow those crops attracting subsidies and maintain home-grown supplies. While price support remains a means of maintaining farm income, payments made directly to producers provide substantially more income support. Subsidies have generally been paid on the area of land growing a particular crop, rather than on the total amount of crop produced.
- **Import levies.** These are set at a level to raise the world market price up to the EU target price. The target price is chosen as the maximum desirable price for those goods within the EU. In

Table 20.1 **Agriculture's share of GDP, 2005**

	%		%
Austria	1.0	Latvia	2.2
Belgium	0.8	Lithuania	2.9
Cyprus	2.5	Luxembourg	0.3
Czech Republic	1.0	Malta	1.3
Denmark	1.2	Netherlands	1.7
Estonia	1.9	Poland	2.5
Finland	0.9	Portugal	1.7
France	1.7	Slovakia	1.2
Germany	0.6	Slovenia	1.8
Greece	4.7	Spain	2.8
Hungary	2.7	Sweden	0.4
Ireland	1.3	United Kingdom	0.4
Italy	1.9	EU-25	1.3

Source: Eurostat

preferential trade agreements, such as those with former colonies and neighbouring countries, the EU tries to balance domestic consumer demand while protecting high domestic prices through import quotas and minimum import price requirements.

■ **Import quotas.** By controlling supply, the CAP can restrict the amount of food imported into the EU. Some non-member countries have negotiated quotas which allow them to sell particular goods within the EU without tariffs. This notably applies to countries with a traditional trade link with a member country.

■ **Production quotas and "set-aside" payments.** These were introduced in an effort to prevent overproduction of some goods (for example, milk, grain, wine) that attracted subsidies well in excess of market prices. The need to store and dispose of excess produce wasted resources and brought the CAP into disrepute. A secondary market evolved, especially in the sale of milk quotas, and some farmers made imaginative use of set-aside – for example, setting aside land which was difficult to farm. Set-aside was suspended, subject to further decisions about its future, following rising prices for some commodities and increasing interest in growing biofuels.

Reforms

The high costs of the CAP were already alarming European leaders as early as 1967. By the 1980s, when EU self-sufficiency was reached, the policy led to almost permanent surpluses of basic farm commodities – the notorious butter mountains and wine lakes. The CAP was subsequently increasingly used for export and storage subsidies. Various reforms over the past two decades have aimed to remedy the surplus problem and take account of the environmental sustainability of agriculture. The aim has been to break the link between subsidies and production, to diversify the rural economy and to respond to consumer demands for safe food, and high standards of animal welfare and environmental protection.

- The first reform, adopted in 1992 – and named after then agriculture commissioner Ray MacSharry – aimed to dismantle the price support system, reduce guaranteed prices and compensate farmers with a "direct payment" less closely related to levels of production. The reforms would, MacSharry said, limit rising production, while at the same time adjust to the trend towards freer agricultural markets. It began the process of shifting farm support from prices to direct payments. The MacSharry reforms reduced support prices and compensated farmers for lower prices with direct payments based on historical yields, and introduced new supply control measures. These reforms affected the grain, oilseed, protein crop (field peas and beans), beef and sheepmeat markets, but farmers had to produce the commodity to receive a payment.

- The second major reform was adopted as part of the Agenda 2000 package in March 1999. It was to prepare for EU enlargement in May 2004. Similar to the first CAP reform, Agenda 2000 used direct payments to compensate farmers for half of the loss from new support price cuts. It divided the CAP into two "pillars": production support and rural development, the latter including things such as trade, tourism, environmental protection and biodiversity. Again, payments depended on production. Agenda 2000 reforms focused on the grain, oilseed, dairy and beef markets. Shortly after, in 2002, EU member states agreed that expenditure on agriculture (though not rural development) should be held steady in real terms between 2006 and 2013, despite enlargement.

- The third, perhaps most significant reform, in 2003, introduced the Single Payment Scheme (SPS) to break the link between farm aid and production. This "decoupling" of agricultural production from subsidy payments would end overproduction and waste. The reform represented a degree of renationalisation of farm policy, as each member state had discretion over the timing (from 2005 to 2007) and method of implementation. The SPS allocated subsidies to indicators such as land size rather than production volume and laid down environmental, food safety and animal welfare standards as a pre-condition for receiving payments. The reform also featured a shift or so-called "modulation" of monies from the first pillar of the CAP (direct aid and market support) to the second (rural development); land not farmed must be maintained in good agricultural condition. Indeed, the 2003 reforms reflect a philosophical change in the approach to agricultural policy. For the first time, much of the pressure to reform the CAP came from environmentalists and consumers. Another important feature is the move from a price support policy to an income support policy through decoupled payments. EU farmers will have more choices in their planting decisions because of decoupled payments. Commodity support prices continue to exist, but at lower levels, and direct payments to farmers without requirements to plant a crop are more widespread.
- The fourth policy review, dubbed the CAP Health Check and launched in 2008, aims to divert more subsidies for food production to rural development, further reducing the traditional incentives for farmers to produce. The reforms, covering the period 2009–13, will make farmers spend 10% of their EU subsidies – double the previous amount – on projects to improve the countryside. Milk quotas will be boosted before being scrapped in 2015. Instead of paying farmers to produce more, the EU now makes payments conditional on farmers meeting environmental and animal welfare standards and keeping their land in good condition. But while large-scale production subsidies and surplus buy-ups were largely consigned to the past, soaring global food prices in 2008 prompted a renewed debate about maintaining sufficient subsidies to the EU farming sector, as some argued that feeding people cannot be left to the mercy of the market.

Table 20.2 **EU agriculture expenditure, 2009 (€m)**

	Commitments	Payments
Administrative expenditure of agriculture and rural development policy area	133	133
Interventions in agricultural markets	3,410	3,410
Direct aids	37,779	37,779
Rural development	13,645	10,226
Pre-accession measures in the field of agriculture and rural development	121	340
International aspects of agriculture and rural development policy area	6	6
Audit of agricultural expenditure	−458	−458
Policy strategy and co-ordination of agriculture and rural development policy area	43	40
Total	**54,680**	**51,477**

Note: Totals may not add up due to rounding.
Source: European Commission

Agricultural costs

The total cost of EU agriculture is around €50 billion a year, around 41% of the EU budget for 2007–13, compared with nearly 70% in the 1970s. But strictly defined, the CAP itself accounts for 34% over the 2007–13 period. About 88% of it is direct aid, the rest is market price support – public purchases to protect farmers from a drop in prices. In addition, about €7.7 billion is spent on rural development.

In the 2008 budget, EU subsidies in the form of market support totalled around €4 billion. Fruit and vegetables and the wine sector were the main recipients, but the EU food programme to the most deprived people also benefited with almost €345m. €395m was used for animal disease eradication and other activities related to feed and food safety.

Only 5% of EU citizens work in agriculture, and the sector generates just 1.6% of EU GDP. Supporters of the CAP say it guarantees the survival of rural communities – where more than half of EU citizens live – and preserves the traditional appearance of the countryside. They add that most developed countries provide financial support to farmers, and that without a common policy some EU countries would provide more than others, leading to pressure for trade barriers to be reintroduced.

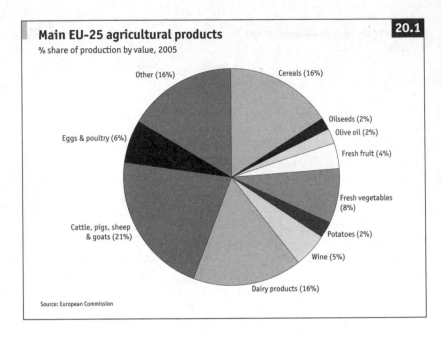

20.1

Main EU-25 agricultural products
% share of production by value, 2005

Cereals (16%)

Oilseeds (2%)

Olive oil (2%)

Fresh fruit (4%)

Other (16%)

Eggs & poultry (6%)

Fresh vegetables (8%)

Cattle, pigs, sheep & goats (21%)

Potatoes (2%)

Wine (5%)

Dairy products (16%)

Source: European Commission

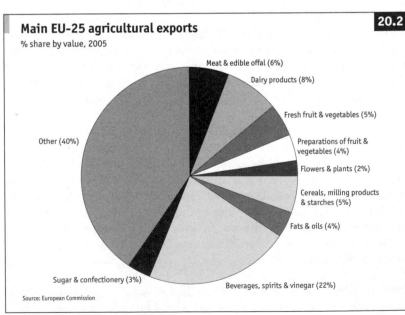

20.2

Main EU-25 agricultural exports
% share by value, 2005

Meat & edible offal (6%)

Dairy products (8%)

Fresh fruit & vegetables (5%)

Preparations of fruit & vegetables (4%)

Flowers & plants (2%)

Cereals, milling products & starches (5%)

Fats & oils (4%)

Other (40%)

Sugar & confectionery (3%)

Beverages, spirits & vinegar (22%)

Source: European Commission

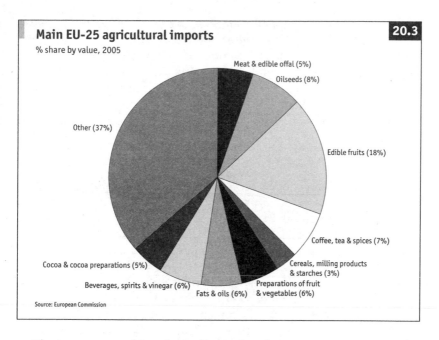

Main EU-25 agricultural imports `20.3`
% share by value, 2005

- Meat & edible offal (5%)
- Oilseeds (8%)
- Other (37%)
- Edible fruits (18%)
- Coffee, tea & spices (7%)
- Cocoa & cocoa preparations (5%)
- Cereals, milling products & starches (3%)
- Beverages, spirits & vinegar (6%)
- Fats & oils (6%)
- Preparations of fruit & vegetables (6%)

Source: European Commission

The importance of farming to the national economy varies across the EU. In Poland, 18% of the population works in agriculture, compared with less than 2% in the UK and Belgium. The number of people working on farms roughly halved in the 15 older EU member states between 1980 and 2003. About 2% of farmers leave the industry every year across the EU, though falls of more than 8% were registered between 2002 and 2003 in the Czech Republic, Hungary, Poland, Slovenia, Slovakia and the UK.

France is by far the biggest recipient of CAP funds, with about 20%, followed by Germany and Spain (13% each), Italy (11%) and the UK (9%). In 2006, France was the biggest agricultural producer in the EU, accounting for 18.6% of total farm production, ahead of Italy (13.2%), Germany (12.6%) and Spain (11.4%). The member states who joined in 2004 initially received CAP subsidies at only 25% of the rate they are paid to the older member states. However, this rate is slowly rising and will reach equality in 2013. Poland, with 2.5m farmers, is likely then to be a significant recipient of funds.

Food safety

After food-related scares such as BSE and foot-and-mouth disease in cattle and dioxin-contaminated chicken, in 2002 EU farm ministers set up a European Food Safety Authority (EFSA). Based in Parma, Italy, the EFSA provides independent scientific advice on all matters linked to food and feed safety – including animal health and welfare and plant protection – and offers scientific advice on nutrition in relation to EU legislation. The watchdog will not only set food safety standards across the EU but also be responsible for ensuring that they are implemented in the field.

GM foods

By the 1990s, confidence in food safety had already poisoned public sentiment towards genetically modified organisms (GMOs), which were mainly being produced in the United States. Many GM crops had received regulatory approval in the United States, but by 1998, the approval process stalled in the EU. Despite threatening to ignite a trade war with the United States, the EU stuck by its effective ban on GM crops. In July 2001, the commission unveiled two regulations proposing new rules on the traceability of GMOs throughout the food chain, and providing consumers with information by labelling all GM food. By 2004, some 25 applications for GM products had been received by the commission, and they are still waiting to go through the authorisation procedure.

21 Research and new industries

The industrial policy of the EU has had two main prongs: to help older, declining industries such as textiles, shipbuilding and steel restructure themselves in such a way as to minimise the inevitable pain and disruption; and to assist in the development and spread of new technologies which provide the foundation for future economic growth.

EC's industrial research began in 1980s

Although the Community had for many years been heavily involved in fundamental and applied research in the nuclear industry, its involvement in industrial research began only in the early 1980s with the growing realisation that the EC was falling seriously behind the United States and Japan, and was also in danger of being outstripped by thrusting new economies such as those of South Korea, Singapore and Taiwan.

European co-operation had already borne fruit in a number of areas where a large capital investment and the capture of a significant slice of the world market were necessary conditions for success. Examples included Airbus and Ariane in the aerospace sector, which received loans from the EIB, and JET (Joint European Torus) in the thermo-nuclear fusion sector, a powerful experimental research institution built and operated by the EU (see page 188). Yet the commission was worried about the wasteful duplication of research expenditure, which, collectively in the EU, compared favourably with both the United States and Japan, but which was too fragmented to produce comparable results.

The commission's objective has been to stimulate co-operation between businesses, laboratories and universities throughout Europe in the development of new technologies and new products fulfilling existing or potential market needs. What needed to be stimulated, in its view, was not so much basic research as joint action in the pre-competitive stage of technological development. It would be up to business to take over at the production and marketing stage, taking advantage of the more competitive and dynamic commercial environment created by the planned completion of the internal market.

Five-year framework research programmes

Despite these increased efforts, the European Commission remained dissatisfied by the degree of commitment of the member states to the co-ordination of their research programmes. In 1986 the president of the commission, Jacques Delors, proposed that the research share of the Community budget (including the amount spent on nuclear research, see page 188) should be more than doubled, from 3% to 8% of the total. As a first step the commission proposed a five-year framework programme for 1987–91, with a total budget of 7.7 billion ecus, although this was eventually whittled down to 5.4 billion ecus by the member states. In 1989, the concept of rolling five-year programmes was accepted, and a simplified framework was approved for 1990–94, with the total increased to 5.7 billion ecus.

The European Council, at the Edinburgh summit in December 1992, stressed the need for the EU's R&TD activities to continue to focus on generic, pre-competitive research with a multi-sectoral impact. Ministers eventually approved a package of research measures, the fourth framework programme, with a budget of 12.3 billion ecus – later raised to 13.1 billion when Sweden, Finland and Austria joined the EU.

A fifth framework programme, covering the years 1998–2002, was adopted by the Council of Ministers in December 1998, with a budget of 14.96 billion ecus.

The sixth framework programme (2002–06) had a budget of €17.5 billion – a 17% nominal increase compared with the previous programme – of which Euratom accounted for €1.23 billion.

The seventh framework programme (FP7), which covers the 2007–13 period (see Table 21.1), has a budget of €50.5 million over seven years. It amounts to a significant jump in investment over previous programmes – and a 41% budget increase on FP6 at 2004 prices.

The core of FP7, representing two-thirds of the overall budget, is the "co-operation" strand, which fosters collaborative research across Europe and other partner countries through projects by transnational consortia of industry and academia. Research will be carried out in ten key thematic areas:

- health;
- food, agriculture and fisheries, and biotechnology;
- information and communication technologies;
- nanosciences, nanotechnologies, materials and new production technologies;

Table 21.1 **Seventh framework programme (FP7) budget, 2007–13**

	€m
Joint Research Centre (EC)	1,751
Co-operation	32,413
Ideas	7,510
People	4,750
Capacities	4,097

Source: European Commission

- energy;
- environment (including climate change);
- transport (including aeronautics);
- socio-economic sciences and the humanities;
- space;
- security.

The other elements of FP7 are "ideas", which aims to establish the European Research Council, provider of funding for frontier science; "people", which covers human resources and includes scholarships for young researchers, fellowships for lifelong training and career development, partnerships between industry and academia and awards for excellence; and "capacities", which involves upgrades for research infrastructures, development of knowledge and science clusters, and promotion of scientific knowledge in general. FP7 also includes support for the EU's Joint Research Centre (JRC), a network of seven research institutes across the EU. In addition to nuclear energy and nuclear safety research, the JRC has developed such technologies as a remote sensing to detect emerging food crises in developing countries where EU food aid will be needed.

European Research Area

The Lisbon European Council in March 2000 identified research and development as essential to make the EU "the most competitive and dynamic knowledge-based economy in the world". As part of this agenda, the leaders backed a commission plan to create a European Research Area (ERA), where think-tanks and university departments from member states work together regularly and effectively, maximising the

EU's potential for innovation. The plan focused on the internet, setting ambitious goals to bring the net into schools, public administration and people's homes.

Telecommunications

Europe could claim a remarkable success in fostering the mobile phone standard known as GSM (Groupe Spéciale Mobile or Global System for Mobile communications). GSM is without rival as a successful example of the merits of a pan-European industrial policy approach to technology research, resulting from an agreement on cellular technology within the European Conference for Post and Telecommunications (CEPT). Where the adoption of analogue cellular systems in Europe was piecemeal, restricting mobile-phone users to their national boundaries, GSM was accepted throughout Europe. It created the possibility of roaming from network to network in different countries and has enjoyed success beyond Europe. It also helped handset manufacturers such as Finland's Nokia and Sweden's Eriksson to emerge from almost nowhere to become two of the most important IT companies in the world.

Although the EU was only indirectly involved in setting the GSM standard, it was implicitly part of a process for speeding mobile-phone use in Europe. The 1993 telecommunications package set January 1998 as the date for opening up the EU's networks to free competition. Overall, the package helped precipitate competition, a new focus on consumers and tumbling prices, and inspired bold new operators, who leapt in to serve the sudden interest in mobile phones. Incredibly, Europe found itself on the cutting edge of technological development, streets ahead of even the United States when it came to developing mobile telephones.

The technology primed to succeed GSM, the third generation (3G), was agreed in 1998 at a European Telecommunications Standards Institute conference in Paris. The Universal Mobile Telecommunications System (UMTS), introduced in the EU on January 1st 2002, offers users advanced features such as moving video images and internet access at rates more than 200 times faster than previous mobile standards. UMTS is an EU-backed initiative described as the Holy Grail of mobile technology, designed to do anything fibre and broadband networks can do.

The Information Society and e-Europe

When new multimedia technologies started taking off in the 1990s, the European Commission quickly realised that it was essential to foster the entrepreneurial spirit needed to let them thrive in Europe. While the

United States was talking about information superhighways straddling the globe, the commission came up with the concept of the "Information Society". In terms of legislation, the Information Society Action Plan covered a wide range of issues, including telecommunications deregulation, the development of trans-European networks (see page 198) in mobile communications and Integrated Services Digital Network (ISDN), standardisation, interconnection, interoperability, intellectual property, privacy and security on the web, and data protection.

At the June 2000 European Council in Feira, EU leaders backed the e-Europe 2002 Action Plan as part of the Lisbon strategy (see page 177–8). Its aims were to:

- develop a cheaper, faster and more secure internet, for example, by unbundling the so-called local loop and making wireless frequencies available;
- invest in people's skills and access (despite having millions of jobseekers, the EU suffers an acute shortage of IT professionals);
- stimulate internet use with confidence-boosting measures such as legislation on copyright, distance-marketing of financial services, e-money.

The plan has chalked up some clear achievements: personal internet penetration in Europe has sky-rocketed and 90% of schools are online. Broadband access is taking hold.

Community patent

Registering a patent in the EU is slow and expensive: it costs an average €49,900 compared with €10,330 in the United States and €16,450 in Japan. Translation accounts for about 40% of the cost in Europe. For the past 30 years, everybody – governments, industry, labour organisations – has concurred that a common, straightforward, less costly system for granting patents in Europe would boost competitiveness by reinforcing and strengthening innovation. But it has been held up as it also touches on issues of justice and language, which many countries consider a matter of sovereignty. The idea of the community patent is to grant inventors automatic legal protection in all EU member states: European Patent Office (EPO) patents can be challenged from one country to another. Otherwise, patents in the EU are awarded either on a national basis or through the EPO in Munich. The EPO awards "European patents" through a single procedure, but to be applicable throughout the

EU it needs translation into the official EU languages. As well as lowering translation costs, the community patent would allow the European Court of Justice to rule on disputes. However, squabbling over languages has held up the plans: although there was a political agreement in 2003, it fell apart over the details. As of 2009, the patent had still to be confirmed.

22 Regional policy

The regional policy of the EC was not originally directly based on the Rome treaty, though the preamble to that treaty refers to the need to "reduce the differences between the various regions and the backwardness of the less favoured regions". (The Single European Act incorporated regional policy into the treaty, and formally recognised it as one of the means of strengthening the Community's economic and social cohesion.) The impetus for developing a regional policy came from the first enlargement, in 1973, when Denmark, Ireland and the UK joined the Community.

Aims of regional policy

The main objectives of the EU's policy for the regions are as follows:

- To ensure that regional problems are taken into consideration in other EU policies.
- To attempt to co-ordinate the regional policies of the member states.
- To provide a broad range of financial support for the development of the EU's poorer regions.

To facilitate the first objective, the commission regularly monitors the economic and social conditions of all the regions and studies the regional consequences of all EU policies. The common agricultural policy, for example, was found to be strongly geared towards helping the more prosperous agricultural areas, and modifications have been introduced which have reduced, but by no means completely removed, this anomaly. The Social Fund (see Chapter 23) has been sharply oriented towards the needy regions and special regional programmes have been designed to back up other EU policies.

So far as co-ordination of national efforts is concerned, an important aim has been to ensure that member states do not indulge in the ultimately self-defeating practice of outbidding each other by increasing the level of aid. Common rules allow the EU to avoid wasting scarce resources and to ensure a more coherent pattern of regional development. The commission has fixed upper limits on the state aids which can be offered to would-be investors in the underdeveloped regions. They range from 10% to 100% of the cost of investments, on a sliding scale according to the gravity of the problems in the particular regions.

Structural Funds

About one-third of the EU's budget is devoted to regional spending. For 2007–13, that amounts to a total budget of €347 billion. It is disbursed through the two Structural Funds (€277 billion) and the Cohesion Fund (€70 billion). The main beneficiary countries are Poland (€67.3 billion), Spain (€35.2 billion), Italy (€28.8 billion), Czech Republic (€26.7 billion), Germany (€26.3 billion), Hungary (€25.3 billion), Portugal (€21.5 billion), and Greece (€20.4 billion).

The Structural Funds are:

◼ The European Regional Development Fund (ERDF), which dominates the funding and covers programmes involving general infrastructure, innovation and investments. Money from the ERDF is available to the poorest regions across the EU. Funding priorities include research, innovation, environmental protection and risk prevention, while infrastructure investment retains an important role, especially in the least-developed regions.

◼ The European Social Fund (ESF), which pays for vocational training projects and other kinds of employment assistance, and job-creation programmes. As with the ERDF, all EU countries are eligible for ESF assistance. Under the 2007–13 programme, the ESF will focus on four areas: increasing adaptability of workers and enterprises; enhancing access to employment and participation in the labour market; reinforcing social inclusion by combating discrimination and facilitating access to the labour market for disadvantaged people; and promoting partnership for reform in the fields of employment and inclusion.

In addition, the Cohesion Fund covers environmental and transport infrastructure projects as well as the development of renewable energy. Funding from this source is reserved for countries whose living standards are less than 90% of the EU average. This means the 12 recent newcomers, Portugal and Greece. Spain, which benefited under earlier Cohesion Fund operations, is being phased out.

Most of regional spending is reserved for regions with a GDP below

75% of the Union average to help improve their infrastructures and develop their economic and human potential. This concerns 17 of the 27 EU countries. However, all 27 are eligible for funding to support innovation and research, sustainable development and job training in their less advanced regions. A small amount goes to cross-border and inter-regional co-operation projects.

Objectives

Regional priorities were formerly arranged around up to seven numbered objectives. But for the 2007–13 period, they have been cut down to three:

- **The "convergence" objective (formerly objective 1):** to accelerate the convergence of the least developed member states and regions by improving growth and employment conditions. It is financed by the ERDF, the ESF and the Cohesion Fund. The co-financing ceilings for public expenditure amount to 75% for the ERDF and the ESF and 85% for the Cohesion Fund. The funding covers 84 regions in 17 member states representing a population of 170m, and – on a phasing-out basis – another 16 regions with 16.4m inhabitants and a GDP only slightly above the threshold owing to the statistical effect of enlargement. The amount available is €282.8 billion, representing 81.5% of the total resources allocated. Areas qualifying for this status include nearly all the regions of the new member states, southern Italy, east Germany, most of Greece and Portugal, much of Spain and some of Ireland. In the UK, Cornwall, Merseyside, South Yorkshire and much of Wales qualify under objective 1. Scotland's objective 1 regions are to be phased out. Northern Ireland, although having a GDP per head above the qualification threshold, benefits from convergence status because of the peace process.
- **The "regional competitiveness and employment" objective (formerly objective 2):** to anticipate economic and social change, and to promote innovation, entrepreneurship, environmental protection and the development of labour markets which include regions not covered by the convergence objective. It is financed by the ERDF and the ESF and accounts. Measures under this objective can receive

co-financing of up to 50% of public expenditure. A total of 168 regions in 19 member states are eligible under this objective, representing 314m inhabitants. The amount available is €54.9 billion, just under 16% of the total resources allocated. Industrial areas can qualify for this status if unemployment is higher than the EU average, a higher percentage of jobs are in the industrial sector than the EU average and the industrial employment is declining. Rural areas qualify if the area has a low population density (less than 100 people per km) or the agricultural employment rate is double that of the EU average. The region must also have either a higher unemployment rate than the EU average or a declining population. Areas dependent on the fishing industry will also qualify if the industry is in decline. Urban areas qualify if unemployment is above the EU average, the crime rate is high and education levels are low, and there is deemed to be a high level of poverty in the area. Areas with regional competitiveness and employment status include much of northern England and parts of Devon, most of the remainder of Spain not covered under objective 1, much of central France and central Italy, parts of Austria, southern Finland and most of Cyprus.

◪ **The "European territorial co-operation" objective:** to strengthen co-operation at cross-border, transnational and interregional levels in the fields of urban, rural and coastal development, and foster the development of economic relations and networking between small and medium-sized enterprises (SMES). It is financed by the ERDF. Measures under this objective can receive co-financing of up to 75% of public expenditure. The population living in cross-border areas is 181.7m (37.5 % of the total EU population), and all EU regions and citizens are covered by at least one of the existing 13 transnational co-operation areas. The amount available is €8.7 billion, representing 2.5 % of the total resources allocated.

Structural Fund and Cohesion Fund support for the three objectives always involves co-financing. The rates of co-financing may be reduced in accordance with the "polluter pays" principle or where a project generates income.

Table 22.1 **Cohesion policy: indicative financial allocations, 2007–13 (€m, current prices)**

	Convergence objective			Regional competitiveness and employment objective		European territorial co-operation objective	Total
	Cohesion fund	Convergence	Statistical phasing-out	Phasing-in	Regional and competitiveness and employment		
Belgium	–	–	638		1,425	194	2,258
Bulgaria	2,283	4,391	–		–	179	6,853
Czech Republic	8,819	17,064	–		419	389	26,692
Denmark	–	–	–		510	103	613
Germany	–	11,864	4,215		9,409	851	26,340
Estonia	1,152	2,252	–	–	–	52	3,456
Greece	3,697	9,420	6,458	635	–	210	20,420
Spain	3,543	21,054	1,583	4,955	3,522	559	35,217
France	–	3,191	–	–	10,257	872	14,319
Ireland	–	–	–	458	293	151	901
Italy	–	21,211	430	972	5,353	846	28,812
Cyprus	213	–	–	399	–	28	640
Latvia	1,540	2,991	–	–	–	90	4,620
Lithuania	2,305	4,470	–	–	–	109	6,885
Luxembourg	–	–	–	–	50	15	65
Hungary	8,642	14,248	–	2,031	–	386	25,307
Malta	284	556	–	–	–	15	855
Netherlands	–	–	–	–	1,660	247	1,907
Austria	–	–	177	–	1,027	257	1,461
Poland	22,176	44,377	–	–	–	731	67,284
Portugal	3 060	17,133	280	448	490	99	21,511
Slovenia	1,412	2,689	–	–	–	104	4,205
Slovakia	3,899	7.013	–	–	449	227	11,588
Finland	–	–	–	545	1,051	120	1,716
Sweden	–	–	–	–	1,626	265	1,891
UK	–	2.738	174	965	6,014	722	10,613
Romania	6,552	12.661	–	–	–	455	19,668
Interregional	–	–	–	–	–	445	445
Technical aid	–	–	–	–	–	–	868
Total	**69,578**	**199,322**	**13,955**	**11,409**	**43,556**	**8,723**	**347,410**

Note: Totals may not add up due to rounding.
Source: European Commission

23 Social policy

ESF is centrepiece of social policy

At the centre of the EU's social policy is the European Social Fund (ESF), established under Article 123 of the Rome treaty. The purpose of the fund was defined as:

> To improve employment opportunities for workers in the
> common market and to contribute thereby to raising the
> standard of living ... it shall have the task of rendering the
> employment of workers easier and of increasing their
> geographical and occupational mobility within the Community.

In its early years the ESF operated on a very small scale, providing assistance for the retraining of workers displaced through structural changes. With the sixfold increase in unemployment between 1970 and 1986, when it reached the record level of 16m people or 12% of the working population, both the finances and the scope of the fund were greatly increased. The ESF planned to grant a total of €75.95 billion across the EU for various schemes between 2007 and 20013.

The ESF aims to help unemployed people find jobs, as well as promoting equality between men and women, sustainable development and economic and social cohesion. Activities that can be supported by the fund include:

- education and vocational training projects;
- schemes to promote and encourage employment and self-employment;
- initiatives to generate new sources of employment;
- improvements to national, regional and local employment services;
- schemes to foster links between the worlds of work, education and research;
- innovative measures and pilot projects to create work in local communities.

Measures funded by the ESF receive aid alongside financial support from the public and/or private sectors in the country concerned – this is known as the "additionality principle".

Support for youth training programmes

Much of the aid earmarked for young people is channelled through major schemes undertaken by several of the member states. For example, in France tens of thousands of young people have benefited from employment/training contracts, enabling them, with the ESF's assistance, to work in a business while continuing their training. In Ireland significant support has been given to the Industrial Training Authority to help set up extensive youth training programmes.

On the other hand, through national governments, the commission receives thousands of applications each year to support small-scale schemes. Normally around half of these applications are approved.

Certain categories of adults

In addition to its efforts on behalf of young people, the ESF gives priority to adults in the following categories:

- unemployed or underemployed workers, and especially the long-term unemployed;
- women who wish to resume work;
- handicapped people capable of joining the labour market;
- migrant workers from within the EU and immigrants who have settled there in order to work, together with their families;
- workers, particularly in small and medium-sized firms, faced with the problem of retraining owing to the introduction of new technologies or the improvement of management techniques;
- people working in the field of employment promotion; experts in vocational training or recruitment, or development agents.

Other specific operations

Lastly, there are specific operations under the ESF, for which 5% of the budget must be reserved. For example, EQUAL was created to help find more and better jobs that would be open to all. It tests new ways of tackling discrimination and inequality experienced by those in work and those looking for a job. The EU's contribution of €3.3 billion over the 2007–13 period will be matched by national funding. The ESF also supports the so-called "Article 6" measures, which include pilot projects, exchanges of experience and information activities.

Table 23.1 **ESF co-funding breakdown, 2007–13 (€m)**

	EU	National	Private	Total
Austria	524	550	110	1,184
Belgium	1,073	1,155	91	2,319
Bulgaria	1,185	209	–	1,394
Cyprus	119	30	–	150
Czech Republic	3,775	661	–	4,435
Denmark	254	170	85	510
Estonia	392	52	19	461
Finland	619	802	–	1,420
France	5,395	3,693	1,188	10,275
Germany	9,381	4,786	1,499	15,666
Greece	4,363	1,362	–	5,726
Hungary	3,629	640	–	4,269
Ireland	375	982	3	1,360
Italy	6,938	8,383	–	15,321
Latvia	550	86	21	657
Lithuania	1,028	106	76	1,210
Luxembourg	25	25	–	50
Malta	112	20	–	132
Netherlands	830	468	407	1,705
Poland	9,707	1,713	–	11,420
Portugal	6,512	2,697	–	9,210
Romania	3,684	651	–	4,335
Slovakia	1,500	265	–	1,764
Slovenia	756	133	–	889
Spain	8,057	3,243	125	11,426
Sweden	691	692	–	1,383
United Kingdom	4,475	4,135	215	8,825
Total	**75,953**	**37,708**	**3,840**	**117,501**

Note: Totals may not add up due to rounding.
Source: European Commission

Employment strategy

At the Amsterdam summit in June 1997, EU leaders agreed a new language in the treaty to link employment and economic policy more closely. While confirming that EU governments have primary responsibility for the design and delivery of employment policies, the treaty provided the legal base for a more strategic framework for co-ordination of EU employment policies. The Luxembourg European Council of November 1997 initiated what is known as the European Employment Strategy (EES). The leaders agreed a set of common objectives and targets for employment policy comprising four pillars: employability; entrepreneurship; adaptability; and equal opportunities for women and men.

Since 2005, the employment guidelines are integrated with the macroeconomic and microeconomic policies and are set for a three-year period. The guidelines are:

- implement employment policies aiming at achieving full employment, improving quality and productivity at work, and strengthening social and territorial cohesion;
- promote a life-cycle approach to work;
- ensure inclusive labour markets for job-seekers and disadvantaged people;
- improve matching of labour-market needs;
- promote flexibility combined with employment security and reduce labour-market segmentation;
- ensure employment-friendly wage and other labour cost developments;
- expand and improve investment in human capital;
- adapt education and training systems in response to new competence requirements.

New agenda

At the Lisbon European Council in March 2000, EU leaders agreed a broad agenda of economic and social reforms (see pages 125–7). They set ambitious targets for raising employment rates in the EU by 2010: to 70% for the labour force as a whole, to at least 60% for women and to 50% for older workers. As part of the so-called Lisbon process, the European Social Policy Agenda was launched to build an active welfare state, invest in human resources, consolidate cohesion, and boost the quality and quantity of jobs. In June 2000, the commission unveiled details of the new agenda, a five-year plan for 2000–05 addressing new social challenges such as introducing labour market flexibility, tackling social exclusion, adopting crucial health and safety laws, addressing pension problems, and improving training and life-long learning. A scoreboard detailing progress on the agenda was set up, and plans were made to co-ordinate the social agenda with the employment package, the broad economic guidelines and the budget.

After five years of limited results, EU leaders relaunched the strategy in March 2005, placing greater emphasis on growth and jobs and transferring more ownership to member states via national action plans. In March 2008, they agreed to shift the Lisbon agenda away from the purely "growth and jobs" focus, putting the environment and citizens in the foreground instead.

By 2009, with the economic turmoil biting, job creation and competitiveness returned to the top of the agenda. The European Commission unveiled a new jobs plan in June 2009, redirecting €19 billion of planned expenditure under the European Social Fund to help people stay in work or move towards new jobs via skills upgrades. In July 2008, the commission also tabled new proposals to tackle discrimination and improve workers' rights and cross-border health care, but both were put on hold because of the recession.

24 Workers' rights

Under Article 117 of the Rome treaty the member states agreed on the need to promote improved living and working conditions for workers, while Article 118 gave the commission the task of promoting close co-operation between member states in the social field, particularly in matters relating to:

- employment;
- labour law and working conditions;
- basic and advanced vocational training;
- social security;
- prevention of occupational accidents and diseases;
- occupational hygiene;
- the right of association, and collective bargaining between employers and workers.

In practice, the EU's impact has been most marked in relation to the rights of migrant workers, equal pay for men and women (see page 234), and safety factors. Despite the activities of the European Social Fund (Chapter 23) and the European Regional Development Fund (Chapter 22), little has been achieved in terms of assuring employment for EU workers, unemployment having risen to 8.9% of the labour force by mid-2009. Attempts to harmonise social security systems have enjoyed only partial success, and commission initiatives to provide a wider framework for worker participation in management decisions have been blocked by the unwillingness of some member governments (notably that of the UK) to agree to legislation in this field.

Rights of migrant workers
Some 18.5m third-country nationals are estimated as working in the EU, or 3.8% of the population. One-third of these are from other EU member states. In 2006 the annual crude immigration rate was 1.6 per 1,000 in the EU. Under EU law, EU migrants must be treated like nationals of the host country. Their right of free movement from one member state to another is guaranteed, and all discrimination on national grounds is forbidden, whether relating to employment, social security, trade union rights, living and working conditions, housing, education or vocational

training. Union migrants going to jobs in another EU country do not need a work permit and can claim a five-year residence permit, which is automatically renewable, even after their retirement.

The right to work is, in theory, subject to only two restrictions:

- for "justified reasons" of public order, health or safety;
- for certain forms of public administration work.

In practice, member states have tried to shut off all public administration jobs from foreign applicants, but a series of decisions by the Court of Justice has gradually reduced the range of posts which can be reserved to nationals of the host country.

Mutual recognition of professional qualifications

It had taken a long time for the member states to agree on the mutual recognition of professional qualifications, so that for many years it was not possible for many workers to practise their professions in EU countries other than their own. However, doctors, nurses, veterinary surgeons, dentists and midwives are now able to do so, provided that they are nationals of an EU country and have obtained their qualifications within the EU. Lawyers established in one member state are able to offer their services in another, as are architects and pharmacists, but only since 1987 as it took the best part of 20 years for agreement to be reached in the Council of Ministers.

Improvement of working conditions

Somewhat more urgency has been shown in dealing with proposals for the improvement of working conditions. In 1975 the European Foundation for the Improvement of Living and Working Conditions was established in Dublin, and since that date it has helped to formulate EC policy in this area. The major emphasis has been on safety and health in the workplace, where more than 100,000 people are killed in accidents each year and millions injured. European Agency for Safety and Health at Work (EU-OSHA) was set up in 1996 in Bilbao, Spain. It is the main EU reference point for safety and health at work. With some 5,720 fatal work-related accidents a year in the EU, the agency aims to make workers and employers aware of the risks that they face.

In its second action programme on work safety, adopted in 1984, the EU concentrated on:

- rules for the use of dangerous substances;
- ergonomic measures and principles for preventing accidents and dangerous situations;
- improvements in organisation, training and information;
- problems posed by new technologies.

Several directives have been adopted on safety signs, on electrical equipment used in mines with firedamp, and on protection against chemical, physical or biological agents such as lead, asbestos, noise and vinyl chloride monomer. Under the Single European Act, agreement on new directives or regulations on improving the working environment and on health and safety provisions no longer requires unanimity within the Council of Ministers. This has led to a speeding-up of decision-making in this area.

Workers' rights in companies

Since the mid-1970s the European Commission has made vigorous efforts to promote the protection of workers' interests in other areas, notably by safeguarding their rights in companies. Directives have been in force since 1977 establishing minimum requirements with regard to mass redundancies, since 1979 guaranteeing established rights in the event of transfer, and since 1983 ensuring payment of salary and other claims when an employer goes out of business.

The Social Charter of Workers' Rights

The other principal element in the EU's social policy is the Social Charter of Workers' Rights, signed at Strasbourg in December 1989 by 11 of the then 12 heads of government. Margaret Thatcher, who was then the UK prime minister, refused to sign on the grounds that it would lead to higher unemployment by deterring employers from creating new jobs.

The Social Charter was originally conceived by Jacques Delors, who argued that the implementation of the 1992 programme would chiefly benefit European companies whose profits would rise as barriers to their operating on a Europe-wide basis would disappear. He successfully persuaded all the governments except that of the UK that the 1992 programme should be buttressed by parallel measures which would improve the working and social conditions of employees.

The charter itself had no more than a declaratory effect, but it was to be followed by a Social Action programme, containing 47 pieces of legislation which, if adopted by the Council of Ministers, would be binding on the member states including the UK.

Much of the Social Action programme could be approved by qualified majority voting and would therefore be adopted despite UK opposition. The draft Treaty on European Union, presented to the Maastricht summit in December 1991, would have made the remaining proposals also liable to majority voting rather than unanimity. John Major refused to accept this, however, so the other 11 member states signed a Protocol on Social Policy (also known as the Social Chapter), which provided that they could decide these matters by qualified majority voting among themselves but that the UK would not take part in the deliberations nor be bound by the outcome. This extraordinary decision, whereby 11 member states could use the institutions, procedures and mechanisms of the EC for the taking of decisions that did not apply to the 12th member, was an unprecedented development and many observers doubted whether it would last long. It was effectively terminated by the victory of the Labour Party in the UK general election on May 1st 1997. The newly elected government lost no time in declaring that it would adhere to the protocol, which in the following month was formally incorporated in the Amsterdam Treaty.

So far the main directives adopted under the Social Action programme have been concerned with protecting the employment rights of pregnant women; restricting the number of hours that employees could be required to work within a fixed period; special provisions for restricting night work; guaranteeing subcontracted workers from other countries the same rights (on health and safety, equal opportunities and dismissal) as local workers; and giving part-time workers the right to written contracts.

Revised European company statute

In 1989 the commission also tried to refloat its earlier proposal for a European company statute. In its revised form this would be a voluntary option for companies, but sweetened with the possibility of more favourable tax treatment. The proposals for worker participation were made a great deal more flexible, with three alternative systems on offer based respectively on French, German and UK practices. Despite this new flexibility the then UK government remained firmly opposed. Part of the statute was, however, adopted under the Protocol on Social Policy, which meant that, initially at least, it was applicable only in the other 14 member states. The commission approved such a proposal in April 1994, under which European Works Councils were to be established in multinational firms within the EU so that employees may be informed and consulted about strategic decision-making by their companies. This proposal, which was adopted as a directive by the Council of Ministers later in 1994, did not apply to workers in the UK, but UK companies with employees in other EU countries were required to comply. In practice, the directive has largely been applied in the UK, despite the "opt-out" insisted on by the government of John Major, which was given up by the newly elected Labour government in June 1998.

The European company statute was formally adopted by EU social affairs ministers in October 2001, after more than 30 years of negotiation. The European Company (known by its Latin name of "Societas Europaea" or SE) will give companies operating in more than one member state the option of setting up as a single company under EU law, operating with one set of rules and a unified management and reporting system. It obliges SE managers to provide regular reports to a body representing the companies' employees, detailing current and future business plans, production and sales levels, implications of these for the workforce, management changes, mergers, divestments, potential closures and lay-offs.

Amsterdam and Luxembourg initiatives

The inclusion of a new chapter on employment in the Amsterdam treaty, which came into force in May 1999, and the convening in Luxembourg of a special EU summit on employment in November 1997 have given a fresh boost to EU action in the employment field. Following the Luxembourg summit, the Council of Ministers adopted a series of guidelines, which the member states were required to incorporate in their own national action plans.

The Working Time Directive

The 1993 EU Working Time Directive, which came into force in June 1996, sets provisions for a maximum 48-hour working week (including overtime), rest periods and breaks and a minimum of four weeks paid leave per year, to protect workers from adverse health and safety risks. It applies to all sectors of activity, both public and private. A number of areas, such as air, rail, road, sea, inland waterway and lake transport, sea fishing, other work at sea and doctors in training, which were exempt from the 1993 directive, were brought within its scope in an amendment agreed in 2000.

Several categories of workers are still excluded from the directive:

- managing directors or other persons with autonomous decision-making powers;
- family workers;
- workers officiating at religious ceremonies in churches and religious communities.

The 1993 directive defines working time as "any period during which the worker is working, at the employer's disposal and carrying out his activities or duties, in accordance with national laws and/or practice". A rest period is defined as "any period which is not working time". The directive does not allow for any interim category. In 2000 and 2003, the European Court of Justice ruled on two cases involving the definition of working time. Both turned on whether time spent on call constituted working time, and both concerned the health-care sector: the SIMAP case in primary health care and the Jaeger case in hospitals. In both cases the ECJ ruled that time spent on call should be regarded as working time.

Although the UK government, along with 14 other member states, negotiated an opt-out from the directive, the European Parliament voted in December 2008 to cancel the opt-out. However, MEPS' conciliation talks with EU ministers later failed to produce a new deal on the directive, so the current directive and opt-out remain in force.

25 Energy

Common energy policy slow to evolve

The coal industry was subjected to detailed supervision under the ECSC since 1951, and the civil nuclear industry, particularly with regard to research and development, under Euratom since 1958, yet the Community was slow to evolve a common energy policy which would enable it to plan and implement a joint strategy to meet all its energy needs. Since the first "oil shock" of 1973, which caught the EC woefully unprepared, there has been a certain convergence in policy and common objectives have been defined without, however, a central machinery being established to ensure that they are pursued in a co-ordinated manner. The result is a "semi-common" policy, with agreement in principle on most objectives, but a patchwork division of responsibility between the different sectors.

This is undoubtedly a significant improvement on the situation in the early 1970s, but the EU remains particularly vulnerable in the energy field. In 2008, external sources of supply accounted for 54% of total consumption (compared with a mere 18% for the United States) and the commission says it could rise to 70% by 2020 if appropriate measures are not taken. Moreover, its internal energy production is likely to remain stable or even to decline, and its demand would surely grow in the event of renewed economic growth. Of the 27 member states, only Denmark and the UK are net exporters of energy.

A programme was adopted in 1974

The 1973 crisis, which saw the quadrupling of oil prices virtually overnight, was followed by the fiasco of the December 1973 Copenhagen EC summit, which singularly failed to produce a joint response to the Arab oil producers, France and the UK in particular preferring to pursue bilateral deals with oil suppliers rather than to present a united front with their EC partners. It was only in September 1974 that the Council of Ministers adopted a programme drawn up by the European Commission called "Towards a New Energy Policy Strategy". This programme has formed the framework for most subsequent discussions on energy policy.

The overriding priority laid down was the importance of reducing dependence on imported oil supplies and the desirability of diversifying

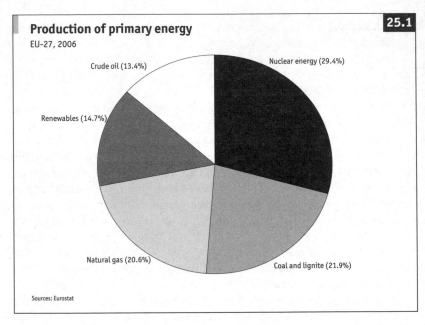

Production of primary energy
EU-27, 2006

25.1

Crude oil (13.4%)

Nuclear energy (29.4%)

Renewables (14.7%)

Natural gas (20.6%)

Coal and lignite (21.9%)

Sources: Eurostat

the sources of supply. This objective was pursued with considerable success. Over ten years the Community cut its oil imports by half. By 1983 it was estimated that the equivalent of 250m tons of oil annually was being saved due to more efficient use of energy: an economy of more than 20%.

Other measures
Completion of the internal market
The market for oil products is already largely open, and little more can practically be done. There is, however, scope for increasing internal trade in the gas and electricity sectors through the encouragement of long-term contracts, cross-border investment and interconnections between national systems, such as France–UK and France–Italy, both of which have been assisted by EIB loans. In 1990 a more comprehensive programme was adopted for linking up energy networks throughout the Community.

Common pricing
The EU has been increasingly active in ensuring that all energy sectors should follow common pricing principles which are transparent and realistic and should not distort competition between industries. For

example, the Dutch gas industry was prevented from supplying cheap gas to horticulturalists which allowed them to heat their greenhouses more cheaply than their competitors in other EU countries. In 1990 a directive was adopted enforcing transparency in the pricing policies of electricity and gas suppliers.

Improved security of supply
This is to be achieved by the development of competitive European production, diversification of imports, greater flexibility of consumption and effective contingency measures. Community legislation provides for the compulsory stocking of fuel at electricity plants, equal to 30 days' consumption and for oil stocks to be maintained at a minimum level equivalent to 90 days' consumption.

External relations
The EU is seeking to capitalise on its bargaining power as a major customer of energy supplies, the Union absorbing some 14% of the world market. In 1989 the EC negotiated an economic co-operation agreement with the Gulf states, which have the world's largest oil reserves, and it maintains close relations with OAPEC, the Organisation of Arab Petroleum Exporting Countries. In the nuclear field long-term agreements with the principal uranium suppliers (Australia, Canada and the United States) assure a certain stability of supply. The commission is seeking to secure a greater degree of co-operation between member states on gas supply contracts. In the developing countries the Union is helping to disseminate new technologies (solar energy, energy saving, and so on) through some 60 aid programmes. (See also European Energy Charter, page 191.)

Environmental protection
Since 1989 the EC, in response to strong pressure from public opinion, has adopted a series of measures designed to reduce environmental damage caused by the energy sector. They concern the introduction of lead-free petrol, the reduction of toxic emissions from automobiles and large combustion plants, and the reduction of the sulphur content of heating oil and diesel fuel.

Regional development
In addition to the grants and loans offered by the ECSC, the ERDF and the EIB for regional development projects, many of which are concerned with

the energy sector, the special Valoren programme for improving the efficiency of energy resources in the less-favoured regions was launched in
1986. This programme, which was allocated 400m ecus, seeks to exploit the
use of indigenous fuels (such as small peat and lignite deposits) as well as to
promote the efficient use of energy. In 1996 the Valoren programme was
incorporated in the EU's SAVE II programme, running from 1996 to 2000, to
promote energy efficiency. Under this programme the commission now
finances some 100 local energy agencies under the responsibility of local
and regional authorities.

Technological innovation
The EU is pursuing a major research, development and demonstration
programme focusing on:

◼ nuclear safety (reactor security, waste management, control of
   fissile materials, protection against radioactivity, and so on);
◼ controlled nuclear fusion;
◼ solid fuels;
◼ new energy resources;
◼ the efficient and environmentally friendly use of energy.

Much of the research is being pursued by firms and institutes in the
different member states. The four research centres directly established
by Euratom, at Karlsruhe in Germany, Ispra in Italy, Geel in Belgium and
Petten in the Netherlands, now known collectively as the Joint Research
Centre (JRC), do important work mainly in the field of nuclear safety
and environmental protection. The EU's most ambitious undertaking,
however, was the establishment at Culham in the UK of the Joint European Torus (JET), where all European research into nuclear fusion is
now concentrated. This is one of only four major programmes in the
world, the others being in Russia, the United States and Japan. Co-operation and exchange of information agreements have been reached with
each of these countries, and the four partners built the International
Thermonuclear Experimental Reactor (ITER) under joint auspices. This is
seen as the next major step in a programme whose ultimate objective is
the generation of electricity by more economic, cleaner and safer means
than those provided by nuclear fission.

Energy white paper
In December 1995 the commission adopted a white paper on energy. The

three pillars of the EU's energy policy in the future were defined as overall competitiveness, security of energy supply and environmental protection. This policy would be implemented mainly by means of integration of the market, management of the external dependency, promotion of sustainable development and support of energy research and technology. The first fruits of the white paper were directives aiming to secure the liberalisation and transparency of the markets for electricity and gas supply. The electricity directive was approved at the end of 1996 and the gas directive early in 1998. It brought many changes to the functioning of the electricity market: it abolished exclusive rights; it required unbundling of network activities from generation and supply activities; and its fundamental objectives were transparency and non-discrimination.

However, with France consistently blocking moves to let foreign companies compete in national markets, the energy liberalisation plans seemed to be heading nowhere. France was only able to sign up to opening the market in 2004, allowing the introduction of a range of measures that would make it easier for the hitherto frustrated power companies of Spain and Germany to get into the market. Under the accord, EU leaders backed opening the market for commercial users of gas and electricity, around 60% of the market, in 2004. The deal maintained, for a while at least, the unique protection enjoyed by Eléctricité de France, a state-owned energy giant.

The deal opened the electricity market for all non-household customers by July 2004, and for all customers by July 2007. The directive also contains further measures concerning the legal unbundling of network activities from generation and supply; establishes a regulator in all member states with well-defined functions; requires published network tariffs; reinforces public-service obligations, especially for vulnerable customers; introduces monitoring of security of supply; and sets up mandatory electricity labelling for fuel mix and for some emission and waste data.

However, in the years since the 1995 commission white paper, there has been fierce resistance to the liberalisation process within the EU, highlighting different attitudes to competition and the notion of protecting national interests in the energy sector. By 2009, the single European energy market was still far from reality. The reforms have not been fully implemented in some parts of the EU, so a handful of former state energy monopolies continue to have a crushing grip on their domestic markets. Former state monopolies have too much market power and there is evidence that consumers in some countries are paying too much for their gas and electricity. To counter this, the commission has proposed splitting the ownership of power providers and the energy distribution grid, and increasing distribution links between countries, allowing competition across borders. It continues to argue, in the face of resistance from countries such as France and Germany, that power producers must not be allowed to own the distribution network because they are then able to hinder competitors.

Energy and climate change

After the Kyoto climate change protocol in 1997, the EU's energy policy was intricately linked with its climate change commitments (for more details, see Chapter 28).

In a green paper written in August 2006 regarding Europe's energy policy, the European Commission identified three main objectives for an EU energy policy. It should:

- be sustainable with an emphasis on environmentally friendly forms of energy;
- allow healthy competition that provides affordable prices for consumers;
- ensure a secure and continuous supply, and decrease the dependence on foreign sources.

The commission also identified six areas in which the EU should focus its work and resources:

- complete the internal market for energy (electricity and gas);
- secure the EU's energy supply;
- promote a coherent and united external energy policy on the international stage;
- seek sustainable energy sources from a variety of sources, exploring possible alternative sources;
- establish an environmentally friendly plan that combats the effects of climate change;
- use Europe's diverse technology to improve European energy.

As a follow-up to the green paper, the commission unveiled a package of energy and climate change proposals in January 2007 in a move which, it said, would "set the pace for a new global industrial revolution" and increase EU resilience to future oil-price shocks. The overall price tag of the plan was estimated at around 0.5% of EU GDP, about €3 a week for EU citizens.

The 2008 package

An energy and climate change package was eventually broadly confirmed at a landmark EU summit in December 2008. Despite lobbying by business and various EU member states, the overall so-called 20–20–20 targets were kept (for more details, see Chapter 28). The package focused on three areas:

- 20% cut in greenhouse gas emissions by 2020;
- 20% increase in use of renewable energy by 2020;
- 20% cut in energy consumption through improved energy efficiency by 2020.

European Energy Charter

This major initiative towards international co-operation in energy supplies was launched in 1989: western know-how and investment would be made available to the Soviet natural gas and oil industries in exchange for the Soviet Union guaranteeing supplies to western Europe over a lengthy period. The European Energy Charter was signed in The Hague in December 1991 by the EC, 37 European and OECD states and 12 former Soviet republics. Its objective is to create a climate favourable to the operation of enterprises and to the flow of investment and technology by applying market-economy principles to the field of energy. Concrete co-operation focused specifically on:

- access to and development of energy reserves;
- market access;
- liberalisation of trade in energy;
- energy efficiency and environmental protection;
- safety principles and guidelines;
- research, technological development, innovation and dissemination;
- education and training.

In 1994 the signatory countries went on to sign a binding agreement, the European Energy Charter Treaty, which set out the general rules on trade in energy, conditions of competition, access to capital, transmission and transit, transfers of technology, environmental protection, intellectual property, conditions for investment and the procedure for settling disputes. The treaty came into force in 1998.

ECSC treaty expires

When the European Coal and Steel Community (ECSC) was established in 1951, the coal and steel industries, which were regarded as the "basic industries", held a dominant place in the west European economy. This is now much less true, though both industries remain significant factors. The steel industry, in particular, has been transformed in the past three decades, and the Community was largely instrumental, first in its rapid growth and subsequently in its sharp decline.

The ECSC treaty expired on July 23rd 2002. Well before the treaty ran out, the levies on coal and steel production were phased out, as they were yielding far more than was needed to meet the social costs of the run-down of the two industries. By 2001, the total budget of the ECSC was €168m, compared with €339m 14 years earlier.

However, the commission decided to maintain the strict rules on state aid for the European iron and steel industry.

The expiry meant the treaty's assets were transferred to the EU, as provided for in a protocol annexed to the Nice treaty. The revenue from these assets and liabilities is now used exclusively for research in the sectors related to the coal and steel industries.

26 Transport

Slow progress on common transport policy

The Rome treaty, in Article 74, envisages the creation of a common transport policy, but for the first 24 years of the EC's existence progress in this direction was so slow that in September 1982 the European Parliament brought proceedings against the Council of Ministers in the Court of Justice for failing to carry out its obligations under the treaty. The action was partially successful. The court held that the council had infringed the treaty by failing to ensure freedom to provide services in international transport and to lay down conditions for the admission of non-resident carriers to national transport in the member states. The court declined, however, to take cognisance of the absence of a common transport policy as such, since the treaty did not define that policy with sufficient clarity to enable the court to pronounce on it. It did, however, recommend the council to work continuously towards the progressive attainment of a common transport policy.

Speed-up after court ruling

Following the court's ruling there was a significant acceleration of council decision-making in the transport field, partly in the context of the adoption of a timetable to complete the EC's internal market by 1992. In 1991 a report entitled "Transport 2000 and Beyond" was adopted, setting objectives for an integrated continent-wide transport system, involving EC assistance in linking national networks and in improving links with central and eastern Europe. Transport is estimated to provide 6.5% of the EU's gross national product. It accounts for more than 6% of total employment, 40% of member state investments and 30% of EU energy consumption. Its importance in the economic integration of western Europe can hardly be overestimated.

Overall transport priorities

In September 2001, the commission unveiled a white paper on a common policy in the transport sector for the following decade. The underlying aim was to reduce congestion on roads caused mainly by increasing freight and to transfer part of it to more environmentally friendly means of transport such as maritime routes and railways. It pinpointed unequal growth in the different modes of transport, congestion on some main roads and busy rail lines, impact on the environment or citizens' health, and lack of road safety. The paper included a range of measures combining pricing, revitalising railways and waterways as alternative modes of transport to roads and targeted investment in the trans-European transport networks. The main objectives were:

- decoupling economic growth and transport growth;
- shifting the balance between modes of transport by 2010, by curbing the demand for road transport via pricing mechanisms and revitalising alternative transport modes such as railways, maritime and inland waterway transport (intermodality);
- having taxation systems reflect the true costs of transport, including external costs such as environmental damage, congestion, or human accidents;
- making transport systems more efficient and safer.

The white paper led to various policy initiatives:

- a regulation reinforcing air passengers' rights;
- improving road safety – the European Road Safety Action Programme was launched and two communications on eSafety and the development of safer and more intelligent vehicles were adopted, with the overall objective of improving road safety and halving the number of road deaths by 2010;
- preventing congestion by promoting intermodality, through the "Marco Polo" programmes;
- revision of the Eurovignette Directive creating a harmonised EU framework for charging heavy goods vehicles on European motorways, so as to reflect the "external costs" of transport, including environmental damage, congestion and accidents and to promote the "modal shift";
- improving infrastructure in the context of trans-European networks and integration of the new member states into the network;
- reinforcing the position of railways, with the adoption of three packages of measures aimed at market liberalisation and harmonisation.

Table 26.1 **Modal breakdown of inland passenger and freight transport, 2006**

	Passenger transport (% of total inland passenger-km)			Freight transport (% of total inland freight-km)		
	Car	Bus	Rail	Rail	Road	Waterway
Austria[a]	79.4	10.3	10.3	33.8	63.2	3.0
Belgium	79.9	13.1	7.0	14.0	71.2	14.7
Bulgaria[b]	64.3	30.4	5.3	27.1	69.0	3.9
Cyprus	–	–	–	–	100.0	–
Czech Republic	75.6	16.9	7.5	23.8	76.1	0.1
Denmark	79.8	11.2	9.1	8.2	91.8	–
Estonia	76.0	22.0	2.0	65.3	34.7	0.0
Finland	84.9	10.3	4.8	27.1	72.7	0.2
France	85.3	5.3	9.4	15.7	80.9	3.4
Germany	85.7	6.5	7.8	21.4	65.9	12.8
Greece	76.3	21.9	1.8	1.9	98.1	–
Hungary	63.2	23.8	13.0	23.9	71.6	4.5
Ireland	76.1	18.8	5.1	1.2	98.8	–
Italy	81.9	12.1	5.9	9.9	90.1	0.0
Latvia[b]	76.2	18.2	5.6	61.0	39.0	0.0
Lithuania	90.5	8.5	1.0	41.6	58.4	0.0
Luxembourg	85.3	10.8	3.9	4.6	91.5	4.0
Malta	–	–	–	–	100.0	–
Netherlands	87.5	3.8	8.7	4.1	63.6	32.3
Poland	82.5	10.6	6.9	29.4	70.4	0.2
Portugal	82.8	12.8	4.5	5.1	94.9	–
Romania[b]	74.0	15.6	10.5	19.4	70.5	10.0
Slovenia	85.6	11.4	3.0	21.8	78.2	–
Slovakia	72.7	21.2	6.1	30.9	68.8	0.3
Spain	82.6	12.0	5.4	4.6	95.4	–
Sweden	84.1	7.5	8.4	35.5	64.5	–
United Kingdom	87.4	6.5	6.1	11.8	88.1	0.1
EU-27	83.4	9.5	7.1	17.7	76.7	5.6

Note: Totals may not add up due to rounding.
a Excluding pipelines.   b Excluding powered two-wheelers.
Source: Eurostat

In June 2009, the commission kicked off a year-long debate on the EU's transport plans when it unveiled a paper outlining how the environment, fuel shortages and other factors would shape policy over the next few decades. The communication identified six trends and challenges: ageing, migration and internal mobility, environmental challenges, the availability of energy resources, urbanisation and globalisation. These will affect policy in different ways. For example, the number of people aged 65 or more will rise from 17% of the population in 2009 to 30% in 2060, putting more pressure on transport services for users with reduced mobility. Globally, the paper says the number of cars in the world will jump from about 700m in 2009 to more than 3 billion in 2050. Households in the EU spend about 13.5% of their income on transport-related goods and services, making these the second biggest budget item after house-related expenditure. The paper notes that more and more vehicles are being driven on Europe's roads: the stock of passenger cars in the EU-27 has surged by around 40% since 1990 to reach a total of about 230m in 2006.

Roads

It is in road transport that the commission has made the most persistent attempts to secure EU policies, and it has often had to wait for many years before the Council of Ministers can agree on the proposals.

Road safety

Some 40,000 people are killed and 1.7m injured each year in road accidents in the EU. A string of directives has harmonised standards for brakes, lighting, windscreens, sound levels, and so on. After a 20-year delay, agreement was reached in 1984 for common standards on weights and dimensions of commercial vehicles. The maximum lorry weight was then set at 40 tons (38 tons in the UK and Ireland). A further agreement on maximum axle weights for articulated lorries was reached in 1986 (11.5 tons, but 10.5 tons in the UK and Ireland). Also 1986 was declared Road Safety Year, and the commission drew up an action programme including infrastructure improvements and measures relating to road signs, vehicle safety and the behaviour and training of drivers. Subsequently, directives were adopted on:

- technical vehicle inspection;
- lorry suspension systems;
- the fitting of speed limitation devices in lorries and coaches;

- limiting the risks involved in the carriage of dangerous goods;
- restricting drivers' hours.

Frontier crossing

Delays and bureaucratic checks at internal frontier crossings had been a major source of expense and an undoubted barrier to intra-EC trade. Under the 1992 programme, steps were taken to remove this barrier.

International transport of goods

This had been restricted by quota and by licence. Up to 1985 only some 40% of road freight was liberalised, but under an agreement reached by the Council of Ministers in June 1986 the remainder of the trade is being progressively opened up to free competition. By 1993 all quota restrictions ended, but it was only by June 1998 that full freedom to operate transport services in other member states (cabotage) was granted.

Employment in road transport industry

Since 1974 the Community has established conditions for employment in the road transport industry, notably in terms of professional ability and training. Maximum driving periods have been established for each day and each week as well as obligatory periods of rest. Observance of these rules is controlled by a tachograph (known pejoratively as "the spy in the cab") which records the driving and resting time and speeds of heavy goods vehicles.

Railways

EU action regarding the railways has mainly focused on their troubled finances, which have steadily deteriorated in the face of increasing competition from road, air and waterway transport. The gap between revenue and costs has caused large deficits. These have been bridged by subsidies, which have placed considerable burdens on national budgets. In many cases these subsidies are a recognition of non-commercial duties imposed by the state, such as low fares and the continuation of loss-making lines in thinly populated areas.

In 1975 the Council of Ministers laid down guidelines for financial recovery and a clearer definition of relations between the railway companies (almost all of which were publicly owned) and government authorities.

In October 2007, EU member states agreed their "third railway package" on railway reforms. It introduced open access rights for international rail passenger services including cabotage by 2010. Operators may pick up and set down passengers at any station on an international route, including at stations located in the same member state. The new European driver licence allows train drivers to operate on the entire European network. The package also strengthens rail passengers' rights.

Transport infrastructure

The EC has played an important role in helping to finance transport infrastructure projects, ranging from roads and motorways to bridges and tunnels, ports and airports, canals, the upgrading or electrification of railways and the purchase of more comfortable and economic equipment (aircraft, high-speed trains, and so on). Nearly 20 billion ecus had been loaned by the EIB up to 1993 and a comparable amount had been expended in grants by the European Regional Development Fund. Projects in the UK which have benefited include Manchester and Birmingham airports, the Tyne-Wear metro, the Manchester light railway, the second Severn bridge and the ports of Ramsgate and Harwich.

Trans-European Networks (TENs)

In 1990 the commission published proposals for assisting the development of TENs in transport, energy and telecommunications. So far as railway development is concerned, a master plan was published for a high-speed network, including 9,000km of new lines, 15,000km of modified track and 1,200km of links between main lines.

The EU, through the EIB, had already assisted in the financing of the Channel Tunnel, a crucial element in the high-speed rail network. The guidelines were reviewed in 2004 prior to the enlargement of the EU, with the aim of integrating the ten new member states' infrastructure into the TEN-T. The number of priority projects, deemed essential for completing cross-border connections among the EU's 27 member states, was raised from 14 to 30, and rules for granting aid were modified to allow for a higher maximum co-funding rate (of 20% rather than 10%) for priority projects which cross borders and natural barriers. The updated list of projects focuses investments in rail and water transport: of the 30 priority projects, 18 are railway projects and two are inland waterways and shipping projects.

Inland waterways

Inland waterways play an important role in heavy industrial trade in several parts of the EU, the most notable of several large waterway systems being formed by the River Rhine and its tributaries. Since 1976 member states have agreed to a mutual recognition of each other's decisions on the navigability of waterways, and since 1982 the Council of Ministers has laid down technical specifications for waterway craft. In 1991 the council adopted a directive liberalising cabotage (international competition for the carriage of goods or passengers within other member states) and others on the mutual recognition of boatmasters' certifications, cockpit crew licences and driving licences.

The commission has taken the initiative in:

- moves to scrap overcapacity, financed by national governments;
- setting up a market monitoring system;
- drawing up an international agreement securing free competition once the Rhine–Main–Danube canal is completed and mutual access is provided for vessels from East European waterways.

Shipping

Few agreements had been reached on sea transport before 1986, despite the importance of this sector to the EC's trade. Around 95% of its external trade is carried by sea, which also plays an important role in intra-EU trade, in part because three member states do not have a common land frontier with the rest of the Union. It is in the interests of the EU to keep the shipping industry open to international competition, but it was only in December 1986 that the Council of Ministers agreed most of the elements of a common shipping policy which should enable the EU to use its collective bargaining power in such a way as to strengthen its opportunities to compete on the world market. Four regulations were approved, which came into effect in July 1987:

- **Competition.** This regulation set out precise directions as to how the EC's general rules of competition should be applied to the maritime transport sector.
- **Predatory pricing by third countries.** This provided for a coordinated response, allowing the EC to take anti-dumping measures against the countries or companies concerned.
- **Cargo reservations.** This regulation provided for a co-ordinated EC response to third countries which reserve a portion of their trade to their own vessels.
- **Freedom to provide services.** EU vessels are now free to ply between member states and between member states and third countries.

In the wake of tanker disasters at La Coruña and the Shetland Islands, the commission and the Council of Ministers mapped out, in 1993, an EU policy on safety at sea to underpin the work of individual member states, and to ensure more effective implementation of international regulations. The commission prepared directives or regulations to:

- lay down common rules for ship inspection;
- enforce a minimum level of training for crews;
- regulate the ballast requirements for oil tankers;
- set up a European vessel reporting system;
- regulate the carrying of dangerous or polluting goods.

Several other EU initiatives were adopted in 1998, including common safety rules for roll-on, roll-off ferries and high-speed passenger craft services; a proposal to improve port reception facilities for ship-generated waste and cargo residues; and directives to impose on all vessels operating within the EU (including those flying the flags of third countries) the working hours laid down by the International Labour Organisation, to apply certain international safety standards for passenger vessels, and to register all persons sailing on board passenger ships.

Tougher shipping rules were announced in 2000 in the wake of the Erika oil tanker spill off the French coast, when the 25-year-old single-hull vessel broke in two, releasing 100,000 tonnes of oil and damaging 400km of the Brittany coast. The first package of measures, known as Erika I, is supposed to toughen up port inspections, introduce better controls for ship classification societies and gradually phase out single-hull tankers, replacing them with safer, double-hull versions. The second package, Erika II, emphasises training for crews, establishes a European pollution damage fund to provide compensation of up to €1 billion for victims and sets up a European Maritime Safety Agency. The main duties of the agency are to support and monitor member states' compliance with maritime safety rules, evaluate the effectiveness of the rules, collect data and audit maritime classification societies.

Airways

Air transport was for many years the sector on which the EU had the least impact, and where its competition rules remained largely a dead letter. The entire system was controlled by a series of inter-governmental and inter-airline agreements, which effectively excluded competition and led to some of the highest air fares in the world, substantially greater, in particular, than on routes of comparable distance in North America. Before 1986 EC action had been largely restricted to the adoption of directives on co-operation in accident inquiries, the reduction of noise from aircraft and helicopters and the opening of routes between certain regional centres.

In April 1986 a ruling from the Court of Justice gave the commission the green light to force the pace. In a case involving the French travel firm Nouvelles Frontières, which had challenged price-fixing regulations under the French Civil Aviation Code, the court ruled that the EC general competition rules were applicable to air transport.

Simultaneously with its legal initiative, the commission sought to secure a political compromise which would enable at least a partial liberalisation of fares to be implemented. After lengthy and tortuous negotiations such a compromise was agreed in 1987 and came into force in January 1988. In 1991 the commission adopted a third liberalisation package designed to introduce full competition between European airlines. Since March 1997 airlines have been free to set their own fares and to operate anywhere within the EU.

The principal beneficiaries of the agreement are the Union's fast-growing private airlines, which have lower overheads and can charge lower prices than most state-owned organisations.

Single European sky

The commission's 1999 plans for a "single European sky" to improve air traffic management aimed to co-ordinate air traffic control as a necessary first step towards liberalisation of the airline market and, it is hoped, fewer delays and cheaper fares. In December 2002, EU transport ministers finally agreed the single sky policy, implemented in 2004, which aims to improve co-ordination of member states' airspace, cut delays and reduce air pollution. It came after the commission released estimates that a quarter of all EU flights were delayed in 2001 at a cost of €4.5 billion.

The legislation created the European Aviation Safety Agency (EASA). Set up in 2002, the agency was initially mandated to guarantee the airworthiness and environmental compatibility of aircraft, but its mandate was progressively extended to cover all other fields of aviation safety to "ensure precise, uniform and binding rules for airport safety, air traffic management and air navigation services" and establish "harmonised rules" regarding air traffic and navigation.

The EU and Eurocontrol, an inter-governmental agency for aviation navigation, also set up the Single European Sky ATM Research (SESAR), a public–private research and development partnership that aims to link all air assets together via common data-exchange networks to form a moving, real-time common operational picture of all assets at all times.

However, despite a series of regulations adopted in March 2004, the European sky remains broadly divided into 27 different pieces of airspace under the control of national governments. In 2007 the commission pushed member states to surrender sovereignty over their national airspace in favour of a European air-traffic management system by 2012, but the proposal was still stalled in 2009.

Attempts by the commission to negotiate liberalisation agreements with third countries, in particular the United States, have been frustrated by the refusal of some member states, notably the UK, to allow it to negotiate on their behalf. Consequently, the United States has been able, to some extent, to pick and choose among EU governments and to play one off against the other, with the prospect that the overall outcome will be less favourable to European airlines and consumers than would otherwise be the case.

Galileo

In March 2002, the €2.5 billion Galileo satellite programme was approved, offering a European and primarily civilian alternative to the dominant American global positioning system (GPS) which was developed largely for military purposes. Galileo, initially based on 30 satellites, will pinpoint the locations of users such as car drivers and airline pilots to within 1 metre, compared with the 100 metres on offer from GPS. The satellite's UN-approved frequencies are adjacent to those of GPS, making US co-operation indispensable if technical conflicts between the systems are to be avoided. However, GPS is free to commercial users whereas Galileo will charge a fee. Galileo should cover extreme latitudes that GPS misses, overcome the poor availability that GPS suffers in urban areas and make it possible to study from space tectonic movements in earthquake zones or analyse the level of rivers and lakes. It is expected to create 150,000 jobs and generate over €11 billion in annual revenue for EU companies.

27 Fisheries

A common fisheries policy was envisaged by Article 38 of the Rome treaty, on similar lines to the common agricultural policy. Yet no proposals for such a policy were produced before 1966, and it was another 17 years before the policy was finally put into place.

Exclusive fishing zones extended

From 1975 onwards a number of countries on the Atlantic coastline, including Iceland, Norway and Canada, extended their exclusive fishing zones to 200 nautical miles. These limits were subsequently to be endorsed by the international Convention on the Law of the Sea. The effect was to turn out of these waters many EC boats and also trawlers from third countries, many of which now concentrated their efforts on the North Sea, which was seriously threatened with overfishing.

In 1977, in self-defence, the Community also extended its fishing limits to 200 miles, leaving itself in charge of a huge expanse of sea, in which competition between member states' fishermen was intensifying. Within these limits there was fierce argument, particularly involving the UK, over the extent to which member states could claim permanent and exclusive rights in their coastal waters.

Common fisheries policy agreed

The European Commission tabled proposals as early as 1976, but it was only at the beginning of 1983, following hard fought negotiations, that a common fisheries policy (CFP) was finally concluded. Its main provisions are as follows:

- **Fishing zones.** In principle the Union's waters are open to all EU fishermen within a 200-mile limit from the Atlantic and North Sea coasts, but within narrower limits in the Mediterranean and Baltic seas. Member states are, however, allowed to retain limits up to 12 miles from their shores, within which fishing is reserved for their own fleets and for boats from other member states with traditional rights. In addition, fishing in an area beyond 12 miles around the Orkney and Shetland islands, for potentially endangered species, is subject to a system of Union licences. These measures apply for 20 years, but may be reviewed after ten.

- **Fish stocks.** These are conserved and managed by fixing total allowable catches (TACS) which are agreed annually by the Council of Ministers for all species threatened by overfishing. They are divided into quotas for each member state.
- **Conservation.** Based on scientific advice, conservation measures consist mainly of limits on fishing in certain zones, minimum mesh sizes for nets and, in certain cases, minimum sizes for fish landed. With the agreement of the commission, member states may apply extra conservation measures of their own, but these must not discriminate against other member states.
- **Surveillance.** Measures such as obligatory logbooks, port inspections, aerial controls, and so on, are applied by the member states, under the supervision of the commission, which has a team of inspectors for this purpose.
- **Marketing.** Standards as regards quality, size, weight, presentation and packing are applied throughout the Union, largely through the agency of producer organisations, but subject to inspection by the commission. Guide prices are set by the Council of Ministers with "withdrawal" prices set at 70–90%, the Union compensating fishermen for catches withdrawn from the market. Export refunds are available when, as is usually the case, the guide and withdrawal prices are higher than world prices. If European supplies prove insufficient, customs duties on imports can be suspended, as has happened in recent years with tuna and cod.
- **International relations.** Reciprocal agreements, permitting limited access to each other's waters and markets have been made with several other countries, such as Norway, the Faeroes, Canada and the United States. Other agreements with developing countries in Africa and the Indian Ocean permit EU vessels to fish in their waters in exchange for financial and technical assistance.

EU is world's fourth largest producer

The accession of Spain and Portugal in 1986 doubled the number of fishermen in the Community (to about 300,000, but by 2007 it was about 190,000), and increased the tonnage of the fishing fleet by about 65% and total catches by 30%. Spain and Portugal were required to adapt their fishing policies to the CFP.

At the same time the EU stepped up its financial aid for restructuring the fishing fleets – with grants available for the scrapping of surplus capacity, the construction and modernisation of boats, the development of aquaculture and improvements in processing and marketing. In 1998 the EU adopted a regulation banning the use of driftnets by all vessels in EU waters except the Baltic and by all EU vessels in other waters. It came into effect on January 1st 2002, and was accompanied by social measures and compensation for the fishermen concerned.

The CFP is based to a large extent on the model of the CAP, but it is far less expensive. The total cost for 2007–13 was around €3.8 billion, or around 0.4% of the entire budget. In the 1990s, all sides – fishermen, fish processors, environmentalists, consumers – agreed that the CFP was wasteful and encouraged cheating. Indeed, from the middle of the 1990s, the commission began pushing for more conservation measures, claiming that if fishing continued at the current rate, stocks would soon be exhausted. The sensitivity of the issue was raised during the "Greenland halibut war" between Spanish fishermen and Canadian authorities off the coast of the Grand Banks, where Canadian fishermen had been forced to stop fishing for cod because of a dramatic collapse in stocks. Within the EU, fleet-cutting programmes were adopted – the so-called multi-annual guidance programmes (MAGPs) – which included tough sanctions for member states that failed to meet their targets.

A radical reform of the CFP was agreed by fisheries ministers in December 2002. The reformed CFP, which came into force on January 1st, 2003, focused more on the sustainable exploitation of living aquatic resources based on sound scientific advice and on the precautionary approach to fishing, as well as on sustainable aquaculture. Specifically, it takes a more long-term approach to fisheries management by setting multi-annual recovery plans for stocks. The commission can take emergency measures where there is a serious threat to the conservation of resources, and member states can adopt conservation and management measures applicable to all fishing vessels within their 12-mile zones. The reformed CFP strengthens control and enforcement by reinforcing co-operation between member states so that each state can control vessels flying its flag throughout EU waters, except in the 12-mile zone of another member state. Fisheries ministers also established an emergency fund to encourage the decommissioning of vessels (the so-called "Scrapping Fund").

By April 2009, a commission green paper on the CFP admitted a catalogue of failure. It came as scientists warned that nearly 90% of stocks were overexploited. Many species – cod and hake, for example – were depleted in certain EU waters after years of chronic overfishing, exacerbated by poor controls and fines that, until recently, were not high enough to deter law-breakers and quota-busters. The commission called for a sweeping policy reform to improve the dire state of fish stocks, saying fleet overcapacity and rule-breakers had brought several species close to collapse. In May 2009, EU fisheries ministers agreed in principle to scrap the rules that decide fishing quotas. The EU has until 2012 to draw up a new CFP, which should be radically decentralised, giving more power to member states and to the industry.

28 Environment

Today, environment policy is seen as one of the most effective in the EU, covering issues as varied as chemical registration, eco-labels and climate change. But it was not considered a priority for the EU's founding fathers. There was no legal provision in the Rome treaty for a common policy on the environment, other than the general authority given by Article 235 enabling the Council of Ministers, acting unanimously, to take appropriate measures to achieve any of the objectives of the Community. This gap, reflecting the lack of interest in environmental matters in the 1950s, was remedied by the Single European Act, which in Article 25 set out a threefold aim for action on the environment:

- to preserve, protect and improve the quality of the environment;
- to contribute towards protecting human health;
- to ensure a prudent and rational utilisation of natural resources.

Programmes adopted from 1973

It is not surprising that, in the absence of any earlier definition of EC competence in this area, environment policy evolved in an ad hoc and incremental manner. It was not until 1985, for example, that the Council of Ministers drew up a work programme for obtaining information on the state of the environment and natural resources. Nevertheless, from 1973 onwards the council adopted a series of five-year action programmes which gradually broadened out from immediate responses to serious pollution problems to an overall preventive strategy for safeguarding the environment and natural resources. The most recent, the ten-year Sixth Environment Action Programme, was agreed in March 2002. The main areas in which EU measures have so far been adopted are described below.

Water pollution

A number of directives have been approved dealing with the protection of water, surface and underground, fresh and salt. Quality standards have been set for bathing water, drinking water, fresh water suitable for fish life and water used for rearing shellfish. The discharge of toxic substances is strictly controlled, with limits set for mercury, cadmium, lindane, DDT, pentachlorophenol and carbon tetrachloride, and specific rules for the control and gradual reduction of dumping of titanium dioxide, which causes "red sludge". The EU is a participant in several conventions designed to reduce pollution in international waterways such as the River Rhine, the North Atlantic, the North Sea and the Mediterranean. The Water Framework Directive of 2000 commits EU member states to achieve good qualitative and quantitative status of all water bodies – including marine waters up to 1km from the shore – by 2015. The directive requires the production of a number of key documents over six-year planning cycles. Most important among these are the river basin management plans to be published in 2009, 2015 and 2021.

Atmospheric pollution

Despite the adoption of a series of directives on such topics as the discharge of sulphur dioxide, the use of chlorofluorcarbons (CFCs) in aerosol cans and the control of pollution from certain industrial premises, progress has been slow in what are widely regarded as the two key areas: pollution from large combustion plants, particularly power stations, and the emission of gases from motor vehicles. Both of these are blamed for widespread damage to forests through acid rain and for a variety of threats to public health. In March 1985 the council reached agreement concerning the lead content of petrol (which provided that unleaded petrol would be generally available from October 1st 1989), but it was only in July 1987, that – under the majority voting provisions of the Single European Act – a series of regulations on automobile exhaust emission was adopted.

Carbon dioxide (CO_2), the main greenhouse gas, is now at the heart of industry and government agendas to curb car emissions as part of the climate change package (see pages 212–4). However, there are other emissions that have been targeted for a long time for their polluting effects. These include nitrogen oxide (NOx), which contributes to smog and acid rain, and carbon monoxide (CO), a product of incomplete combustion, which reduces the blood's ability to carry oxygen and so is dangerous for people with heart disease. Hydrocarbons (HC) are an important ingredient of acid rain, as are sulphur oxides, and particulate matter (PM) can cause respiratory diseases and lead to cancer. The first attempts to curb these exhaust emissions originate from the 1970s; the latest EU standards, Euro 5, apply from September 2009 for new models of cars and from January 2011 for all new cars. The Euro 6 standards have already been defined, cutting exhaust emissions even further, and will apply from September 2014.

Noise
Directives have been adopted fixing maximum noise levels for cars, lorries, motorcycles, tractors, subsonic aircraft, lawnmowers and building-site machinery. The noise level of household equipment must be stipulated on its packaging, and proposals are under consideration concerning helicopters and rail vehicles.

Chemical products
Particularly since the Seveso accident in northern Italy in 1977, which resulted in the contamination of a large area by a highly toxic dioxin, increasingly stringent measures have been taken to reduce the risks arising from the manufacture and disposal of chemical substances. As long ago as 1967 a directive was adopted relating to the classification, packaging and labelling of dangerous substances. Two 1973 directives control the composition of detergents, while since 1986 there has been a European Inventory of Existing Chemical Substances, which lists all chemical products on the market, enabling them to be subject to a general procedure for notification, evaluation and control. Other measures ban the use of certain substances in pesticides, and strictly control the manufacture and use of PCBS and PCTs (the substances involved in the Seveso accident), and of asbestos. In an attempt to prevent further major accidents and to limit their consequences, a directive of June 1982 imposes on manufacturers in all member states the obligation to inform the authorities about substances, plants and possible locations of accidents.

Following the Bhopal tragedy in India there has been strong pressure, particularly in the European Parliament, for a further tightening up of control measures. Concern about the depletion of the ozone layer, which protects the earth from ultraviolet rays, led the EU to adopt a series of measures to bring about a substantial reduction of CFCs and other substances thought to be responsible for this phenomenon.

Another environment initiative is the commission's 2003 proposal to tightly regulate the chemicals found in many everyday household items. Under the plans, companies would be responsible for checking the safety of chemicals used in their products. The commission said the move is necessary because of growing concerns over a rise in cancers, birth defects and other illnesses which may be caused by exposure to chemicals. But manufacturers argue that the planned measures would be a bureaucratic nightmare and would cost jobs. Under the proposals, some 30,000 substances would have to be registered with a new EU chemicals agency.

In December 2008, EU member states and the European Parliament agreed to tighten rules on pesticide use and ban at least 22 chemicals deemed harmful to humans. The law will ban substances that can cause cancer or that can harm human reproduction or hormones. In addition, any use of pesticides near schools, parks or hospitals would be either banned or severely restricted. Large-scale aerial crop-spraying would also be banned.

However, the most important legislation in this area is REACH, a regulation on Registration, Evaluation and Authorisation of Chemicals, which took effect in June 2007, replacing 40 other pieces of legislation. About 30,000 substances will have to be registered with the new Chemical Agency in Helsinki by 2018. The new law puts the onus on the chemical industry to prove that its products, including those that have been on sale for years, are safe. Previously it was up to the national authorities to prove that a given substance was hazardous. A safety report now has to be drawn up for chemicals produced or imported in quantities of more than 1 tonne per year.

Waste disposal

Since 1975 rules have been in force concerning the collection, disposal, recycling and processing of waste, of which the EU produces more than 2 billion tons a year. Specific measures have also been taken in individual areas, such as waste from the titanium oxide industry, waste oils, the dumping of waste at sea and radioactive waste. Recommendations have been made on the reuse of paper, cardboard and drinks containers.

Two recent pieces of legislation concern the collecting, treating, recycling and recovering of cars and household appliances. The Waste Electrical and Electronic Equipment (WEEE) Directive ensures electrical goods manufacturers will have to pay for the recycling of their products and prevent them from ending up in landfill sites and incinerators. The End of Life Vehicle (ELV) Directive involves taking back and recovering the annual 9m tonnes of ELVs, and requires all hazardous substances such as oil, brake fluid and coolant to be removed from all vehicles before they are scrapped.

Nature protection

The EU is a member of the 1979 Berne Convention on the conservation of wildlife, and has also recommended member states to adhere to the 1950 Paris Convention on the protection of birds and the 1971 Ramsar Convention on Wetlands. The Council of Ministers has adopted several directives on the conservation of wild birds, on banning the importation of products made from the skins of baby seals (following a mass campaign in which the European Parliament played a crucial role) and on the control and restriction of scientific experiments on animals.

Broadening the scope of environmental policy

By the early 1990s there was a widespread feeling that the EC should adopt a much more determined and systematic approach to environmental management. The June 1990 summit in Dublin called for action to be developed on a co-ordinated basis, in keeping with the principles of sustainable development and giving priority to preventive measures. The creation of a European Environmental Agency was agreed, but its establishment was delayed by failure among the member states to agree on where it should be sited.

In 1991 there was a considerable broadening of the scope of EC environmental policy, which became inextricably linked to overall economic policy-making. Commission initiatives were seen to be necessary to bring about the integration of environmental considerations into other policy areas including agriculture, the internal market, transport and energy.

Also in 1991 the Council of Ministers adopted the LIFE programme, designed to provide financial incentives for priority projects in the environmental field. The most recent LIFE programme, for 2007–13, is worth a total of €2 billion. The EU has also recently adopted measures on:

- the Norspa project (to protect the environment in the coastal areas and waters of the Irish Sea, North Sea, Baltic Sea and north east Atlantic Ocean);
- waste water;
- an EU eco-label;
- the protection of natural habitats;
- pollution by lorries.

The Treaty on European Union agreed at the Maastricht summit in

December 1991 incorporated a new section on the environment in the Rome treaty, substantially extending EU competence. The Amsterdam Treaty of June 1997 elevated the promotion of "a high level of protection and improvement of the quality of the environment" into a specific EU objective.

Climate change

The EU's most ambitious environmental policy covers climate change and related issues, such as emissions and energy efficiency. This has long been a priority, and as early as the June 1992 UN Earth Summit in Rio de Janeiro, the EU was already taking a leading role in arguing for a worldwide approach to cutting carbon dioxide emissions. By the time of the 1997 UN climate change convention in Kyoto, the EU made the most ardent calls for cuts in greenhouse gases.

The Kyoto Protocol established a legally binding commitment for the reduction of greenhouse gases. The EU subsequently launched its European Climate Change Programme (ECCP) in June 2000 to identify, develop and implement all the necessary elements of a strategy to implement the protocol. The main element of the ECCP, the EU's pioneering Emissions Trading Scheme (ETS), is the largest greenhouse gas trading scheme in the world.

The EU launched the ETS in 2005, setting up a market to trade pollution permits for carbon dioxide (CO_2), the main so-called greenhouse gas of concern. Under the ETS, permits for emitting Co_2 are distributed under a system of national allocations. The permits are traded, so big polluters can buy extra ones from greener enterprises. The ETS covers about 10,000 heavy industrial plants across the EU – notably power plants, oil refineries and steel mills – which together account for almost half the EU's CO_2 emissions. All major industrial emitters of CO_2 are expected to be brought under the ETS eventually and the scheme will also include other greenhouse gases such as nitrous oxide and perfluorocarbons. In the first and second ETS trading periods (2005–12), the EU decided to give most of the CO_2 permits to power plants and energy-intensive industries for free.

But the Kyoto Protocol commitments only run until 2012, so a UN conference in Copenhagen in December 2009 will set new targets for the post-Kyoto world. With this in mind, the European Commission began mapping out proposals from 2006 to build on Kyoto and make further EU commitments. An energy and climate change package was broadly confirmed at a landmark EU summit in December 2008. Despite lobbying by business and various EU member states, the overall so-called 20–20–20 targets were kept.

The 20–20–20 plan focused on three areas: emissions cuts and the Emissions Trading Scheme (ETS), renewables and energy efficiency.

Emissions cuts and the Emissions Trading Scheme

The package sets a target of cutting greenhouse gases by at least 20% by 2020, compared with 1990 levels. The target will rise to 30% if an international agreement is reached committing other developed countries and the more advanced developing nations to comparable emission reductions.

The package aims to reduce the ETS allocations by 21% from 2005 levels by 2020, and there will be one EU-wide cap on the number of permits, rather than individual national allocation plans. Poland and other former communist countries still heavily reliant on fossil fuel will get about 12% of the revenues from the ETS to help clean up their heavy industry. They will have to buy only 30% of their CO_2 permits in 2013, and full auctioning will not apply until 2020.

Much of the emissions cuts will be through carbon "offsets", whereby enterprises in the EU get carbon credits by sponsoring green projects in developing countries. The projects have to comply with the mechanisms set up by the Kyoto Protocol. Credits not already used up in the 2008-12 ETS period can be "banked" and carried over into the 2013-20 period. The commission says that more than one-third of the required 20% emissions cuts will be achieved in this way.

Sectors not covered by the ETS account for about 60% of all EU greenhouse gas emissions. Chief among these are road and sea transport, buildings, services, agriculture and smaller industrial installations. The package calls for cuts of 10% in emissions overall in these sectors in 2013-20 – a contribution towards the total 20% cut. These sectors face binding national targets for emission cuts in what is called "effort sharing". Gradually they will also be brought into the ETS.

The whole car industry – which accounts for about 14% of CO_2 releases – has been set an average emission target of 120g of CO_2 per kilometre by 2012 for new cars, compared with current levels of 160g/km. The target for 2020 is 95g/km. But CO_2 emissions vary from car to car, and manufacturers have been given until 2015 to meet their specific targets for each model.

A key area of green innovation is carbon capture and storage (CCS) – new technologies that allow industrial CO_2 emissions to be captured and stored underground, where they cannot harm the climate. There are plans to build 10–12 big pilot plants in the EU by 2015, with a view to making CCS commercially viable by about 2020. The plants would be funded by revenue from the ETS.

Renewables

The package sets the goal of increasing renewable energy's share of the market to 20% by 2020, from around 8.5% in 2008. Within that goal, 10% of transport fuels will have to come from renewables, including biofuels. The commission wants a strict certification system to ensure that only biofuels achieving a real cut of at least 35% in CO_2 emissions will be allowed. The use of food-based biofuels is under review because of concern about deforestation and food shortages in developing countries. The renewables targets for member states differ because they are at different stages in their use of wind energy, solar power, hydroelectric power and other green sources.

The commission says the EU must embrace renewables not only to slow climate change but also because of its reliance on imported energy and the creation of new jobs in renewable energy technologies.

Energy efficiency

Energy consumption is to be cut by 20% by 2020 through improved energy efficiency. The commission says state aid can legitimately be used to promote emissions cuts and increase take-up of renewables, so long as it does not breach EU competition rules. If the plan is adopted, the EU will help member states install double glazing, wall insulation and solar panels in housing, especially targeting low-income households. The residential sector accounts for 25% of Europe's energy consumption, the commission says. This ties in with the 2002 directive on the energy performance of buildings, requiring member states to ensure that new buildings, as well as large existing buildings undergoing refurbishment, meet certain minimum energy requirements.

Other environmental initiatives

The EU has been involved in other environmental initiatives. After more than a decade in development, the Directive on Environmental Liability was agreed in 2004. Its purpose was to make polluters pay for the damage they cause. Member states are required to prevent and restore environmental damage by ordering the economic operator to take full liability, or by suing. The directive aims to prevent and remedy environmental damage defined as damage to protected species and natural habitat. However, it does not require polluters to repair economic loss or damage relating to private property, and marine pollution incidents and nuclear damage are excluded.

In 2006, the European Commission produced an action plan to halt biodiversity loss by 2010, setting out concrete actions and outlining the responsibility of EU institutions and member states. However, by the end of 2008, the commission admitted that despite the further extension of the Natura 2000 network of protected areas and important investments in biodiversity, the integration of biodiversity and ecosystem issues into other sectoral policies remains a challenge.

29 Justice and home affairs

Until the Delors era, the Community steered clear of justice and home affairs issues, accepting these were essentially the prerogative of member states. The Maastricht treaty changed this: the creation of the EU – erected on three supposedly separate pillars – implied a specific role for justice and home affairs. It reflected concerns that as internal frontiers disappeared, external borders would be strengthened, and that implied increased co-operation between the interior and justice ministries. The Maastricht treaty provided a framework for this co-operation. It provided a new structure with a permanent secretariat and named the actors and joint instruments for dealing with sensitive issues.

Although some working structures are unwieldy, consistency has been improved. With the entry into force of the Treaty of Amsterdam, civil law matters, asylum and immigration became Community matters, with police and judicial co-operation in criminal matters remaining within the third pillar. Since then, co-operation has developed fast, accelerated by continuing debates on immigration and security concerns following the September 11th 2001 attacks in the United States. The rules now try to guarantee the free movement of EU citizens and non-EU nationals, while promising public security by combating terrorism and all forms of organised crime, including human trafficking, sexual exploitation of children, vehicle, arms and drug trafficking, corruption and fraud. With regular council meetings of justice and home affairs ministers, it is easy to forget that this was once a no-go area.

Informal beginnings

In 1957, the Treaty of Rome set the free movement of persons as one of its objectives, but it failed to deal with border crossings, immigration or visa policy. Freedom of movement was viewed in purely economic terms and concerned only workers. But by the 1970s, the desire to extend this freedom to everyone and the growing importance of certain problems – such as cross-border organised crime, drug trafficking, illegal immigration and terrorism – encouraged member states to seek informal co-operation in justice and home affairs.

Member states were already co-operating at various levels: bilaterally, regionally (within the Council of Europe, for example) and globally

(Interpol and the UN). The 1967 Naples convention on co-operation and mutual assistance between customs administrations set out the first framework for dialogue between member states. From 1975 onwards, intergovernmental co-operation slowly began to develop outside the Community's legal framework for dealing with immigration, the right of asylum and police and judicial co-operation. Informal arrangements were set up to swap experiences, exchange information and expertise, and develop networks to improve contacts between member states. The Trevi Group met initially to discuss terrorism and internal security, but it extended its scope in 1985 to cover illegal immigration and organised crime. In parallel, 1984 saw the first regular informal meetings of justice and home affairs ministers, every six months, to discuss issues such as police, judicial and customs co-operation, and the free movement of people.

The Single European Act in 1986 marked a turning point in intergovernmental co-operation. Article 8a (renumbered Article 7a in the Maastricht treaty and Article 14 in the Amsterdam treaty) creates a single market based on four fundamental freedoms: the free movement of goods, capital, services and persons. But freedom of movement for all – European citizens and non-European nationals – obviously implied scrapping border controls. Resistance from certain member states on this issue was overcome by promises of flanking measures to strengthen external frontiers and draft European asylum and immigration policies. New working parties were set up after the Single European Act: the ad hoc immigration group in 1986, the European Committee to Combat Drugs (CELAD) in 1989 and the Mutual Assistance Group (MAG) on customs in 1992.

However, they were still outside the Community framework, and progress on developing the justice and home affairs policy stuttered. This prompted France, Germany and the Benelux countries to sign the Schengen Agreement in 1985 and the Schengen Convention in 1990. This was designed to abolish internal border checks, improve controls at external borders and harmonise arrangements relating to visas, asylum and police and judicial co-operation (see pages 123–5).

The Maastricht treaty

It was the Maastricht treaty that revived the process, establishing justice and home affairs as a third pillar to the structure of the EU (see pages 47–8). The new form of co-operation covered nine areas considered to be of common interest: asylum policy; the crossing of external borders; immigration; combating drug addiction; combating international fraud; judicial co-operation in civil matters; judicial co-operation in criminal matters; customs co-operation; and police co-operation. It incorporated the existing working parties into a complex five-tier structure: specific working parties, steering committees, a co-ordinating committee set up under Article K4 of the EU treaty, the Committee of Permanent Representatives, and the Council of Justice and Home Affairs Ministers.

But the third pillar's decision-taking mechanisms, based on those of the common foreign and security policy, quickly created problems, owing to a blurred distinction between the provisions contained in the Treaty of Rome and EU treaty. Should drugs issues fall into the net of Community health policy or that of co-operation on justice and home affairs, which covers trafficking and drug dependency? Should questions of asylum, immigration and external frontiers be dealt with in the context of freedom of movement of persons, in a Community framework?

The Amsterdam treaty

From an institutional perspective, the third pillar as constructed by the Maastricht treaty offered only a limited role for the institutions and no real control over decisions taken by the member states. So changes were made by the time the Treaty of Amsterdam was negotiated in 1997. The new treaty defined the area of freedom, security and justice more precisely, as well as trying to improve the balance of the various institutions. It boosted the areas of common interest and inserted a new title in the treaty: "Visas, asylum, immigration and other policies related to the free movement of persons". This covers external border controls, asylum, immigration and judicial co-operation in civil matters, bringing these areas under the first pillar, where they can be the subject of EU directives, regulations, decisions, recommendations and opinions.

Police and judicial co-operation remain under the reshaped third pillar, however, to which the Amsterdam treaty added the prevention and combating of racism and xenophobia. Some changes were made to decision-making: joint actions were replaced by the framework decisions, which are legal instruments similar in spirit to directives and the corresponding implementing measures.

Co-operation in the field of justice and home affairs, unlike other policies, puts more weight on the member states and limits the powers of the European Commission, the European Parliament and the Court of Justice. The commission does not have sole right of initiative, sharing this role with the member states. The treaty does, however, give it the right of initiative in all justice and home affairs areas. The Treaty of Amsterdam creates a distinction between the free movement of persons and the establishment of an area of freedom, security and justice. This means that policies on visas, asylum, immigration and judicial co-operation in criminal matters have been made Community matters, making it possible to use Community instruments such as regulations, directives, decisions, recommendations and opinions.

The area of freedom, security and justice enables the Schengen agreements to be brought within the framework of the EU. To avoid the repetition of exclusive inter-governmental collaboration on the lines of Schengen, Title VI of the EU treaty provided that member states intending to establish closer co-operation between themselves may be authorised to do so within the EU framework. The UK, Ireland and Denmark indicated in various protocols to the Treaty of Amsterdam that they do not wish to participate fully in all the measures relating to the area of freedom, security and justice (all have since adopted the Schengen rules). Conversely, Norway, Switzerland and Iceland have concluded an association agreement to co-operate with the Schengen area.

The Vienna European Council of December 1998 endorsed a council and commission action plan which stressed the need for a European law-enforcement area, improved co-operation between national judicial and police authorities, a more effective Europol and an overall strategy on migration, asylum and the reception of refugees. At the Cologne European Council of June 1999, it was decided to draw up a charter of the basic rights of EU citizens which was adopted at the Nice summit in December 2000, although it was not formally incorporated into the Rome treaty.

At the Tampere European Council in October 1999, EU leaders asked the commission to produce a scoreboard listing all the measures to be taken in the next five years and keeping progress under review. The aim is to develop an open and secure EU, compliant with the Geneva Refugee Convention and other relevant human rights instruments, and to improve European citizens' access to justice throughout the EU.

There were further changes when the Treaty of Nice was negotiated in December 2000. This shifted voting to qualified majority on asylum, civil law, the free movement of legal third-country nationals, frontier controls, illegal immigration and repatriation. In 2000, the EU also set up a €216m four-year European Refugee Fund to help member states cope with the influx of displaced people. In May 2001, justice and home affairs ministers agreed penalties of no less than eight years in prison for people convicted of smuggling and harbouring illegal immigrants. They also agreed to swap information among criminal investigation agencies to combat money-laundering, allowing foreign investigators access to bank accounts in countries with strong banking secrecy laws if they can demonstrate the information they are looking for has substantial value.

Recent developments

The difficulties surrounding asylum revolve around the inability of member states to agree on the very concept of political refugee. So far there has been little movement on questions of minimum guarantees to be granted to asylum applicants in the event of expulsion and their rights during examination of an asylum application or an appeal. Naturally, these are sensitive political questions, perceived as directly affecting the sovereignty, security and people in member states, especially since political cultures, legal systems and administrative traditions can vary enormously. The different interpretations of rules at the end of 2001 led to dramatic attempts by immigrants gathered in Calais to try to seek asylum in the UK by jumping on Eurostar trains travelling into the Channel tunnel.

Earlier, in 2000, the discovery of the bodies of 58 Chinese immigrants in a truck in Dover led to a more intense discussion on issues of human trafficking. By March 2002, justice and home affairs ministers had adopted a new EU-wide fingerprint database for asylum seekers. This is seen as an important instrument in stamping out illegal immigration and so-called asylum shopping. The new Eurodac system should allow immigration services to check the fingerprints of asylum seekers against records held by other EU countries.

One of the most visible results of co-operation in justice and home affairs is the European Police Office, Europol, to improve police co-operation between the member states in order to combat serious international crime. Based in The Hague, Europol enables personal information to be exchanged, collected and analysed at European level. This has been followed by the creation of new co-operation bodies, such as the European Police College and the Police Chiefs Task Force.

A judicial counterpart to Europol is Eurojust, set up to co-ordinate national investigations into serious cross-border crime. In 2001 a European Crime Prevention Network was set up to fight urban, juvenile and drug-related crime, including football hooligans and war criminals. In June the same year a European Judicial Network in civil and commercial matters was created to promote smooth operation of cross-border litigation and the practical application of EU legislation on judicial co-operation. (A European Judicial Network in criminal matters was set up in 1998.)

In 2007, the commission proposed a new "blue card" scheme that will make it easier for skilled workers from outside the EU to get jobs in Europe. Like the American green card, the EU blue card will operate on a points system for skills and languages, with some weight given to family ties. An engineer who speaks English and French, and who has family in France, would have a better chance of getting a permit than an unskilled labourer who speaks only a little English and has no family in the EU. The subsequent legislation was passed in May 2009. The legislation also allows member states to set quotas on blue card holders or to ban them altogether if they see fit.

Rules establishing an EU-wide procedure for handling illegal immigrants were approved by MEPs in June 2008 and were to become law in 2010. The rules say illegal immigrants can be detained for up to 18 months and face a five-year re-entry ban. However, they will not automatically apply in Denmark, Ireland and the UK because these countries have negotiated opt-outs.

In October 2008, EU leaders signed up to an immigration and asylum pact paving the way for new laws to harmonise policy. The pact itself has political rather than legal force – but related EU directives are likely to enshrine some of the principles in law. The pact says the EU "does not have the resources to decently receive all the migrants hoping to find a better life here". It says it is "imperative that each member state take account of its partners' interests when designing and implementing its immigration, integration and asylum policies". At the same time, the commission called for fairer and more efficient procedures across the EU for asylum seekers – more than 200,000 applications for asylum were made in 2008 – and set a 2012 deadline for a single EU asylum procedure.

Programmes and budgets

As the legal scope has increased, so have programmes and budgets, in particular for managing immigration. The Hague programme, adopted by EU leaders in November 2004 by the European Council, set the overall objectives in justice, freedom and security (commission officials often preferred this heading to "justice and home affairs") for the period 2005-10. However, from a budgetary perspective, justice, freedom and security are covered by three framework programmes for the 2007-13 period: solidarity and management of migration flows (€5.87 billion); security and safeguarding liberties (€743m); and fundamental rights and justice (€543m). In addition, the civil protection financial instrument

(€190m) protects people against disasters. The migration flows framework, which dominates the budget, includes four programmes: the European Refugee Fund (€670m); the External Borders Fund (€2.15 billion); integration of third-country nationals (€1.77 billion); and the European Return Fund (€676m)

Anti-terrorism measures

In the wake of the September 11th 2001 attacks in the United States, ambitious plans were announced for sweeping anti-terrorist measures, including Europe-wide arrest warrants. Proposals for a new network of anti-terrorism liaison officers, a bigger role for Europol and closer collaboration on security precautions were backed by EU leaders who met in Brussels at an emergency summit on September 21st 2001.

Until then, efforts to combat terrorism inside the EU were hampered by differences in law in member states: only six had laws referring to terrorism or terrorists; the rest used more general laws to prosecute suspects. The new agreement defined terrorism broadly, covering cyber and environmental attacks, and included a two-tier penalty system of eight years' imprisonment for those who commit terrorist acts and 15 years for the leaders of terrorist groups. The EU also agreed measures to force courts to freeze and transfer criminals' assets on request from a court in another member state.

The European arrest warrant was agreed at the Laeken European Council in December 2001. This speeds up extradition within the EU; it also differs from the current system in that there will be a minimal role for ministers. It applies to 32 diverse crimes, including terrorism, trafficking in human beings, corruption, rape and racism. EU member states agreed in June 2006 on a system to speed up the transfer of evidence needed for criminal investigations from one member state to another. The agreement created an "evidence warrant" – an order that would be issued by a judicial authority in one member state and recognised in another. This was hailed as an important step in fighting terrorism and organised crime.

A recent institutional development was the creation of an EU counter terrorism co-ordinator in March 2004, just weeks after the Madrid train bombings that killed some 200 people – the single biggest terrorist attack on European soil. EU leaders appointed Gijs de Vries, the Dutch deputy interior minister, to the post – he was dubbed the EU's "Terrorism Czar". The role is to co-ordinate the activities of the EU institutions on terrorism and to persuade member states to implement EU anti-terrorist legislation. Lack of implementation of already agreed measures has been a problem in relation to terrorism.

Amid all the institution building, one notable absentee is a European intelligence agency. Although the idea of an FBI or CIA for the EU has been floated, it has yet to attract solid support. Lack of mutual trust seems to be the problem, but there is at least an acknowledgement in the post-September 11th era of the need to share more intelligence.

30 Consumers

Cinderella of the EU

To some extent consumer policy has been the Cinderella of the EU. It was not mentioned in the Rome treaty, and it took years of campaigning by consumer organisations, often backed by pressure from the European Parliament, before practical steps were taken to ensure that consumer issues were considered on a serious continuing basis. The turning point came at the summit meeting in Paris in 1972, when the leaders decided that economic development must be accompanied by an improvement in the quality of life. This meant that the Community should pursue an active consumer policy. Three important steps followed over the next few years:

- The creation of a service, and then a directorate-general, for the environment and consumer protection, within the commission.
- The creation of a Consumers' Consultative Committee (CCC).
- The adoption by the Council of Ministers, in April 1975, of a first consumer information and protection programme. Five basic consumer rights were enunciated: the right to safeguards for health and safety; the right to economic justice; the right to redress for damages; the right to information and education; and the right to consultation. These rights were to be implemented by concrete measures and also taken into account in other Community policies, such as agriculture, the economy, social affairs and the environment.

Consumer consultation

The body that deals with the consultation process for engaging with consumer organisations has changed titles over the years, but remains essentially the same. Initially the Consumer Consultative Committee (CCC), it was reconstituted as the Consumer Committee in 1995, and in 2003 became the European Consumer Consultative Group (ECCG). The ECCG gives opinions on consumer issues, advises the commission when it outlines policies, and acts as a source of information and a sounding board on EU action. It consists of:

- one representative of national consumer organisations per country;
- one member from each European consumer organisation (BEUC and ANEC);
- two associate members (EUROCOOP and COFACE);
- two EEA observers (Iceland and Norway).

Extending consumer choice

An important judgment by the Court of Justice in 1979 had a major significance in extending consumer choice. This was in the "Cassis de Dijon" case, and it reaffirmed in principle that all goods legally manufactured in a member country must be allowed into others. The judgment found that national technical regulations, even if applied equally to domestic and imported goods, must not be allowed to create a barrier to trade except for overriding reasons such as the protection of public health or consumer interests.

It was not until 1983 that ministers responsible for consumer affairs met for the first time. They are now established participants in the Council of Ministers, meeting several times each year and addressing themselves to a steady stream of proposals put up by the commission. Decisions taken so far in the consumer field can be divided into three broad categories:

- the health and safety of consumers;
- protecting consumers' economic interests;
- consumer information and education.

Health and safety

It is in this category that most progress has been made. Measures adopted have covered the following areas:

- **Foodstuffs.** European lists of permitted substances and purity standards have been established for foodstuff additives, such as colourings, anti-oxidants, preservatives, emulsifiers, stabilisers and gelifiers. Pesticide residues in fruit and vegetables and erucic acid in oils and fats for human consumption have been limited to maximum levels. Regulations also govern the production of honey, fruit juice, tinned milk, cocoa and chocolate, coffee and chicory extracts, mineral waters, jams and marmalades and chestnut purée, and specialist foodstuffs such as products for special diets. Directives are in force relating to the labelling of foodstuffs, specifying ingredients, quantity and the date by which they should be consumed. A ban has been imposed on the use of animal growth promoters which contain certain substances with hormonal or thyrostatic effects.

- **Dangerous substances.** Directives control the classification, marketing and labelling as well as the use of many toxic substances such as pesticides, solvents, paints, varnishes, printers' ink, glues and asbestos.
- **Pharmaceuticals.** The testing, patenting, labelling and marketing of pharmaceutical products are all controlled by EU directives.
- **Other products.** EU directives regulate, for safety reasons, such products as cosmetics, textiles (where the main concern is to prevent the use of inflammable material), toys and a number of other manufactured products. Several hundred directives have been approved for the purpose of standardising tools, component parts and finished products in manufacturing industry, with a view to increasing the efficiency and competitiveness of European firms, but since 1985 a new approach to standardisation has been adopted. Since then new directives have concentrated only on laying down safety specifications and have relied on the mutual recognition of national standards where no European standards exist. The commission does, however, give financial support to the two bodies responsible for setting European standards, CEN and Cenelec, and has given them remits to draft European standards concerning, in particular, toys, pressure vessels, gas appliances and information technology.

Warning system

In March 1984 the Council of Ministers established a system for the rapid exchange of information on dangerous products, allowing the authorities of one member state rapidly to draw the attention of all the others to serious incidents and take action to protect the health and safety of consumers. The 2001 directive on general product safety created the rapid alert system for non-food dangerous products (RAPEX). There were 1,866 notifications in 2008: 498 for toys, 169 for electrical appliances and 160 for motor vehicles. Some 909 notifications concerned products made in China.

Protection of consumers' economic interests

Action to protect the economic interests of consumers has been slower because of difficulty in achieving agreement within the Council of Ministers on proposals put forward by the commission. A number of directives have, however, been adopted in recent years on the following:

- **Misleading advertising.** Consumers can complain to the courts, which are empowered to require advertisers to prove the accuracy of their claims.
- **Consumer credit.** All credit agreements are to be in writing, be easily understandable and clearly indicate the real interest rate charged.
- **Door-to-door sales.** This directive is designed to protect consumers against hard selling techniques, and allow them time to have second thoughts.
- **Airlines.** A regulation which came into force in April 1991 requires airlines to pay financial compensation to passengers who are delayed through being "overbooked" on commercial flights. A package of airline passenger compensation rules came into effect in 2005, providing greater compensation for cancellations, delays and overbooking. Since 2007, the EU has taken action against websites that fail to clearly indicate the total price of airline tickets (for example, not mentioning taxes, or imposing mandatory insurance). In 2008, the commission threatened airlines with legal action if their websites continue to "mislead and rip off" consumers.
- **Product liability.** Potentially the most important EC decision affecting consumers was the adoption in August 1985 of a directive on product liability, which came into force in 1988. It imposed a strict liability on producers for damage caused by defects in their products, and it was adopted only after several years of campaigning on behalf of the victims of unforeseen side-effects of pharmaceutical products. Under the directive member states may impose a limit to the liability, but this must be at least €70m.
- **Excessive charges.** The commission's flagship regulation on mobile phone roaming charges came into force on August 1st 2007 in time for the summer holidays, meaning holidaymakers had the EU to thank for being able to make cheaper calls home

from the beach. Accompanied by a widespread publicity campaign, it was dismissed at the time by mobile phone operators as being driven by the EU executive's "populist agenda".

Consumer information and education

In addition to the directives controlling the labelling of foodstuffs and dangerous substances, others require electrical household equipment to be marked with its estimated energy consumption and food to be marked with unit prices (by the kilogram or litre). Measures are also proposed to extend price marking to goods other than food.

Multi-annual action plans have been launched over the years. The most recent is the EU consumer policy strategy 2007–13, which has three main objectives:

- to empower EU consumers, that is, to give them real choices, accurate information, market transparency and the confidence that comes from effective protection and solid rights;
- to enhance EU consumers' welfare, in terms of price, choice, quality, diversity, affordability and safety;
- to protect consumers effectively from the serious risks and threats that they cannot tackle as individuals.

Meanwhile, three new directives were adopted: on product price indication, injunctions and consumer credit.

The commission is active in promoting a wider awareness of the results of comparative tests on consumer goods, better co-operation between the testing organisations and more information for consumers on the action taken on their behalf. It sponsors frequent conferences on consumer issues, supports experiments on consumer education in schools and gives subsidies to national consumer groups to support local consumer information programmes.

One area of particular action is in combating smoking. In 2002, the EU agreed a wide-ranging ban on tobacco promotion that prevents cigarette companies using ashtrays, umbrellas and other goods to promote their products. It also applies to publicity on the internet and has put an end to sponsorship by tobacco companies of cross-border events such as Formula One motor-racing. The commission also launched a €72m campaign against smoking that included a series of hard-hitting images showing the damage it can do to people's health.

Another area is digital rights. The commission has been active in setting guidelines for business over the internet, and offering guidance for consumers in areas like online shopping and auctions, social networking and digital downloads.

A third area is food labelling. Legislation was approved in 2006 to standardise food product labels to prevent misleading claims. The new rules target the use of health or nutritional claims, such as "low fat", "high fibre" and "helps lower cholesterol". The legislation bans vague claims for foods, such as "preserves youth", along with slimming or weight control claims and health claims on beverages with more than 1.2% alcohol content.

Corporate social responsibility

Corporate social responsibility (CSR) is a concept whereby companies integrate social and environmental concerns in their business operations and in their interaction with their stakeholders on a voluntary basis. The commission's policy in support of this has two facets:

- raise the profile of corporate social responsibility among stakeholders;
- focus on moving from best practice towards common standards for CSR and its reporting based on the triple bottom line approach.

In March 2006, the European Commission launched an Alliance on Corporate Social Responsibility, bringing together mainly industry actors. However, the commission's attempts to bring together all interested parties have been marred by boycotts by a number of key non-governmental organisations (NGOs).

31 Education

Education has always been regarded as an area where national traditions and methods – which are extremely varied – should be respected and, indeed, fostered. Any attempt to standardise teaching, structures, methods or syllabi, it is accepted, would be misplaced. There was little reference to education in the Rome treaty, except for the need for mutual recognition of diplomas (Article 57) and vocational training (Articles 41 and 118).

Six-point programme adopted in 1976

Since 1974, however, there has been increasing recognition of the need for closer co-operation between the member states in educational matters. Accordingly, in February 1976 the Council of Ministers adopted a six-point programme which covered the following:

1 Improved cultural and vocational training for migrant workers and their children.
2 Better mutual understanding of the different European educational systems.
3 The collection of basic documentary information and statistics.
4 Co-operation in higher education.
5 The improvement of foreign-language teaching.
6 The equality of opportunity of access to all forms of education throughout the Community.

Subsequently, the programme was extended to include measures to improve the vocational training of young people and to ease the transition from school to workplace. Since 1980 there has been increasing concern about youth unemployment.

Policy mostly takes form of recommendations

With a few notable exceptions EU policy has taken the form of recommendations to member states rather than of legislation requiring action by them. The main exception concerned efforts to ease freedom of movement in jobs and professions with training and other requirements, where a long series of directives ensured that by the beginning of 1993 a comprehensive formula existed for the mutual recognition of educational diplomas and the right to practice any trade or profession in all member states. Another directive, adopted in 1977, concerned the schooling of the children of migrant workers.

More typical, however, was promoting a wider knowledge of EC languages. In June 1984 ministers from the member states committed themselves to a programme that aimed at encouraging a working knowledge of two languages apart from the mother tongue before the statutory leaving age. There was no guarantee, however, that all member states would make an equivalent effort to achieve this objective. Similar agreements have been reached to promote:

- student and teacher mobility;
- education in European current affairs;
- the transition from school to working life;
- education for the handicapped;
- literacy campaigns;
- new information technologies.

Education and training programmes

Many education and training programmes have been launched since the first student exchange programme, Erasmus, was conceived in 1985. The various initiatives are now integrated under a single umbrella, the Lifelong Learning Programme, which has budget of nearly €7 billion for 2007–13. There are four sub-programmes focusing on different stages of education and training:

- **Erasmus.** This €3.1 billion flagship programme enables 200,000 students to study and work abroad each year, as well as supporting co-operation actions between higher education institutions across Europe. It caters not only for students, but also for professors and business staff who want to teach abroad and for university staff who want to be trained abroad. Around 90% of European universities take part in Erasmus and 2m students have participated since it started in 1987.
- **Comenius.** Designed for schools, the €1.05 billion programme aims to improve the quality and maintain the European dimension of school education by supporting transnational co-operation between schools and institutions active in the field of education. The main goal in the current programme is that at least one pupil in 20 – around 3m pupils – will become involved in joint educational activities during the programme.

- **Leonardo da Vinci.** All aspects of the vocational training are concentrated within this €1.725 billion programme, which aims to improve mobility, make participation more accessible and boost co-operation between businesses, unions, NGOs, research centres and other groups.
- **Grundtvig.** With a €358m budget, this programme aims to strengthen the European dimension in adult education and lifelong learning across Europe.

A few other projects are worth mentioning.

The European Training Foundation

Established in 1990, operational since 1994, the European Training Foundation (ETF) is located in Turin, Italy, and helps improve vocational training systems in non-EU countries, mostly in neighbouring regions such as the countries preparing for EU accession, North Africa, the Middle East, the Balkans and the former Soviet Union.

The European Institute of Innovation and Technology

The European Institute of Innovation and Technology (EIT) aims to be a flagship research university for excellence in higher education, research and innovation. The initial concept was based on the example of the Massachusetts Institute of Technology (MIT) and its combination of world-class education, research and deep engagement in effective innovation processes. The regulation came into force in April 2008. The project will operate mainly by building networks of universities and research institutions, without building any new education or research institutions or granting EU diplomas.

Eurydice

This information service network has been in operation since 1980, with access to educational administrators in all member states. It consists of a computer-based databank, containing a mass of information about educational developments throughout the EU. It now covers the EU's 27 member states, plus Iceland, Liechtenstein, Norway and Turkey.

Lingua

Started in 1990, Lingua contributes to the financing of scholarships, exchanges and teaching materials in order to promote the training of teachers in foreign languages as well as the learning of languages in higher education, vocational training and industry.

European University Institute
This post-graduate institution, set up in Florence in 1976, offers courses in history and civilisation, economics, law and political and social sciences.

European Centre for the Development of Vocational Training
Established in Berlin in 1975, the purpose of the European Centre for the Development of Vocational Training (Cedefop) is to foster the development of vocational training and in-service training of adults.

The European Schools
Fifteen schools offer an international syllabus, in which part of the teaching is in a language other than the pupil's native tongue, leading to a European baccalauréat, which provides admission to universities throughout the EU. Although mainly intended for the children of people working in EU institutions, the schools are open to other pupils. The schools are in Luxembourg (two); Brussels (four) and Mol in Belgium; Varese in Italy; Frankfurt, Karlsruhe and Munich in Germany; Bergen in the Netherlands; Alicante in Spain; Strasbourg in France; and Culham in the UK.

32 Women's rights

The position of women within the Union has substantially improved since the EEC was first established, although they are still some way from removing all the disadvantages from which they suffer, and from achieving full equality with men. By 2007, the employment rate for women was 58.3% (up from 53.6% in 2000), while that of men was 72.5% (up from 70.7% in 2000). Over the preceding 35 years the proportion of women in the workforce had steadily risen, from under 35%, but women are still concentrated in certain sectors and job categories that were often vulnerable, less highly qualified, lower paid and with fewer promotion prospects. Women account for just 32% of managers, 10% of board members and 3% of chief executives of large enterprises in the EU. Above all, women predominate in part-time employment (30.7%, compared with 6.5% for men), and there is a higher proportion of women among those unemployed than among the working population as a whole.

EU has helped improve women's status

There can be little doubt that the Union itself has been instrumental in improving the status of women. Article 119 of the Rome treaty stipulates that "each member state shall ... ensure and subsequently maintain the application of the principle that men and women should receive equal pay for equal work". It goes on to spell out the principle in some detail, stipulating that "pay" means "the ordinary basic or minimum wage or salary and any other consideration, whether in cash or in kind, which the worker receives, directly or indirectly, in respect of his employment from his employer". The article goes on to state that:

> "Equal pay without discrimination based on sex means:
> - that pay for the same work at piece rates shall be calculated on the basis of the same unit of measurement;
> - that pay for work at time rates shall be the same for the same job."

Despite the seeming lack of ambiguity in these provisions, it was necessary for the Council of Ministers to adopt several further measures before all the member states took adequate action to ensure their implementation. Here are some of the most important directives:

- **February 1975.** Member states are obliged to revise their laws so as to exclude all discrimination on grounds of sex, particularly in systems of occupational classification. Workers believing themselves to be victims of discrimination must have the right and the possibility to take their case to a tribunal, and be protected against any wrongful dismissal if they do so.
- **February 1976.** The Equal Treatment Directive requires that there shall be "no discrimination whatsoever on grounds of sex, either directly or indirectly by reference in particular to marital or family status". In 2002, it was amended to include definitions of sexual harassment, harassment, and direct and indirect discrimination.
- **December 1978.** Any discrimination in statutory social security schemes is rendered illegal.
- **End 1986.** Direct or indirect discrimination against independent women workers (including agricultural workers) was to be eliminated by the end of 1989 (or 1991 in some cases). The directive also included further provisions regarding maternity and social security.
- **November 2000.** The Employment Equality Directive prohibits discrimination, harassment and victimisation in employment and training on the grounds of race or ethnic origin.
- **December 2004.** A directive implementing the principle of equal treatment between women and men in the access to and supply of goods and services aims to provide clearer information, for example on how insurance premiums and benefits are calculated.

Series of action programmes put forward

In addition to these directives, the European Commission has put forward a series of action programmes to the Council of Ministers, which have been adopted in the form of recommendations (that is they are not mandatory on the member states).

The latest, covering 2006–10, is a new six-point "roadmap for equality between women and men" which targets areas such as the work/life balance, pay and gender-based violence. With women in the EU earning 15% less than men compared with 17% in 1995 – despite being better educated – the commission admitted that progress in closing the gap was slow. The pay gap is 20% or above in six countries: Cyprus, Estonia, Finland, Germany, Slovakia and the UK.

The roadmap includes a European Institute for Gender Equality to help raise awareness. Based in the Lithuanian capital, Vilnius, and inaugurated in 2007, it has a budget of €52.5m for the period 2007–13. It is tasked with promoting gender equality, combating sex discrimination, and gathering reliable research data and information.

At a broader level, the EU opened a Fundamental Rights Agency in Vienna in 2007 to help combat discrimination on the basis of race, gender or religion. It replaced the EU's Monitoring Centre on Racism and Xenophobia. With a budget of €30m, its purpose is to collect data on violations of fundamental rights, provide advice to the EU and its member states and raise public awareness. At the same time, 2007 was named the European Year of Equal Opportunities for All. Some 430 national actions were launched and there were over 600 events raising awareness about non-discrimination.

In 2008, the commission set up an advisory committee on equal opportunities for women and men, with 68 government and NGO members.

Educational initiatives to encourage equal opportunities

In the belief that the roots of sexual discrimination may lie in the educational system, the commission has launched several initiatives to encourage sexual equality by removing elements which stereotype the sexes from an early age and cut off girls from career choices more readily open to boys.

Violence against women

In 1997 the European Parliament adopted a resolution on the violation of women's rights and another on the need for a Europe-wide campaign of zero tolerance of violence against women. It called for 1999 to be designated "European Year against Violence against Women" and for respect for women's rights to be written into all agreements with non-member countries. The EU's Daphne III programme, from 2007 to 2013, has a budget of €117m and tackles all forms of violence against women and children.

Sexual harrassment

In April 2002, tough new rules to combat sexual harassment at work were agreed, and a number of other changes were made to the EU's sex equality laws. The new rules oblige employers to introduce preventative measures against sexual harassment in the workplace and to provide information to workers about equal treatment of men and women in the organisation.

A dearth of women commissioners

Given the apparent devotion of the EU to sexual equality, it is surprising that no women members at all were appointed to the European Commission until 30 years after its creation. The second Delors Commission, which took over in January 1989, did have two women members – Vasso Papandreou and Christiane Scrivener – as well as 15 men. The two-year commission appointed for 1993–94, however, included only one woman – Mrs Scrivener – and 16 male members. The Santer Commission, which took office in January 1995, included four women among its 20 members. It established a special group of commissioners, chaired by Jacques Santer himself, with the specific task of ensuring that an "equal opportunities" element was incorporated into the full range of EU policies. The Prodi Commission, which took office in September 1999, included five women. The Barroso Commission that followed in 2004 included eight women among its 25 commissioners, one more than the expanded 30-member Prodi Commission had when it stepped down. The second Barroso Commission, appointed in late 2009, contained nine women among its 27 members: exactly one-third. This, however, included Catherine Ashton, who was appointed to the prestigious post of high representative for foreign and security policy, potentially the most powerful position within the EU.

33 Culture and the media

The work of the EU in the cultural sphere was for many years minimal, partly because of a desire to avoid duplicating the activities of the Council of Europe, which has always seen the protection and development of the European cultural heritage as one of its principal functions. The development of new technologies, which are revolutionising the television and film industries and making a mockery of purely national boundaries, caused a reassessment. The commission concluded that it must henceforward play the pivotal role in marshalling a European response to the commercial and cultural challenge in this sphere, which is spearheaded by American and Japanese interests.

Culture programmes

With more than 5m people working in culture, the cultural sector makes a substantial contribution to the EU's economy, growth and employment. According to one commission-funded study, it contributed approximately 2.6% to the Union's GDP in 2003, with growth in this sector being significantly higher than that of the economy in general between 1999 and 2003.

However, it was only in 1998 that the EU agreed its first culture programme. The most recent programme (2007–13) has a budget of €400m for projects and initiatives to celebrate Europe's cultural diversity and enhance its shared cultural heritage through the development of cross-border co-operation between cultural operators and institutions. The programme has three main objectives:

◪ to promote cross-border mobility of those working in the cultural sector;
◪ to encourage the transnational circulation of cultural and artistic output;
◪ to foster intercultural dialogue.

It has three strands of activities:

◪ Cultural actions (around 77% of the budget). These enable a wide range of cultural organisations from various countries to co-operate on cultural and artistic projects. This strand includes three subcategories: multi-annual co-operation projects; co-operation measures, running over a maximum period of two years; and special measures, which relate to high-profile actions of considerable scale and scope (for example, support to European capitals of culture).

◪ Support for cultural organisations and networks of European interest (around 10% of the budget). This aims to co-finance the operating costs of the long-term work programmes of cultural groups.

◪ Support for activities maximising the impact of projects, analysis, statistics, studies on cultural co-operation and cultural policy development (around 5% of the budget).

At the same time, the EU is active globally. Its defence of the concept of "cultural diversity" has been criticised by the United States, which suspects cultural diversity measures aim to create new international rules to limit imports of movies on the grounds that they diminish local content at cinemas or on TV. Nonetheless, the EU was the driving force behind the 2005 UNESCO convention on the protection and promotion of the diversity of cultural expressions, a text that forms the basis of a new pillar of world governance in cultural matters.

Support and training for artistic workers

Apart from films and television programmes, the EU has been mainly concerned with removing barriers to artistic workers exporting their talents and output from one EU country to another. The temporary tax-free export of the tools of an artist's trade (musical instruments, cameras, and so on) has been facilitated, and the commission is drawing up proposals to ensure the free export of works of art, except for strictly defined "national art treasures" which would be exempted. It is also seeking to establish a European information centre to keep a record of stolen works of art, making it more difficult for thieves to dispose of stolen items.

Research sponsored by the commission has revealed that a large number of cultural workers are unemployed, and that many others earn less than they need to live. They are forced to take a second job or abandon their art. It has proposed a number of measures to strengthen their economic position. These include:

◪ the harmonisation of national laws governing copyright to creative artists and performers;

- a share in public subsidies for playwrights and composers;
- "resale rights" to artists guaranteeing them a percentage of the proceeds every time their works are sold;
- the payment of royalties on works in the public domain to funds which could be used for welfare payments to artists or for arts sponsorship.

The commission has used the limited funds at its disposal to support a number of schemes for training young artists, including assistance for young musicians in Siena and Dublin, violin makers in Cremona, composers at the University of Surrey and dancers in Brussels.

Efforts to widen the cultural audience

In recognition of its responsibilities towards a wider Europe, European Cultural Months were held in Cracow (Poland) in 1992 and other cities such as Basel (Switzerland) and Riga (Latvia) in 2001. The commission also acted as a sponsor of the Quincentenary exhibition held in Seville in 1992, and similarly supported Expo '98 in Lisbon in 1998. Other efforts include:

- financial support since 1982 for the translation of great works of contemporary literature, mainly from the lesser spoken languages such as Danish, Dutch and Greek;
- a European Film Festival held each year in a different city;
- a variety of events held in the city that the commission designates each year as European culture capital, starting with Athens in 1985. In 2009 it was Vilnius (Lithuania) and Linz (Austria); and in 2010 Essen (Germany), Pécs (Hungary) and Istanbul (Turkey). From 2011, there will be two cities per year: 2011 Turku (Finland) and Tallinn (Estonia); 2012 Guimarães (Portugal) and Maribor (Slovenia); and 2013 Marseille (France) and Kosice (Slovakia).

Conservation of monuments and buildings

Largely as a result of pressure from the European Parliament, funds have been made available, in the form of interest-rate subsidies and capital grants as well as loans through the EIB, for conservation work on monuments of EU-wide importance or buildings in underdeveloped regions whose restoration would bring economic benefits, especially through tourism. The first beneficiaries, in 1982–83, were the Milos Museum in Greece, the Doges' Palace in Venice and the Parthenon in Athens.

Prizes and "years"

The EU supports various culture prizes that put the spotlight on artists, music groups, architects, authors and those working in the field of cultural heritage and on their work. The prizes are:

- the European heritage awards, with categories ranging from building restoration to landscape rehabilitation, archaeological site interpretations and care for art collections;
- the EU prize for contemporary architecture;
- the European border breakers awards, which reward musicians who succeed in reaching a broad audience with their debut album outside their home country;
- the EU prize for literature.

The EU also sponsors years dedicated to specific issues. The European Year of Intercultural Dialogue was in 2008, and 2009 was the European Year of Creativity and Innovation.

Films and television

The commission's initiatives regarding films and television were prompted chiefly by the prospects offered by the development of direct broadcasting by satellite and the extension of cable networks.

In 1989 a directive entitled "Television without Frontiers" was adopted, which came into force in October 1991. This directive, which is mandatory for member states, made it illegal for them to impede the transmission of programmes from other EC countries provided they conform with the requirements of the directive. The directive covers:

- advertising breaks;
- the duration of advertising;
- ethical questions;
- sponsorship;
- protection of minors;
- the right of reply;
- the production and distribution of European audiovisual works.

The directive, which was denounced as discriminatory by the US government, also calls on member states to try to ensure that at least 50% of air time is devoted to programmes originating within the EC and that at least 10% of their programming budgets is devoted to

European works from independent producers.

The directive was revised in 2006 to reflect and encompass the enormous pace of change in broadcasting and the internet. Now renamed the Audiovisual Media Services Directive, it covers the growing market of video-on-demand services and internet-based broadcasters. It now supports new forms of advertising, such as split-screen, virtual and interactive advertising. And it aims to create a "level playing field" between traditional TV-based broadcasts and online broadcasts.

The commission also introduced the Media programme to support the European film industry, in relation to both production and distribution. Since it first began offering grants in 1991, the Media programme has supported the development and distribution of thousands of films, as well as training activities, festivals and promotion projects throughout Europe. It backs around 300 European films annually, and has supported more than 50 European films distributed outside their countries of origin – including *Le Fabuleux Destin d'Amélie Poulain*, *Volver*, *La Vita e Bella*, *La Môme* and *The Wind that Shakes the Barley*. The latest Media programme, from 2007 to 2013, has a budget of €755m.

The audiovisual sector is also the main target for two directives, on copyright and enforcement. The 2004 enforcement directive for intellectual property is designed to clamp down on music, movies and software copying, with provisions for pirates and counterfeiters to be jailed, fined and have their bank accounts frozen. It also allows legal attacks on internet file-sharing networks. The 2001 copyright directive aims to improve protection across the EU in the digital environment, allowing companies to defend their products with copy-protection technology and makes it illegal for anyone to circumvent such technology.

Sport

The EU has become increasingly involved in sport. The 1995 Bosman ruling on football transfers is the most widely known ruling by the European Court of Justice. It outlawed transfer fees for out-of-contract players, thus aligning football rules with standard EU employment contracts. UEFA and FIFA, respectively the European and world football authorities, were slow to accept the ruling and initially hinted that EU law had no jurisdiction over them. But they eventually accepted the ruling, and in March 2001, FIFA's package covering transfers, training and compensation for breached contracts was approved by the commission. The Bosman ruling also ended the quotas of national players in club teams, heralding a spectacular growth in foreign-player transfers throughout Europe.

Other EU actions in sport include:

◪ becoming involved in the launch of the World Anti-Doping Agency (WADA), the body set up by the International Olympic Committee to drive out drug cheats. As well as being instrumental in providing funding, the commission took observer status in the agency;

◪ designating 2004 as the European Year of Education through Sport;

◪ examining the licensing and management of motor racing, which the commission's competition authorities have suggested is a closed shop;

◪ working with UEFA to ensure that the broadcasting rights for the Champions League are sold on a fair basis and do not constitute a market-sharing arrangement.

34 Citizens' rights and symbolism

The EU continues to be a remote concept to most people. In so far as they think about it at all, it is regarded as a matter for governments, specialist committees and for experts. Although there is a fairly general appreciation (which is stronger in the original six member states than in the others) of the economic benefits that the Union has brought, there is little feeling that the EU affects citizens in their everyday life.

Committee for a People's Europe formed

It was in order to help create such a feeling, and to foster sentiments of loyalty and solidarity among the mass of the population in the member states, that the EC heads of government, at the Fontainebleau summit in June 1984, decided on the appointment of a Committee for a People's Europe, which would suggest ways of strengthening the identity and improving the image of the Community. The committee was chaired by an Italian, Pietro Adonnino, and it produced two reports with a series of proposals for actions.

The reports put forward both specific proposals and longer-term objectives which would make the Community more real in the eyes of its citizens. These proposals cover special rights for citizens, culture, information, youth, education, exchanges and sport, voluntary work to assist developing countries, health, social security, drugs and twinning schemes.

Among the proposals were:

- **The right to participate in Euro-elections under equal conditions.** Electoral procedures should be made uniform, as is required under Article 138 of the Rome treaty.
- **Permanent residents in another member state.** Numbering about 5m, these people should have the right, after a period of time, to vote and stand in local elections.
- **Border region residents.** Taken in the widest sense, they should have the right to be consulted when the neighbouring country is contemplating developments which could affect them such as major public works, reorganisation of transport or measures affecting ecology, safety or health.
- **The right of all Community citizens to enjoy full benefits of**

Community policies. In cases where these conflict with national regulations, the citizen can seek redress in the courts.

◪ European passport holders. The holders of EU passports (see below) should have the right to benefit from the assistance of the embassy or consulate of another member state when visiting a foreign country where their own country is not represented.

During 1986 and 1987 the commission tabled proposals to meet most of the points listed in the two Adonnino reports, and the major part of the programme was implemented by the target date of 1992 which the Community set for the completion of the internal market.

Areas of particular difficulty

Frontier controls

Fears about drug peddlers, terrorism and illegal immigrants have made some member states, particularly the UK, reluctant to ease or abolish controls at internal EU frontiers. This led five countries – France, Germany and the three Benelux states – to sign the Schengen Agreement (see pages 123–5) to eliminate their own frontier controls before the 1992 deadline and to align their immigration and visa requirements for citizens of non-EU countries. The majority of member states, and even countries such as Iceland and Norway which are outside the EU, subsequently subscribed to the Schengen Agreement, although Ireland and the UK remain outside, and are likely to continue to do so for the foreseeable future. Under the Amsterdam treaty, the Schengen Agreement was incorporated in the European Community and it is now mandatory on all member states except the UK and Ireland, which have secured opt-outs.

Euro-election procedures

The demand for a uniform procedure for elections to the European Parliament has still not been met, largely because of the refusal of former UK Conservative governments to agree to introduce proportional representation. The Labour government elected in May 1997 conceded the point, and the elections to the European Parliament in June 1999 and subsequently have been held under different systems of PR in all the member states. This development has removed the pressure for a uniform system, and it seems unlikely that one will be adopted in the near future.

EU citizenship

Despite the progress made in implementing the Adonnino proposals, the Spanish government argued that a specific treaty commitment should be made establishing the right of all persons holding the nationality of a member state to citizenship of the European Community. The Treaty on European Union, agreed at Maastricht in December 1991, accordingly contained provisions establishing citizenship of the EU. It guaranteed the rights of free movement and residence, the right of EU citizens to vote and stand as candidates in municipal elections and European Parliament elections, in countries of residence other than their own, and to equal consular protection in third countries where their own countries were not represented.

Ombudsman

Another Adonnino proposal, for a European ombudsman (or Euro-ombudsman), was eventually adopted in the Maastricht treaty. Appointed by the European Parliament, the ombudsman is empowered to receive complaints from any EU citizen or any person residing or having a registered office in a member state concerning maladministration in the activities of the EU institutions.

Attempts to introduce common symbolism

One factor which has retarded the development of popular loyalties to the EU has been the absence of common symbolism, a lack which the commission and the national governments have made increasing attempts in recent years to rectify.

An EU flag

Since 1986 the EU has had a common flag, which is flown at national and international functions and ceremonies, as well as on other occasions when public attention needs to be drawn to the existence of the Union. This flag, which contains a crown of 12 five-pointed stars on an azure background, had already been used since 1955 by the Council of Europe. It is now shared with the Council of Europe.

Anthem

The Council of Europe also shares the European anthem, for which the words of Schiller's "Ode to Joy", set to the last movement of Beethoven's Ninth Symphony, have been chosen. (This is a cut above most national anthems – of which both words and music are almost uniformly banal

– but it remains to be seen whether it will catch the public imagination.) May 9th, the date of Robert Schuman's birth in 1886, was also chosen in 1986 as Europe Day, with the hope that it would be celebrated as a public holiday in each member state.

Passport

Since 1974 slow progress has been made towards achieving a common European passport. In 1981–82 the member states reached agreement on a uniform model. The format is 88mm × 124mm, the colour is Burgundy red, and the heading is now "European Union", followed by the name of the member state. The date set for its introduction was January 1st 1985, but only three countries, Denmark, Ireland and Luxembourg, respected this deadline. Most other member states started issuing the new style passports (which will progressively replace the old national passports on renewal) later on in 1985, but it was not until 1989 that European passports were being supplied in all member states.

Driving licence

In 1980 the Council of Ministers adopted a directive on the introduction of a Community driving licence, which was implemented in two stages. Since 1983 there has been mutual recognition in each member state of each others' licences, which since then have been issued on the basis of theoretical examinations, practical tests and medical requirements conforming to common specifications. Since January 1st 1986 driving licences issued by member states conform to a Community model, which meets the requirements of the 1968 Vienna International Road Traffic Convention, so that they are valid in non-EU countries which subscribe to this convention.

A 1991 directive harmonised the categories of driving licences among member states. In 2006, ministers adopted a directive to create a single European driving licence to replace the 110 different models then in existence throughout the EU. Its provisions, to take effect in 2013, are for a single credit-card-style, plastic-coated document. Member states will have the option to include a microchip containing information about the card holder.

35 Aid and development

Part Four of the Rome treaty, comprising Articles 131–136, provided for the association with the Community of the former colonial territories of Belgium, France, Italy and the Netherlands. It said:

> This association shall serve primarily to further the interests and prosperity of the inhabitants of these countries and territories in order to lead them to the economic, social and cultural development to which they aspire.

EU–ACP relations are governed by conventions

Initially, this provision applied mainly to former French territories in Africa, nearly all of which became independent in the early 1960s; subsequently, former UK, Spanish and Portuguese territories also became eligible. At first only 18 countries were involved, and they were known collectively as the Associated African States and Madagascar (AASM). Now 79 in number (Cuba does not take part in EU-ACP activities, however), they have been known since the mid-1970s as the African, Caribbean and Pacific (ACP) states (see Appendix 7).

Relations between these countries and the EU have been regulated by a series of conventions concluded at periodic intervals. The first two were signed at Yaoundé (capital of Cameroon) in 1963 and 1969, and they set the pattern for the four subsequent ones, signed at Lomé (capital of Togo) in 1975, 1979, 1984 and 1989. On the one hand, provision was made for duty-free access to the EU for almost all the products of the ACP countries, without any reciprocity being required; on the other, development aid was made available, both in the form of grants from the European Development Fund (EDF), which was set up for this purpose, and of low-interest loans from the EIB. About 10% of the total aid programmes of the EU member states is channelled through the Union, and the bulk of it goes to the ACP countries, although India is the largest single recipient.

The EU-ACP conventions have broken new ground in four ways. They have:

- given stability to co-operation links by creating a legal framework, based on a contract negotiated for a fixed period of years between two groupings, each comprising a large number of independent states;

◪ established a single contract between regional blocs, excluding economic and ideological discrimination and taking account of the special problems of countries which are severely under-developed and those of enclaves and islands;
◪ created common institutions allowing a permanent dialogue and largely responsible for the implementation of the development programmes: a joint assembly of MEPs and ACP representatives, an ACP–EU Council of Ministers and a Committee of Ambassadors;
◪ instituted a global approach covering all aspects of co-operation: financial aid, trade concessions, stabilisation of export earnings, agricultural and industrial assistance.

The changing relationship with ACPs

In June 2000, the 20-year EU–ACP Agreement was signed in Cotonou, Benin, after 18 months of negotiations. The deal, known as the Cotonou Agreement, replaced the Lomé Convention, and focused on poverty alleviation, aid and stronger political, economic and trade co-operation. Its four main principles are as follows:

◪ **Equality of partners and ownership of development strategies.** In principle, it is up to ACP states to determine how their societies and their economies should develop.
◪ **Participation.** In addition to the central government as the main actor, partnership under the Cotonou Agreement is open to others (for example, non-state actors and local authorities).
◪ **Dialogue and mutual obligations.** The Cotonou Agreement is not merely a pot of money. The signatories have assumed mutual obligations which will be monitored through continuing dialogue and evaluation.
◪ **Differentiation and regionalisation.** Co-operation agreements will vary according to each partner's level of development, needs, performance and long-term development strategy. Special treatment will be given to countries that are considered least developed or vulnerable (landlocked or island states).

The Cotonou Agreement is adapted every five years and the next revision will take place in 2010. The Stabex and Sysmin instruments designed to help the agricultural and mining sectors under the Lomé

Conventions were abolished by the new partnership agreement signed in Cotonou in June 2000 and replaced by the FLEX mechanism, aimed at remedying the adverse effects of instability of export earnings.

Cotonou also streamlined the European Development Fund (EDF), an intergovernmental body, and introduced a system of rolling programming, making for greater flexibility and giving the ACP countries greater responsibility. The ninth EDF was allocated €13.8 billion for 2000–07; and the tenth for the period 2008–13 was allocated €22.7 billion. The geographical co-operation with the ACP (with the exception of South Africa) is not integrated in the EU budget but continues to be funded through the existing intergovernmental EDF. As well as managing part of the EDF's resources under the investment facility, the EIB will contribute up to €2 billion from its own resources for the period covered by the tenth EDF.

In April 2002, the commission adopted a negotiating strategy for Economic Partnership Agreements (EPAS) between the EU and 76 ACP countries, designed to translate the EU's relations based on unilateral preferences – provided for by the Cotonou Agreement – into more "balanced relations". The strategy outlined EPA negotiations between September 2002 and January 2008, the resulting agreement entering into force in 2008, but with a 12-year transition period, to 2020. The new EPAS would enhance duty-free access to the EU market for exporters in the ACPS, while simultaneously dismantling barriers that prevent European goods and services from entering their markets.

Aid goals

The EU, which provides over half of all official development assistance worldwide, has made a number of commitments to meet the 2002 Monterrey Consensus (the partnership between rich and poor countries to find ways of financing development that will meet the Millennium Development Goals). It agreed to increase its official development assistance (ODA) to achieve 0.39% of gross national income (GNI) by 2006 (as a step towards the 0.7% target set by the UN). This collective pledge was based on individual promises by some member countries to donate at least 0.33% and others to maintain their already high(er) aid levels. Other commitments concerned innovative sources of financing, more predictable and stable aid mechanisms, debt relief, aid effectiveness, untying aid, aid for trade, reform of international financing institutions and global public goods. The EU has also set a target that by 2015 "old" member states should give 0.7% and "new" member states 0.33% of GNI in ODA.

Over the years, EU aid levels have fluctuated. They increased by more than 30% from 2004 to 2005, and the target of 0.39% GNI in 2006 was exceeded with a record €47.7 billion in ODA, or 57% of the global total. That amounted to 0.41% of GNI, or €100 per EU citizen, while €7.5bn was distributed directly by the EU. In 2007 EU aid levels fell back to 0.38% of GNI (some €46.4 billion). Based on existing commitments, OECD forecasts suggest that the EU will have contributed more than 90% of the global increase in ODA from 2007 to 2010.

Aid distributed directly by the EU to ACP countries is managed and distributed by EuropeAid, a commission department. This aid comes from either the EU budget or the EDF.

The EU (bilateral aid by member states and Community aid combined) is by far the largest donor in the world, representing around 55% of global ODA. But only 51% of ODA from the EU goes to ACP countries. The remainder goes largely to countries either negotiating membership of the EU or part of the European Neighbourhood Policy (ENP).

Within the framework of the EU's regular budget 2007–13, the number of external action instruments has been rationalised and reduced from more than 30 to nine: the instrument for humanitarian aid and eight new financing instruments.

Horizontal and geographical instruments of particular relevance to development co-operation are as follows:

- **The Development Co-operation Instrument.** The DCI covers geographic co-operation with South and Central America, Asia, Central Asia and South Africa, as well as the thematic programmes benefiting all developing countries: investing in people (social sectors); non-state actors (civil society) and local authorities; environment and sustainable management of natural resources including energy; food security; migration and asylum. Over 2007–13, roughly €16.9 billion will be spent under the DCI.
- **The European Neighbourhood and Partnership Instrument.** The ENPI covers geographical co-operation with countries of the Mediterranean and eastern Europe. It has a budget of €11.2 billion for the period 2007–13.
- **The European Instrument for Democracy and Human Rights.** The EIDHR is a global financing instrument which contributes to the development and consolidation of democracy and respect for human rights in third countries. It has a budget of €1.1 billion for the period 2007–13.

◪ **The Instrument for Stability.** This contributes to stability in situations of crisis or emerging crisis, thereby preserving, establishing or re-establishing the conditions for development co-operation; it also helps build capacity to address threats and prepare for pre- and post-crisis situations. Over 2007–13, €2.1 billion has been earmarked under this instrument.

Emergency aid
The EU sends foodstuffs to countries which request assistance in coping with serious food shortages. Emergency aid is also sent to countries devastated by natural catastrophes or other crises. Such aid, much of it channelled through NGOs, is administered by the European Community Humanitarian Office (ECHO), created in 1991. In 2008, a total of €937m was distributed through ECHO for humanitarian aid. In recent years numerous emergency aid operations have been launched, particularly to assist the victims of famine and war in countries such as Afghanistan, Kosovo, North Korea, Rwanda, Burundi, Ethiopia, Sudan, Somalia, Angola, Mozambique and Liberia, as well as in former Soviet republics such as Tajikistan, Armenia, Azerbaijan and Georgia. The assistance is not entirely disinterested: it helps to reduce the surplus food stocks of the CAP. Funds are, however, provided for special programmes to help poor countries overcome their food production problem, and to assist the work of NGOs.

36 Foreign, defence and security policy

The Rome treaty made no mention of foreign policy, as distinct from foreign-trade policy, and progress towards co-ordinating the foreign policy of the member states was – for long – slow and largely informal. It is, however, one of the few fields where progress, however limited, has been virtually continuous – at least since 1969 – and each year has seen somewhat closer co-operation among the member states than the previous one.

Davignon Report provided basic framework

Foreign policy co-operation (long known as "political co-operation" in EU circles) really dates in an organised sense from The Hague EC summit of December 1969, when it was decided to ask top national officials to report on the possibilities of achieving a degree of co-operation in foreign affairs. A committee presided over by Etienne Davignon (then a Belgian foreign office official, later a leading EC commissioner) drew up a report which recommended a system to "harmonise points of view, concert attitudes and, where possible, lead to common decisions".

The Davignon Report was accepted, and with a number of adaptations over the years it provided the basic framework for "political co-operation" by EC countries during the 1970s and 1980s. It proposed that the EC foreign ministers should meet at least twice a year to discuss foreign policy matters. In practice, they now normally meet at monthly intervals, and more often at times of crisis. For a number of years, largely due to French insistence during the Gaullist and post-Gaullist period, a sharp distinction was drawn between meetings held on political co-operation (which were normally convened in the capital city of the country currently holding the presidency of the Council of Ministers) and those on "normal" EC business,¹ which were in Brussels or Luxembourg. Over the years this distinction has become looser, and it is now normal for both types of business to be transacted at the same meeting.

As well as the foreign ministers, each member state has designated a leading diplomatic official, known as the political director, who is specifically responsible for foreign policy co-operation between the 27 member states. The political directors meet every month, and each is assisted by a more junior official, known as the European correspondent, who is responsible for day-to-day communications. With the development of e-mail, the interaction has become a great deal more intense and can best be described as a continuous process. The organisation of political co-operation was assumed by the foreign ministry of the country currently holding the presidency. However, under the Single European Act, which formalised political co-operation for the first time, a small secretariat was established in Brussels in 1987 to provide back-up support and ensure greater continuity. Since the coming into force of the Lisbon treaty, it is the high representative for foreign and security policy who is responsible and who presides over meetings of the foreign ministers.

Commitment to joint foreign policy formalised

The Single European Act formally committed the member states to "endeavour jointly to formulate and implement a European foreign policy" (Article 30). It also (Article 2) regularised the position of the European Council, or the regular series of summit meetings of heads of government, which had been meeting three times a year since 1973, and twice yearly since 1986. The European Council meetings had played a considerable role in promoting political co-operation, and foreign policy issues invariably occupy a prominent, and sometimes the predominant, place on the agenda. To a significant extent, they have provided an opportunity for the European members of the Western alliance to co-ordinate their positions, and thus enable them to adopt a more equal posture vis-à-vis the United States, which dwarfs each of them on a one-to-one basis.

Development hindered by member states' own interests

A number of factors, however, seriously inhibited this development. One has been the neutrality of Ireland, which has largely prevented the EU from playing the role of the European end of NATO (there is also the fact that three European NATO members – Norway, Iceland and Turkey – are not members of the EU). Furthermore, both Denmark and Greece, although they belong to NATO, had severe inhibitions about discussing matters of western security within an EU framework.

Three of the larger EU members – Germany, France and the UK – have also on occasion been reluctant to subordinate their independent interests to those of the Union. Before German unification in 1990 the West German government, because of its economic links with East Germany and its desire to keep open doors to closer co-operation with the East German regime and to do nothing to hinder prospects, however remote they then seemed, of eventual unification, often took a slightly softer position in relation to eastern Europe than the other member states. After unification it continued to be notably more willing than its allies to accommodate the former Soviet Union and to consider economic aid on a large scale. By 1992, however, the cost of unification had become so great that German resistance hardened to paying the lion's share of aid to the rest of eastern Europe. France and the UK both have worldwide interests, largely arising from their colonial pasts, and each has shown itself rather more nationalistic in its approach than the majority of other member states.

For these reasons, the European Council – and the EU foreign ministers' meetings – have not formally assumed the role of the "general staff" of the European end of the western alliance that might otherwise have been expected. Informally they have come rather nearer to it. For example, defence matters are supposed to be excluded from the agenda (as distinct from the "political and economic aspects of security"), but there is no doubt that they have been discussed several times. On these occasions, the Irish prime minister or foreign minister has kept silent. He might more logically have left the meeting temporarily, but nobody has wished to make an issue of the matter, and in practice the neutral status of Ireland has not been noticeably compromised by the attendance of its ministers. Nevertheless, the Community felt inhibited from shouldering responsibilities in the defence field, and this led in 1984 to an attempt to breathe new life into the moribund Western European Union (WEU) as a forum for discussing defence in a west European context.

Co-operation has been achieved in some respects

In practice foreign policy co-operation within the EU has manifested itself in three main aspects.

Presenting a common EU position

A serious effort has been made for the member states to speak with one voice in international fora. Thus the foreign minister of the country holding the presidency now speaks on behalf of all the member states in the general debate which opens each session of the UN in September. During the course of the year the 27 EU ambassadors to the UN are in constant conclave and take a lot of trouble to ensure that all the EU countries vote together in divisions in the General Assembly. As well as in the UN, it has become the practice for the country holding the presidency to present a common EU position at other international conferences, notably the

Conference on Security and Co-operation in Europe (CSCE), arising out of the 1975 Helsinki agreement. Since 1992 this body has been known as the Organisation for Security and Co-operation in Europe (OSCE). Its membership of 56 states includes all European countries, plus the United States and Canada.

Imposing sanctions

Common action has been taken in the imposition of economic sanctions. These have been imposed by all or most EU members, in concert, on several occasions. Some of them are:

- against Southern Rhodesia in 1965, following a UN resolution;
- against Iran after the taking of American hostages in 1980;
- against the Soviet Union and Poland after the imposition of martial law in Poland in 1981 (Greece declined to apply the sanctions);
- against Argentina during the Falklands War in 1982 (Italy and Ireland discontinued the sanctions halfway through the war);
- against Israel after the invasion of Lebanon in 1982;
- against South Africa in 1986 (the UK was initially unwilling to participate, but eventually agreed to do so after the original package of measures had been considerably watered down);
- against Iraq, following its invasion of Kuwait in August 1990, in accordance with the resolutions of the UN Security Council;
- against Serbia and Montenegro during the fighting in Croatia and Bosnia-Herzegovina in 1991–95;
- against Serbia before, during and after the Kosovo conflict, from 1998 onwards;
- against Zimbabwe in 2002, following evidence of violence and massive irregularities in the presidential election.

It is arguable that few of these attempts at applying the EU's economic clout for a political purpose had the desired effect. What they perhaps did achieve was to cement the EU countries' habit of working together in foreign policy and to strengthen their sense of common purpose.

Taking initiatives

The EU heads of government have taken a number of initiatives during their periodic meetings in the European Council. Statements and declarations have been made on East–West relations, the Middle East, the

Iran–Iraq war, Afghanistan, Poland, Central America and South Africa, with no apparent effect at all, even though some of them (such as the Venice declaration on the Middle East, which was taken to imply a role for the PLO in the peace process) were widely publicised at the time. A persistent weakness of these statements is that they have generally been purely declaratory, and little serious attempt has been made to follow them through.

New impetus towards common foreign policy

The collapse of communism in eastern Europe, which had as one of its many consequences the unification of Germany, followed by the 1991 Gulf war against Iraq, gave a fresh impetus towards a common foreign policy. On the one hand, the then German chancellor, Helmut Kohl, felt that it was necessary to tie Germany into a closer European federation if its neighbours' fears about unification were to be allayed. On the other hand, the serious differences that emerged among the member states before and during the Iraq war emphasised how far the EU had to go before it presented a single face to the outside world.

Reinforced by Maastricht treaty

Steps towards a common foreign, defence and security policy were thus major items on the agenda of the inter-governmental conference on political union, which opened in December 1990 and reported to the Maastricht summit in December 1991. The Treaty on European Union, which was agreed at the summit, did contain far-reaching provisions, although they did not go as far as Germany and most of the other member states would have preferred. A more cautious approach, based substantially on the principle of unanimity rather than majority voting, prevailed, largely at the bidding of the UK government. It was, however, agreed that the whole question should be reviewed at a further conference beginning in 1996, when Germany and its supporters hoped that a more thorough-going approach would be adopted. When this inter-governmental conference reported in June 1997 to the Amsterdam summit it was not in a position to put forward any radical proposals, and the Amsterdam treaty (see page 48) did not represent a conspicuous advance on that of Maastricht.

The Maastricht treaty pledged the "Union and its member states" to put into effect a common foreign and security policy (CFSP). This was to be pursued by establishing systematic co-operation between member states, gradually implementing joint action. The member states were required to inform and consult each other within the Council of Ministers on matters of foreign and security policy, and the council would adopt common positions where necessary. Member states were to ensure that their national policies conformed to the common positions, and to co-ordinate their action within international organisations. The European Council was to define general guidelines for "joint action" and the council would decide, by unanimity, whether an area or issue should be the subject of joint action. The detailed arrangements for the implementation of joint action would be decided by qualified majority.

The treaty stated that the CFSP should include all questions relating to the security of the EU, including the eventual framing of a common defence policy, which might in time lead to a common defence. Decisions on security with defence implications would, in the meantime, be implemented on request by the WEU. Previously, although there had been a substantial overlapping of membership, relations with the WEU had been complicated by the fact that not all the EC member states belonged to it. At Maastricht a parallel meeting of WEU ministers agreed to admit any EC member states that applied.

The treaty specifically gave authority to the country holding the rotating presidency of the Council of Ministers to act on the EU's behalf, which it had often done informally in the past. It gave it the responsibility for organising the CFSP, assisted where appropriate by the preceding and successive presidencies (the so-called "troika") and by the commission. It also laid down that the European Parliament must be kept regularly informed by the presidency, be consulted on broad policy questions and be permitted to question the council and make recommendations. The actual decision-making process of the CFSP would, however, be entirely inter-governmental, with the other EC institutions excluded. This process became known as Pillar Two of the EU.

The treaty also provided for co-operation between the member states on the following matters relating to security:

- asylum policy;
- rules governing crossing of member states' external borders;
- immigration policy;
- conditions of entry and movement by third-country nationals;
- conditions of residence including family reunion and access to employment for third-country nationals;
- combating unauthorised immigration and residence by third-country nationals;

- combating drugs;
- combating fraud;
- judicial co-operation in civil matters;
- judicial co-operation in criminal matters;
- customs co-operation;
- police co-operation on information exchange within a European Police Office (Europol).

These subjects, known collectively as Pillar Three, were also to be dealt with on an inter-governmental basis.

There was widespread disappointment that the Maastricht treaty provisions did not prove effective, and a number of changes were incorporated in the Amsterdam treaty in June 1997. They included the following:

- The appointment of a high representative, intended to be a major political figure, for the CFSP. He would act as secretary-general of the Council of Ministers, with a deputy to take charge of day-to-day management, and would have at his disposal a new Policy Planning and Early Warning Unit.
- A new "troika", consisting of the president of the Council of Ministers, the high representative and the president of the commission (or his nominee).
- Unanimity would be retained for substantive decisions, but there would be a possibility for "constructive abstention by member states which do not want to participate in a joint action, but have no wish to prevent a 'willing majority' from acting together".
- Many of the issues consigned to Pillar Three would be transferred back to Pillar One, and would in future be subject to normal EC procedures. The Prodi Commission established a separate directorate-general for Justice and Home Affairs, and at the Tampere summit in October 1999 EU leaders called for the creation of an area of "freedom, justice and security".

Javier Solana

The appointment in September 1999 of Javier Solana, formerly secretary-general of NATO and foreign minister of Spain, as the EU's high representative, gave a new impetus to the development of the CFSP. This was followed up at the Helsinki summit the following December with a series of decisions that should have led to an increase of the overall power and influence of the EU in international affairs.

The principal decision was that the EU should take over the responsibilities of the 50-year-old WEU, which was largely defunct, although it still existed on paper. The EU leaders decided that the Union needed its own military force to back up the CFSP. The aim was to assemble within three years a rapid reaction force (RRF) of 60,000 troops, which would be available within 60 days for deployment to a crisis area up to 2,500 miles away with the ability to stay in place for at least a year.

The missions that the force would fulfil were the so-called Petersberg tasks, enumerated at a WEU conference at Petersberg, Germany, in June 1992:

- humanitarian and rescue tasks;
- peacekeeping tasks;
- tasks of combat forces in crisis management, including peacemaking.

Such missions are normally carried out by NATO. The largely unspoken justification for having a separate EU force was to cover situations in which NATO (and, more particularly, the United States) did not wish to be directly involved, but was nevertheless sympathetic.

A new institutional basis was established for controlling the RRF. The Political and Security Committee (PSC) was established at ambassadorial level, with twice-weekly meetings in Brussels. It replaced the former Political Committee, which met far less frequently and whose members were based in their own capital cities. The PSC is flanked by a military committee, chaired for a three-year term by a four-star general, initially General Gustav Haglund from Finland. The 140-strong military staff was headed by General Rainer Schuwirth from Germany.

The objective was to have the RRF operational within three years, but, despite a dispute with Turkey about the conditions under which NATO equipment and planning resources could be loaned to the new force, it was declared "partially operational" at the Laeken summit one year early, in December 2001. The first operations were expected to be in the Balkans.

The member states held two "capabilities conferences" in 2000 and 2001, at which pledges were made of troops and equipment for the force. There was little difficulty in finding the numbers of troops needed, but there were significant shortfalls on the equipment side, mainly of air-lift and sea-lift capacity, communications equipment and headquarters units, intelligence-gathering satellites and aircraft, and precision-guided weapons. It was clear that, for the foreseeable future, the RRF would be heavily dependent on NATO assistance in any large-scale combat missions.

Further changes

The changes effected since the Amsterdam treaty, and those currently proceeding, should help to bring greater coherence to European foreign policy. So long as the unanimity rule is maintained for the CFSP, however, it is unlikely that the EU will be able to play as effective a part on the world stage as its economic power, military potential and wealth of democratic experience would warrant. This became embarrassingly clear in the run-up to the US intervention in Iraq in 2003, when the EU failed to reach a common position: the UK, Spain and Italy led those supporting the US plans, while France and Germany were the most vocal opponents. Amid bitter exchanges within the EU, Donald Rumsfeld, the US defence secretary, was able to characterise France and Germany as "Old Europe" and the US allies – including most of central and eastern Europe – as "New Europe".

Although EU leaders were unable to patch up their differences, they did confirm a 15-page European Security Strategy in December 2003 outlining areas where they felt the EU should be a more effective actor in world affairs and prevent divisions of the sort that rocked it over Iraq. Although the document, the so-called "Solana doctrine", says nothing about the use of force, and references to pre-emption were excised from the final text, it focuses on "effective multilateralism" and containing proliferation through export controls and other political pressures. Also in December 2003, the EU's main military powers – France, Germany and the UK – agreed a deal on a military planning cell for crisis management operations. It showed that despite high political tensions, there was strong co-operation on foreign and defence policy between London, Paris and Berlin.

CFSP to Lisbon treaty

In the ten years between the appointment of Javier Solana as high representative for foreign and security policy and the coming into force of the Lisbon treaty in December 2009, the EU embarked upon no fewer than 22 overseas operations of a military or civilian nature, many of them in the immediate neighbourhood of the EU, but some many thousands of miles away, reflecting greater interest in, and sense of responsibility for, the outer world. Among these interventions were:

- the civilian monitoring mission in the Indonesian province of Aceh in 2006 that oversaw the successful implementation of the peace agreement negotiated by the former Finnish president, Marti Ahtisaari;
- the military operation in the Democratic Republic of the Congo in support of the UN mission during the election process in 2006;
- the deployment of 3,000 soldiers to Chad and the Central African Republic to protect refugees from the Darfur region of Sudan;
- the dispatch of 300 monitors to Georgia in 2008 to oversee the ceasefire negotiated by President Nicolas Sarkozy in his capacity as president the EU Council of Ministers;
- the stationing in Kosovo of 1,800 police, judges and customs officers to help build an effective justice system and to protect the Serb minority;
- the deployment of a naval force (EUNAVFOR) off the coast of Somalia to protect international shipping from pirate attacks;
- the dispatch of police missions to Afghanistan and the Palestinian territories, including manning the Rafah crossing point between the Gaza strip and Egypt.

The EU also continued to apply sanctions or other "restrictive measures" against governments or individuals, usually because of gross abuses of human rights. In the period since 2006, this has included Uzbekistan, Myanmar (Burma), North Korea, the Democratic Republic of the Congo, Somalia, Sudan, Ivory Coast, Liberia, Zimbabwe, Macedonia, Belarus and Transnistria (the breakaway territory from Moldova). As on earlier occasions, there have, unfortunately, been few cases where these actions have led to measurable improvements.

The changes to be effected by the Lisbon treaty, and in particular the recruitment of the European External Action Service (EEAS), due to become fully operational in 2012, will probably result in an increase in the number of EU operations under the CFSP, and certainly an improvement in their efficacy.

Note

1 The foreign ministers form the so-called "general affairs council", which is regarded as the most senior of the various manifestations of the Council of

Ministers. As such they often meet to discuss matters unrelated to foreign affairs, sometimes arbitrating on issues which overlap the competences of departmental ministers, sometimes discussing particularly knotty problems, sometimes acting as direct deputies to the heads of government.

4
SPECIAL PROBLEMS

37 Enlargement

It was, from the outset, envisaged that other European countries besides the original six member states would subsequently be admitted into the European Community. Article 237 of the Treaty of Rome stated, in part: "Any European state may apply to become a member of the Community." This general invitation was, however, qualified by the preamble to the treaty which referred to the original members' resolve to strengthen peace and liberty and called upon "the other peoples of Europe who share their ideal to join in their efforts". This wording has subsequently been taken to mean that only countries with a democratic form of government are eligible to join. A further implied condition is that the economies of applicant states should be sufficiently developed to enable them to meet the obligations of membership and to be able to compete effectively within a free market.

Successful applicants

In 1961, and again in 1967, the UK, Denmark, Ireland and Norway made applications to join. On both occasions the UK was eventually vetoed by France, and the other three countries withdrew their applications. In 1969 a third approach was made, and new negotiations began with the four applicants which resulted in treaties of accession being signed in 1972. The three smaller applicant countries submitted the treaties to referendums, which produced majorities in favour in both Denmark and Ireland. France also held a referendum which showed a majority in favour of enlargement, but the Norwegian referendum resulted in a narrow majority against joining the Community (53:47 per cent). Denmark, Ireland and the UK became full members on January 1st 1973, although a transitional period of five years was allowed for adjusting tariffs, and for staggering various other membership provisions regarding, for example, agriculture and budgetary contributions. The UK did not hold a referendum on its entry to the Community, but following the election in 1974 of a Labour government the entry terms were partially renegotiated, and membership was subsequently confirmed by a majority of more than 2:1 in a referendum held on June 5th 1975.

Greece, Portugal and Spain were effectively excluded from membership during the years that they languished under dictatorships. Greece, which had already negotiated associate status with the EC several years before the military coup which overthrew its democratic regime in 1967, lost no time in applying for full membership after democratic government was restored in 1974. Its application was tabled in 1975, and Greece became the Community's tenth member on January 1st 1981. There was a five-year transition period for aligning import duties and for most parts of the common agricultural policy. A seven-year period, ending on January 1st 1988, was allowed for peaches and tomatoes, and also for the free movement of workers.

Portugal and Spain also applied for membership within a year or two of the Portuguese revolution of 1974, and the death of General Franco in 1975. Their membership negotiations were a great deal longer and more complicated than those with Greece, partly because of initial French reluctance but also because Spanish membership, in particular, was likely to cause greater problems for the existing member states. Agreement was finally reached in May 1985 and treaties of accession were signed on June 12th 1985, to take effect, after ratification by all the existing members as well as by Spain and Portugal, on January 1st 1986. In this case the transitional period was for seven years, ending on January 1st 1993, but for a number of sensitive agricultural products it lasted for ten years up to January 1st 1996. Freedom of movement for workers was not to come fully into effect for seven years, and in the case of Luxembourg (which already had a large population of immigrant Portuguese workers) for ten years.

Unsuccessful applicants

Turkey, which is recognised as a European state despite having 96% of its land area in Asia, and which signed an association agreement as long ago as 1963, officially applied for membership in April 1987, as did Morocco, which had made an unofficial approach three years earlier, in July 1987. Morocco claimed to be a democratic state with organic links with Europe, but was politely told that it was not eligible. The Turkish application was officially referred to the commission, for an opinion on its acceptability, as provided by the Rome treaty and as had occurred with all previous applications. In the past the commission verdict had always been favourable and membership negotiations had subsequently been opened. In this case, however, the commission reported that Turkey was not yet ready for membership, both because its economy was insufficiently developed and because its democracy had not been fully established. It was politely suggested to Turkey that its application should be shelved indefinitely. This rebuff did not deter the Turkish government, which in November 1992 announced that it wished to proceed to a full customs union with the EU, as had been foreshadowed in the original association agreement. The target date that the Turks set themselves was 1995.

Despite much scepticism, and some reluctance by the European Parliament to give its approval, the customs union came into effect on December 31st 1995. It would be a severe test for Turkish industry, which would have to face the full effect of competition from manufacturers within the EU. Yet the Turkish government welcomed this challenge as it believed that it would give an essential spur to the efficiency of Turkish enterprises. A provisional report by the commission on the working of the customs union, after the first ten months in October 1996, concluded that it was too early to assess the long-term effects, but the early indications seemed promising. There had been a sharp rise of EU exports to Turkey in the early months of 1996, while Turkey's exports to the EU had also risen, but not so sharply. Turkey had attracted a considerable amount of west European investment in recent years, and – since the end of the cold war – had been seen as an important trading link with the countries of the former Soviet Union and its satellites in the Balkans, the Caucasus and Central Asia. The Turks believed that the more their country became economically involved with the EU the more difficult it would become for the Union to refuse it full membership. In practice, however, Turkish accession was not regarded by the EU as a feasible option unless and until three conditions were met:

1　A sustained improvement in Turkey's human rights record.
2　A solution to the Cyprus dispute, involving the withdrawal of Turkish troops.
3　The consolidation of Turkish democracy.

Two other Mediterranean countries which had association agreements with the EU – Malta and Cyprus – applied for membership in 1990. Both could probably have adapted easily enough to the requirements of membership, but they were given no early opportunity to do so. As far as Cyprus was concerned, there was a strong feeling that membership would be inappropriate so long as the northern part of the island continued to be under Turkish military occupation. Both countries also suffered from EU doubts as to whether such small nations could effectively take on the burdens of membership. However, as Luxembourg, a founder member, has a similar population to Malta and a much smaller one than Cyprus, it was difficult to advance this as an argument against admitting them. The Copenhagen summit, in June 1993, adopted a more encouraging approach, and approved the sending of positive signals to both countries. These foresaw that the membership application of Cyprus would be re-examined in January 1995, in the light of the progress made in settling the Turkish Cypriot problem, and that an intensive dialogue would be held with Malta which would help prepare it for integration into the EU. Later, both countries received an assurance that negotiations on membership could commence within six months of the conclusion of the inter-governmental conference of 1996–97. The Maltese application was, however, put on ice by the newly elected Labour government in December 1996, only to be reactivated in September 1998 following its defeat in a subsequent election.

Two events gave a strong impetus to expanding EU membership, which had looked as though it would stabilise after the accession of Spain and Portugal in 1986: the 1992 programme to complete the single European market and the collapse of Soviet communism.

Negotiations with EFTA countries

The launch of the 1992 programme (see Chapter 16) caused immediate ructions in the seven EFTA countries. These had all negotiated industrial free trade agreements with the EC in the 1960s, but they were afraid that they would be left out of the opportunities that the creation of a single European market would provide.

A two-year negotiation led to an agreement to form a European Economic Area (EEA), due to come into effect on January 1st 1993. Yet in the process of the negotiations most of the EFTA countries concluded that they were being asked to make so many concessions that they might as well go the whole hog and apply for full membership. Austria had already decided to do this before negotiations began and Sweden put in its application in 1991. Finland and Switzerland followed suit early in 1992. Norway still had traumatic memories of the 1972 referendum which narrowly rejected membership at the same time as Danish, Irish and UK entry. Its government, in the face of sharply divided public opinion, hesitated before taking the plunge, but finally put in an application at the end of 1992. Meanwhile, the Swiss voters narrowly rejected membership of the EEA in a referendum in December 1992. This led to a minor renegotiation of the terms of the agreement enabling it to come into effect after a delay of one year, on January 1st 1994, without Swiss participation. Consequently, the Swiss application for membership of the EU was put on ice, much to the chagrin of Swiss industry which believed it would have great difficulty in competing if Switzerland remained outside.

This left two EFTA countries: Iceland and Liechtenstein. The latter, with a population of 28,000 (less than one-tenth of Luxembourg's), can hardly aspire to full membership although since April 1995 it has been a member of the EEA. Iceland was obsessed with the need to retain full control over its fisheries resources and was not then thinking of membership.

Negotiations with Austria, Finland, Sweden and Norway started early in 1993 and were successfully concluded in March 1994. Referenda were subsequently held in Austria in June, in Finland in September and in Sweden and Norway in November 1994. The first three produced majorities in favour, but Norwegian voters for the second time rejected EU membership (by 52.5% to 47.5%), so the number of member states increased from 12 to 15 in January 1995.

Few problems arose during the negotiating process. Each of the four applicant countries had high per head incomes and all eventually became net contributors to EU funds. The main contentious issues related to agriculture, the environment, regional policy, transport (in particular the transit of goods vehicles over mountain roads in Austria), alcohol monopolies (in the three Nordic countries) and, in Norway's case, fisheries. Eventually final agreement was reached on the basis that the applicant states would conform to EU legislation, but with varying transition periods and a small number of special provisions to meet specific difficulties.

The problems anticipated by the traditional neutrality policies of Austria, Finland and Sweden largely disappeared with the end of the Cold War. In the event, each of these countries declared that, from the time of its accession, it would "be ready and able to participate fully and actively in the Common Foreign and Security Policy as defined in the Treaty on European Union" (the Maastricht treaty).

Obstacles for new members

New members who join the EU are required to accept not only all the provisions of the treaties (see Chapter 3), but also the entire *acquis communautaire* (that is, all the secondary legislation – directives, regulations and decisions – that has already been adopted under the treaties). Consequently, membership negotiations, which are nonetheless normally exhaustive and long drawn out, are mostly concerned with the length and nature of the transitional period during which the applicant state will have to modify its existing laws in order to conform, and which provisions shall be included in such transitional arrangements. If an accession treaty is concluded it must then be ratified by the parliaments of all the existing member states before it can come into effect. Since the Single European Act came into force in 1987 it has also been necessary for the European Parliament to ratify new accessions by the vote of an absolute majority of its members. The first time this occurred was on May 5th 1994 when, by a large majority, the membership applications of Austria, Finland, Sweden and Norway were approved.

Central and eastern Europe

No sooner had the countries of central and eastern Europe broken free from the Soviet yoke in 1989–91 than they started to show a keen interest in joining the European Union. Some EU voices were raised against this, but in December 1991 association agreements were reached with Czechoslovakia, Hungary and Poland which specifically foresaw eventual membership. Similar agreements were later negotiated with Albania, Bulgaria, Romania, Slovenia and the Baltic states of Estonia, Latvia and Lithuania. The agreement with Czechoslovakia was later replaced by separate agreements with the Czech Republic and Slovakia. Slovenia also negotiated a similar agreement.

At the Copenhagen summit in June 1993 it was specifically affirmed that any central or east European country that so wished could become a member of the EU "once it was able to fulfil the obligations associated with membership and meet the economic and political requirements". The first countries to apply were Hungary and Poland in March 1994, and over the next two years they were followed by Bulgaria, the Czech Republic, Estonia, Latvia, Lithuania, Romania, Slovakia and Slovenia.

The commission reacted by producing a white paper in May 1995, setting out the preliminary steps the applicant countries should take to prepare themselves for membership. This bulky document, which contained hundreds of recommendations under 23 different policy headings, was intended largely as a checklist for the applicant countries to help prepare their administrations and adapt their legislation. At the same time, a great deal of technical assistance was provided to each of the countries under the Phare programme, to help minimise the pain that the process would inevitably entail. It was subsequently decided at the Florence summit in June 1996 that membership negotiations with the central and east European applicants could start, at the same time as those with Cyprus, six months after the conclusion of the inter-governmental conference. The commission was asked to prepare its opinion on the suitability and preparedness of each of the candidates immediately after the conclusion of the IGC.

Accordingly, in July 1997 it published its opinion on the relative preparedness of the 11 candidate countries, concluding that membership negotiations should begin early in 1998 with six of them but that the other five were not yet ready to accept the obligations of membership. The commission's opinion was accepted by the EU heads of government at the Luxembourg summit in December 1997, and negotiations were opened with Cyprus, the Czech Republic, Estonia, Hungary, Poland and Slovenia the following March. Bulgaria, Latvia, Lithuania, Romania and Slovakia were encouraged to continue with their preparations and were assured that these would be monitored on an annual basis and that if they made sufficient progress they too could be included in the process. In the meantime they were invited to an annual European conference of all EU member and applicant states, the first of which was held in London in March 1998. Turkey was also invited, but was offended at not being given the same assurances as the other candidates, and boycotted the conference.

Separate, but parallel, negotiations were started with the six favoured candidates, and at the Helsinki summit, in December 1999, EU leaders gave the go-ahead for entry talks with Bulgaria, Latvia, Lithuania, Malta, Romania and Slovenia to begin early in 2000. Long and laborious negotiations continued, and by the end of 2001 four of the second batch of candidates had caught up with the earlier starters. Bulgaria and Romania, however, were significantly behind. At the Laeken summit in December 2001, a target was set to complete negotiations with the ten leading candidates by the end of 2002, with the aim of bringing them into membership in time to participate in the European Parliament elections in 2004.

This target was successfully attained at the Copenhagen summit, in December 2002, after last-minute difficulties about the level of financial aid to be made available to the new member states were overcome. The EU insisted – and the candidate states reluctantly agreed – that the level of subsidies paid to them under the Common Agricultural Policy should start at only 25% of that accorded to existing members, rising in stages to 100% only in 2013, and that total financial assistance under the structural funds – for any member state – should not exceed 4% of GDP in any one year. All the new member states, except Cyprus, held referendums during 2003 to ratify the membership terms. This enabled them to enter the EU on May 1st 2004, and to take part in the elections for the European Parliament one month later.

Only in the case of Cyprus did things go wrong. It had been hoped that the imminent prospect of accession to the EU would stimulate efforts to agree on the reunification of the island, on the basis of a compromise plan put forward by Kofi Annan, the UN secretary-general. This plan was put to voters in Cyprus in two separate referendums held on April 24th 2004. The Turkish Cypriots accepted the plan by a two-to-one majority, but the Greek Cypriots, largely influenced by a negative campaign led by the recently elected left-wing president, Tassos Papadopoulos, rejected it by a margin of three to one. So one week later only the Greek controlled part of the island was able to join the Union. In retrospect, it can be seen that the EU made an error of judgment in agreeing in advance to the entry of the Republic of Cyprus in the absence of an agreement on reunification. Its bargaining power with the Greek Cypriots has been reduced now that EU membership has been granted.

That EU foreign ministers were displeased with Papadopoulos became clear within two days of the referendums. They agreed to show their appreciation of the more conciliatory attitude of the Turkish Cypriots by making economic aid available to them at the level that would have applied if reunification had gone through and opening the Union to Turkish Cypriot exports, despite the fact that the Turkish Republic of Northern Cyprus remained unrecognised internationally. Papadopoulos responded by threatening to veto these proposals when the formal regulations approving them were presented to the Council of Ministers, and by late 2009 they had still not been implemented. On their side, the Turkish Cypriots, who had rejected the anti-reunification stance of their long-serving president, Rauf Denktash, continued to seek an agreement under UN auspices under their new leader, Mehmet Ali Talat. The election, in February 2008, of Dimitris Christofias as successor to Papadopoulos, sparked new hope that agreement on the reunification of both parts of the island might yet be achieved. Christofias was much more forthcoming than Papadopoulos had been, and was personally friendly with the Turkish Cypriot president. Negotiations between the two men opened, under UN auspices, in March 2008, and quickly led to the reopening of the Ledra crossing point, which had divided the two halves of the city of Nicosia. Subsequently, however, they proceeded in a desultory fashion, and by the end of 2009 most of the steam seemed to have gone out of the initiative.

At the 1999 Helsinki summit, it was finally signalled to Turkey that it, too, was a candidate for eventual membership, while spelling out the conditions it would have to meet before negotiations could begin. The Turkish government announced early in 2002 that it was embarking on an ambitious programme of political and economic reforms to meet the EU's prerequisites for membership and aimed to begin negotiations during 2003. This proved too optimistic, but the sweeping victory in the general election of November 2002 of the moderate Islamic Justice and Development Party (AKP) brought the energetic Recep Tayyan Erdogan to power. His government pursued the reform programme with greatly increased vigour, and at the December 2004 summit EU leaders agreed that negotiations would begin in October 2005. This target was reached, but the serious bargaining began only in June 2006, when an agenda setting out 35 chapters for the negotiation was formally agreed. The first of these, on science and research, was opened and quickly concluded, but in December 2006 the negotiation came to a juddering halt as Turkey had not fulfilled its obligation to open its ports to ships from the Republic of Cyprus. The Turks retorted that they had not done so because the EU had not fulfilled its promise to open up trade with Northern Cyprus. The EU negotiators – prodded by the Greek Cypriots – then decided to partially suspend the negotiations, refusing to proceed on eight chapters that were ready for opening. The following June the talks restarted, but initially on only two chapters, and it seems unlikely that serious progress will be made until agreement is reached on the reunification of Cyprus. Even then, the Turks face an uncertain future, as several member states – notably France, Austria and Germany (which favours a "privileged relationship" with Turkey rather than full membership) – are extremely unenthusiastic. Even if things go unexpectedly well, it will be 2015, at the earliest, before Turkey is admitted.

Before the Turkish negotiations are concluded, several more countries, mostly from the western Balkans, may have joined the EU. Negotiations with Bulgaria and Romania were concluded in late 2004, and, on January 1st 2007, they became the 26th and 27th members of the Union. It was agreed, in principle, at the Thessalonica summit in June 2003 that Albania, Bosnia-Herzegovina, Croatia, Macedonia and Serbia-Montenegro would be eligible for membership if they fulfilled the necessary conditions, and both Croatia and Macedonia applied during 2004. Negotiations began with Croatia in October 2005 but were held up by a territorial dispute with Slovenia. Following mediation, this appeared to have been settled in late 2009, and there seemed a good prospect that the negotiations would be concluded in 2010, enabling Croatia to join the Union in 2011. So far as the Former Yugoslav Republic of Macedonia (FRYOM) was concerned, although it was accepted as a candidate, negotiations were not started, pending settlement of a dispute with Greece over the country's name, which the Greek government insisted implied a claim on its own province of Macedonia. The change of government in Greece, following the general election in October 2009, led to optimism that a compromise would finally be reached, enabling negotiations to begin in 2010. The other west Balkan states are less prepared – either politically or economically – for membership, but if they can get their act together they, too, may well precede Turkey into the Union. Montenegro, which voted in 2006 to end its union with Serbia, applied for membership in December 2008, and Albania followed suit in April 2009. If the commission reports favourably on their readiness for membership, negotiations may begin in 2010. In December 2009 Serbia submitted its own application. Bosnia-Herzegovina and Kosovo (which has been recognised as a potential candidate) may not be ready to apply for several years. Meanwhile, Iceland, which had been heavily hit by the 2008 recession, when its major banks and currency crashed, applied for membership in June 2009, and within a month had received a nod of approval from the commission. Negotiations were expected to begin early in 2010, and could be completed rapidly, enabling the country, which is already a member of the EEA and is participating in several EU programmes, to join the Union at the same time as Croatia.

The Community, which started with six members in 1958, now has a membership of 27 and a population of nearly 500m. Ten years later, if all goes well, there could be over 40 members, not including Russia but otherwise embracing the entire continent of Europe, and a total population approaching 700m. This may seem scarcely credible, and many would no doubt deeply regret the sea change in the nature of the Union which such an expansion would imply. Yet the logic of the Treaty of Rome and the way in which the EU has conducted itself so far point inexorably to a gradual but accelerating increase in membership.

38 The UK and the Union

The UK was a late entrant into the EC, and it has had an uneasy relationship with its partners for much of the time since it became a member state in 1973.

A history of distrust

Even before 1973 there was a long history of distrust and disappointment, despite the evident desire of the original six members of the Community for UK membership. At the end of the second world war the popularity and prestige of the UK was probably higher in western Europe than at any time before or since, and there was little doubt that had the UK taken the lead in the movement for closer integration it would have had a predominant influence on the shape and form of any association that was formed. In the event, there was widespread dismay and incomprehension at the UK's lack of interest in joining the Coal and Steel Community in 1951 or in attending the 1955 Messina conference which led to the creation of the EEC. The reasons behind this aloofness – the continuing belief that the UK was a global rather than a European power, that it had a special relationship with the United States, and that its major trading as well as political links were with the Commonwealth – were little appreciated beyond the English Channel. Furthermore, the UK initiative in founding the European Free Trade Association (EFTA) in 1959 was widely seen as a spoiling device to reduce the impact of the EEC, which had been established the previous year.

Nevertheless, the UK's application to join the EC, when it finally came in 1961, was warmly welcomed, and there was regret in all the member states (including France itself) when President de Gaulle twice vetoed its entry, in 1963 and 1968. It was only at the third time of asking that terms of accession were finally agreed, in June 1971, following renewed negotiations between Edward Heath's Conservative government and the six existing members.

Opposition to EC membership in the Labour Party

The long years of haggling had taken their toll in the UK, and a substantial degree of opposition to membership had built up. This affected both major political parties, but in the Conservative Party, where it was largely confined to a narrow, right-wing, nationalistic fringe, the party leadership had little difficulty in isolating and containing its anti-EC members.

In the Labour Party internal divisions were more serious. The EC was depicted by left-wingers as a capitalist conspiracy opposed to the party's most basic objectives, while many trade unionists feared that food prices would rise as a result of the impact of the CAP. The pro-EC elements in the party, led by Roy Jenkins, held their ground against strong pressure to abandon their own deep convictions; 69 Labour MPs (including the author) defied the party whip and enabled the membership terms to be approved by a good majority in the House of Commons. The damage done to the Labour Party by this dispute, particularly by the intolerant way in which it was conducted, was considerable, and undoubtedly contributed to the split which occurred a decade later when the Social Democratic Party (SDP) was formed. Hostility within the Labour Party continued, but it was successfully defused, at least for a time, by the commitment that a Labour government would hold a referendum to determine whether the UK would remain a member. Following Labour's election victory in 1974, the terms of membership were renegotiated, the main change being the institution of a financial mechanism designed to prevent excessive UK budgetary contributions (although in the event it proved to be ineffective, see pages 13–14). A majority of the cabinet led by the prime minister, Harold Wilson, and the foreign secretary, James Callaghan (both of whom had voted against membership in 1971), were able to recommend the acceptance of the revised terms, despite the opposition of a large section of the Labour Party. In the referendum which followed, on June 5th 1975, a majority of just over 2:1 favoured continued UK membership, and the dispute seemed to be over.

It flared up again in 1979 when it was discovered, in the closing months of James Callaghan's Labour government, that – despite the renegotiated terms – the UK, which had now reached the end of its transitional stage of membership, was liable to pay an unacceptably high net contribution to the EC, probably exceeding 1 billion ecus in the following year (see pages 18–19). It fell to Mrs Thatcher's Conservative government, elected in May 1979, to attempt to secure a permanent abatement of the UK contribution. Mrs Thatcher played the leading part in the negotiations, which dominated the life of the Community and particularly the meetings of the European Council until a settlement was reached at the Fontainebleau summit in June 1984 (see page 20). In the meantime Labour Party hostility to UK membership was rekindled, and in the June 1983 general election campaign the party proposed a unilateral withdrawal, without even the possibility of a further referendum. Following Labour's heavy defeat in that election, and the replacement of Michael Foot by Neil Kinnock as party leader, the issue was quietly dropped. There was no mention of withdrawal in the Labour Party manifesto for the 1987 general election.

A year or so later, following a highly successful visit to the Trades Union Congress in 1988 by Jacques Delors, who fired the delegates with a vision of a Europe in which trade unionists would share fully in the fruits of the Community's future development, including the 1992 programme, both the trade unions and the Labour Party finally came round to see the EC in a positive light.

Mrs Thatcher reduced UK influence in the EC

This welcome development was balanced by a perverse reaction in the Conservative Party, which, under the leadership of Mrs Thatcher, became steadily more hostile to the EC from September 1988 onwards, when she delivered a widely reported speech at Bruges. This was hailed as a rallying call by all those who looked nostalgically back to the days when the UK was a world power and who were psychologically incapable of adjusting to current realities. Mrs Thatcher became especially hung up over questions of "sovereignty", which she and her supporters saw as a zero-sum concept, assuming that any accretion of power to EC institutions constituted an equal diminution of that of the member states. This ran directly counter to the prevailing view within the Community, which was that national sovereignty had been declining for many years, for reasons which had little to do with the growth of the EC, and that it was only by pooling their resources in a number of fields that the member states would be able collectively to achieve objectives which would be beyond their individual capacity.

In fact it is clear that Mrs Thatcher substantially reduced UK influence within the EC during her final years as prime minister by insisting that the UK took a negative or minimalist position on most proposals for new EC initiatives, even including those, such as the Lingua programme on foreign language teaching (see page 232), which would be of particular benefit to the UK. She seemed to glory in being in a minority of one at meetings of the European Council, and it was her behaviour at and after the Rome meeting in October 1990, which set a date for the beginning of stage two of EMU, that led to her being challenged for the leadership of the Conservative Party and her replacement by John Major.

John Major did not do any better

Major evidently did not share Mrs Thatcher's deep distrust of the Community, and spoke of his desire "to bring the UK into the heart of Europe". He promptly dropped her abrasive criticisms of the EC, but, conscious of her continuing influence within the Conservative Party, he continued to approach the proposals for EMU and "political union" with circumspection. By adopting a more reasonable negotiating approach, he was able to secure considerable changes in the two inter-governmental conferences, particularly in that on "political union", and a year after becoming prime minister he agreed to the Maastricht Treaty on European Union, but only on the basis of two opt-out clauses. One of these reserved the right of the UK not to take part in the third stage of EMU, with a European Central Bank (ECB) and a common currency. Few observers believed at the time that there was any serious possibility of the UK not participating in stage three, and the only lasting consequence of Mr Major's obduracy at Maastricht was likely to be the undermining of the otherwise strong claim of the City of London to house the ECB. This prediction proved correct when Frankfurt was subsequently chosen as the site for the European Monetary Institute, which was the forerunner of the bank. The other opt-out concerned the Social Charter.

These opt-outs were double-edged so far as Major was concerned. While not really appeasing the Eurosceptics in his own party, they were profoundly unwelcome to the Labour Party and the Liberal Democrats, which otherwise were enthusiastic supporters of the Maastricht treaty. It was not, therefore, possible to depend on wholehearted support from the opposition parties during the long and difficult process of getting the ratification bill through both Houses of the UK Parliament. This was completed only in July 1993, after repeated alarms and a real risk that the government, with its slender parliamentary majority, might be swept away in the process. Major and his colleagues emerged shell-shocked from the experience and thereafter seemed to give overriding priority to keeping Tory Eurosceptics happy. This led to a resumption of Thatcherite anti-EU rhetoric by ministers, and the UK once again allied itself with those wishing to obstruct further progress towards European integration. Major unwisely attempted to play to the anti-EU gallery in his party in March and April 1994, when he sought to maintain the size of the blocking minority in votes in the Council of Ministers at the same level as for 12 member states when the rules were being revised for the extension of membership to 16, with the anticipated accession of Austria, Finland, Sweden and Norway. He encountered determined opposition from all the other member states except Spain, as well as from the European Parliament, and eventually had to make a humiliating climbdown in order not to jeopardise the accession of the four applicants, which had been a long-term UK aim.

Worse was to follow in June 1994, when at the Corfu summit Major vetoed the appointment of the Belgian prime minister, Jean-Luc Dehaene, as successor to Jacques Delors as president of the commission. This caused real offence, not only in Belgium but in the other member states as well, all of which had backed his appointment. The ostensible reason given for Major's action was that Dehaene was a "federalist", who believed in an important role for the state in economic decision-making. Actually, it was intended as a "macho" action to impress Tory backbenchers. It was to little avail: a few weeks later Major agreed without demur to the appointment of the Luxembourg prime minister, Jacques Santer, who blandly announced that his own views were identical to those of Dehaene.

Subsequently, the Conservative Party got itself into a hideous mess over the question of economic and monetary union, with a determined attempt by the Eurosceptics to rule out UK membership definitively. Major resisted this pressure but at the cost of engaging in more and more anti-EU rhetoric, spurred on by large sections of the press, which, although mostly foreign-owned (by Rupert Murdoch and Conrad Black), took an increasingly obsessive nationalistic line. Major's government also took a negative position in the inter-governmental conference, making it impossible for it to reach any agreed positions on serious issues before the UK general election on May 1st 1997.

Last chance for the UK?

The newly elected Labour government lost no time in emphasising that it intended to make a "fresh start" in relations with the EU, and that although it would defend vital UK interests it would adopt a much more positive approach than its predecessors. Its first initiative, within a couple of days of the election, was to announce that it would end the UK opt-out and sign up to the Social Chapter at the earliest opportunity. This was probably the UK's last chance to end the damage caused by its previous semi-detached attitude to the Union, and to restore its influence as a leading player. Tony Blair and his ministers followed this up by adopting a much more conciliatory attitude in negotiations within the inter-governmental conference, enabling agreement to be reached at the Amsterdam summit in June 1998. The fact that the Amsterdam

Treaty did not go so far towards greater EU integration as many people had hoped was not, for once, the fault of the British negotiators. Blair succeeded in dispelling within a few weeks the bad blood which had existed between the UK and its European partners over the preceding years, but there was great disappointment when later in the year Gordon Brown, the British Chancellor of the Exchequer, announced that the UK would not be one of the founder members of economic and monetary union (EMU). British ministers were subsequently reluctant to concede – what was evident to everybody else – that their influence in EU decision-making was bound to be reduced until such time as they finally took the plunge. It was especially painful for them to accept their exclusion from the ministerial Euro-11 (later Euro-16) committee set up to oversee the EMU process.

It is far from certain when, and even if, the UK will join the single currency. The Blair government declared itself in favour in principle, but repeatedly said that it would recommend entry in a referendum only when five economic tests set by Gordon Brown had been satisfied. These tests were as follows:

- Would joining EMU create better conditions for firms making long-term decisions to invest in the UK?
- How would adopting the single currency affect the UK's financial services?
- Are business cycles and economic structures compatible so that the UK and others in Europe could live comfortably with euro interest rates on a permanent basis?
- If problems do emerge, is there sufficient flexibility to deal with them?
- Will joining EMU help to promote higher growth, stability and a lasting increase in jobs?

Few, if any, of these tests were susceptible to precise measurement, and there was a large subjective – if not cosmetic – element to them. The government's decision was, in fact, to be made on political rather than economic grounds.

Its overcautious attitude had been affected by three important factors. First, opinion polls, which consistently showed majorities of two to one, or even more, against entry, even though 80% of voters expected the UK to have adopted the single currency by 2010. Second, the hostility of large parts of the press, particularly the *Sun* and the *Daily Mail.*

Third, the opposition of the bulk of the Conservative Party. The last factor was somewhat mitigated by the rout of the Conservatives in the 2001 general election after William Hague, then its leader, had made "save the pound" a central feature of his campaign. At this stage – or certainly in January 2002, after the extraordinarily smooth introduction of euro notes and coins throughout the 12 member states of the euro zone – the government should have pressed home its advantage and launched a full-blooded campaign to win over public opinion in a referendum campaign. Yet both these opportunities were let slip, and in the absence of any serious initiative on the government's part, the hostile lead in the opinion polls continued to build up. In June 2003, the government announced that, of its five economic tests, only one had been fully and one partially met, and that therefore it would not be recommending euro membership in the near future. It was painfully evident that the real reason for backing off was not its reading of the economic tests but its lack of confidence in winning a referendum.

A common interpretation was that Blair, who clearly believed that joining the euro would be in the UK's interest, had allowed himself to be outmanoeuvred by the more sceptical Brown, but it was becoming obvious that Blair too was becoming averse to risking unpopularity by adopting a pro-European stance. This became evident in the search for a new EU constitution during the convention and inter-governmental conference of 2003–04. The UK contribution was largely confined – with considerable success – to retaining national vetoes over as wide a field of policy as possible, even though this negated the main purpose of the exercise, which was to make decision-making easier in an EU with 25 or 27 members. Blair achieved his objective, confounding the ludicrous suggestions in the tabloid press that the Constitutional treaty which emerged would lead to the creation of a European "super-state". He then, quite unnecessarily, put the proposed constitution at risk by promising to hold a referendum on it, despite the fact that he would have had no difficulty in having it ratified by Parliament. Blair has often been described as the most pro-European prime minister since Edward Heath, but his record hardly sustains this. Instead of trying to confront an increasingly sceptical public opinion and attempting to convert it, he ran scared and progressively surrendered the initiative he had won by his high popularity during the earlier years of his government.

The constitution ... and the Lisbon treaty

The constitutional treaty met all the requirements that Blair had set out during the preceding negotiations. It was designed to make the EU more transparent and more effective and to ease decision-making when its membership increased from 15 to 27. Yet all the "red lines" that Blair had set out were respected, and the UK received a number of specific opt-outs or opt-ins. Even so the Conservative Party, and much of the popular press, immediately condemned it as a forerunner of a super-state, and began a highly emotional campaign to defeat it in the promised referendum. Whether the Labour government would have been able to carry it through if it had fought a spirited campaign in the referendum will never be known, as the defeats it suffered at the hands of French and Dutch voters in May–June 2005 led to its demise.

It was eventually replaced by a watered down version, the Treaty of Lisbon (see Chapter 3). With the exception of the Irish, who had constitutional problems of their own, the EU heads of government agreed that their countries should seek to ratify the treaty by a parliamentary rather than popular vote, and this was the view taken by the new British prime minister, Gordon Brown, and his ministers. The earlier pledge, they maintained, applied only to the Treaty Establishing a Constitution for Europe (TCE), and as this was a different document, if similar in its effect, there was no obligation to put it to a popular vote. They were, no doubt, influenced by opinion polls indicating that the treaty would be defeated, and by their knowledge that referendums proposed by unpopular governments were almost invariably voted down, whatever the subject. By this time anti-European feeling within the Conservative Party had built up so much – under the successive leaderships of William Hague, Iain Duncan Smith, Michael Howard and David Cameron – that the once powerful pro-European element within the party had been reduced to derisory dimensions. Virtually the whole party was now converted to a Eurosceptic, if not Europhobic, view – a sad commentary on a party once led by such convinced Europeans as Winston Churchill, Harold Macmillan and Edward Heath.

Even Cameron himself, who had successfully pointed the party in a more liberal direction over many domestic political issues, took a consistently negative view towards the EU. Whether this was from conviction or a determination not to be outflanked by the United Kingdom Independence Party (UKIP) in his appeal to Eurosceptic voters is a matter for conjecture. He vehemently denounced the treaty, and said that a future Conservative government would hold a referendum on it, while recommending a "no" vote. He emphasised his anti-EU position by withdrawing the British Conservative MEPs from the centre-right European People's Party group (EPP), and linking them instead with a motley collection of extreme right-wingers, several of whom were alleged to be anti-Semites, homophobes or admirers of the Waffen SS. This action greatly reduced the influence of Conservative MEPs within the Parliament and infuriated the main centre-right leaders within the EU, such as Nicolas Sarkozy and Angela Merkel. When the Irish voters finally endorsed the treaty, in their second referendum in October 2009, opening the way to its coming into force a few weeks later, Cameron conceded that there would be no referendum in the UK despite his "cast-iron" guarantee. However, he said he would seek to reopen the question by attempting to "repatriate" certain unspecified powers that had been transferred to the Union. This would require the unanimous consent of all the member states, and most independent observers concluded that it would be doomed to failure, and would serve only to poison relations with the UK's European partners for years to come.

Is there something in the British psyche that leads people to take leave of their rationality when considering the EU? This seemed to be the case with a majority of the Labour Party during the 1970s and early 1980s, and the same bug seems to have bitten the Conservatives even more virulently in the early years of the 21st century. If a Conservative government should be elected in the UK in 2010, it is greatly to be hoped that the new ministers will savour their victory, calm down, and take a more realistic view of the EU and the enormous opportunities it offers for a UK that participates wholeheartedly in its activities rather than standing sulkily on the sidelines. If not, it will, of course, be a loss to the Union, but an even greater loss to the British people.

39 The future

On March 25th 2007 a special meeting of the European Council was held in Berlin. It issued a ringing declaration calling for reform and renewal within the Union to celebrate the 50th anniversary of the signing of the treaty to set up the European Economic Community (EEC). This was a very different gathering from the one 50 years earlier, when the heads of state and government of France, West Germany, Italy, the Netherlands, Belgium and Luxembourg first assembled in the Italian capital. That cosy club of six west European neighbours had expanded to 27 member states by 2007, and the population of the Community had grown from less than 200m to nearly 500m. The expansion in the scope of its activities had been equally impressive. What started out as an embryonic customs union, with a Common Agricultural Policy tagged on, had emerged as a leading economic actor on the world stage, whose policies had proliferated into many fields not mentioned in the original treaty.

The more recent achievements of the EEC, and its successor the EU, are too numerous to list in detail, but on the economic side two, in particular, stand out. First, the 1992 programme for completing the single market (see Chapter 16) was substantially concluded on time, and the bulk of the internal barriers that prevented the Community from operating as a single trading area were removed. Second, the member states committed themselves to economic and monetary union. The successful launch of the euro at the beginning of 1999 and the astonishingly smooth introduction of notes and coins in January–February 2002 left little doubt that it will act as a further spur to European integration and may well, in time, come to challenge, if not surpass, the American dollar as the principal world currency. The value of the euro connection became apparent during the recession of 2008–09, when the Irish banks and economy were saved from disaster by the country's membership of the euro zone. The contrast with Iceland, whose banks had met similar difficulties and whose currency crashed, was widely observed, and prompted the hitherto Eurosceptic Icelanders to apply for EU (and euro-zone) membership without delay. It was also noteworthy that the euro zone recovered from the recession more quickly than the UK (which had chosen to keep its own currency), despite the energetic steps the UK government took to bail out its grossly overextended banks.

A third major economic initiative was that launched at the Lisbon summit, in March 2000, to turn the EU into "the most competitive and dynamic knowledge-based economy in the world". It is a ten-year programme, which is being monitored each spring by special meetings of the European Council. Although considerable progress was made in some areas, the overall result after the first five years – assessed at a summit in Brussels in March 2005 – was disappointing. The target date of 2010 was abandoned, and it was decided to relaunch the initiative, with a greater concentration on more limited objectives, mainly economic growth and job creation.

Progress has been mixed, too, in the EU's objective of forging a common foreign and security policy, with sufficient military clout to back it up, without being heavily dependent on the United States. The EU's response to the end of the cold war was highly positive. It took the lead in providing moral and material support for the newly free countries of central and eastern Europe, to which it clearly acted as a powerful magnet. It was the EU that took the initiative in setting up the European Bank for Reconstruction and Development and subscribed more than half its $12 billion capital, while establishing the Phare and TACIS programmes, which have dispersed a substantial amount of economic, financial and technical aid. In so far as this has represented a continuation of the Marshall Plan, which rejuvenated western Europe, it is the EU and not the United States that is providing the great bulk of the material assistance. The EU also opened up the prospect of membership for the countries of central and eastern Europe. Eight of them (together with Malta and Cyprus) became full members in May 2004, with Bulgaria and Romania joining in 2007 and the prospect of Turkey, Croatia, Macedonia and other countries in the Balkans, and further east, eventually also joining the Union.

The uncertain EU response to the break-up of Yugoslavia in 1991–92, when the combatants looked to the EU rather than to the Organisation on Security and Co-operation in Europe (OSCE, formerly the CSCE) to broker a peaceful settlement, underlined how unready the Union and its member states were to assume such a role. This story was largely repeated in Kosovo in 1998–99, and in both cases it required massive intervention by NATO, with the American contribution predominant, before the conflicts were resolved.

Since then the momentum towards a common European defence effort has significantly speeded up. The wastefulness of competing national research and manufacturing concerns, most of which are too small to compete successfully with their American rivals, has produced a spate of mergers, which will certainly continue. The moves to develop a European Defence and Security Policy, with its own Rapid Reaction Force (RFF), described in Chapter 36, offer a hopeful prospect. But the member states will have to do a great deal more – in terms of contributing to the equipment as well as the manpower of the RFF – before it is able to play an effective role in peacekeeping, let alone peacemaking, operations.

As the second decade of the 21st century began the EU stood at a crossroads. A large part of the previous decade had been taken up with disputes about the institutional structure of the Union as it struggled to update the Treaty of Rome and its successor treaties to enable the EU to operate successfully with a much larger membership and the prospect of further enlargement. The Treaty of Lisbon, which finally came into force on December 1st 2009, is far from being perfect, and it is unfortunate that – unlike the TCE, which it replaced – it does not set out clearly the aims and purposes of the Union. But given the will of Europe's leaders to make it work, and a spirit of give-and-take among them, it should just about meet the purpose for which it was designed. It will not be the last word in EU governance, and future changes will no doubt be made in the EU's institutional structure, but for the moment it will have to do.

It is likely to be another decade or so before the issues fought over since the Laeken summit of December 2001 are re-examined. When they are, it is to be hoped that one of the most important lessons will have been learnt: that the holding of referendums is a wholly inappropriate method for seeking approval for complex and detailed changes to EU treaties. New member states joining the Union usually feel the need to put a straight "yes" or "no" question to their citizens, as EU membership profoundly affects their international status. But to submit a series of often petty amendments to largely uninterested and uninformed electors is a negation rather than an affirmation of democracy. The proper forums for examining such details are popularly elected parliaments, whose members have the opportunity to consider legislative proposals on behalf of their electors. To take this responsibility away from them is to undermine the basis of representative democracy. Traditionally, referendums were used by dictators – such as the two Napoleons and Hitler – to manipulate their electors, and were thus widely distrusted. They have a more respectable history in Switzerland and several American states, but recent experience from other European countries has not been encouraging. The evidence is that many voters use their vote to indicate their approval or disapproval of the national government in power rather than the question on the ballot paper. To get 27 or more national electorates to vote the same way at any one time would be the triumph of hope over experience. To rely on referendums in the context of institutional change within the Union would be a formula for stagnation.

The first half-century

One thing that has held the EU back – and has diminished its influence in the outside world – has been its reluctance to use the means already at its disposal to further its professed aim to secure a peaceful world based on the rule of law and a willingness to accept mediation rather than force in settling disputes. A particularly unfortunate incident has been pinpointed by a think-tank, the European Council on Foreign Relations, in a comment on the Russo-Georgian war in 2008:[1]

> In 2005 Russia terminated a 150-person strong OSCE Border Monitoring Mission on the Russian-Georgian border and Georgia invited the EU to take over. The EU response was to send three persons (later extended to twelve) to help Georgia to reform its border management system. In January 2007, an EU fact-finding mission suggested a number of modest steps such as financing for civil society, the opening of European Information Centres, and the appointment of EU police liaison officers in Abkhazia and South Ossetia. Even these small-scale measures were blocked and delayed by a minority of EU member states afraid of irritating Moscow.

Had these steps been taken, it is unlikely that the festering dispute would have led to open hostilities in August 2008.

Charles Grant, director of another influential think-tank, the Centre for European Reform, summed up the basic reason the EU fails to punch its weight in international affairs in his magisterially argued essay, *Is Europe doomed to fail as a power?*,[2] published in July 2009. It is the refusal of the leaders of member states to sink their differences and present a united front to the outside world, particularly in their dealings with the United States, China and, especially, Russia. One of the most spectacular failures has been the lack of agreement on a common energy policy. This means that Russia, on which several member states have become unduly dependent for their energy supplies, is able to play off one state against another in negotiations over pipelines, for example, with a less than optimum outcome for the EU as a whole. As unanimity is required for all substantive decisions under the common foreign and security policy, it is not enough to get all the major players on side in coming to a decision; even the smallest member states can thwart proposed actions, as the Republic of Cyprus has shown in preventing progress being made in membership negotiations with Turkey. There is no realistic possibility of scrapping the unanimity rule in the foreseeable future, as the painful passage of the Lisbon Treaty has virtually assured that there will be no further institutional changes to the Union for many years. Is it too much to hope that the useful device of "constructive abstention" will become the normal recourse of countries that are unable to associate themselves with a particular policy, but have no fundamental reason to oppose it?

It is sadly the case that the vanity of certain European leaders has on more than one occasion been a factor in preventing agreement from being reached. This may well have played a role in the selections made in November 2009 of a permanent president of the European Council and a high representative for foreign and security policy. For the first of these posts, the only high-profile candidate seriously considered was Tony Blair. He probably would not have been the best person for the job because of his role in launching the war on Iraq, which grievously offended many, particularly, but by no means exclusively, on the left side of the political spectrum. Yet there is no evidence that any serious attempt was made to find an alternative figure with a strong but less controversial international record. In particular, Martti Ahtisaari, a former Finnish president, whose outstanding accomplishments as an international mediator won him the Nobel Peace Prize in 2008, does not seem to have been approached, despite a widely publicised article by Timothy Garten Ash putting forward his claims. Similarly, present or former foreign ministers who had made a strong international impact, such as Germany's Joshka Fischer or Sweden's Carl Bildt, were conspicuously ignored in the search to find an effective high representative. Both Herman Van Rompuy and Catherine Ashton may turn out to have been inspired choices, but the suspicion remains that they were chosen, at least in part, because of their relative obscurity, so as not to overshadow the leaders and foreign ministers of national governments.

G2 or G3?

More than half a century ago, Paul-Henri Spaak, a former Belgian prime minister and foreign minister, reportedly said of the original six members of the EEC: "We are all small countries now – but not all of us realise this." In the second decade of the 21st century, this has become a truism, and former "great powers" such as France and Germany are increasingly aware of their limited clout in the world, unless they act together within the umbrella of the EU. This is equally true of the UK, which risks becoming even less influential if it continues to be only a "semi-detached" member of the Union. The recession of 2008–09, and the relative success of China and other Asian states in avoiding its worst consequences, has underlined the increasing marginality of Europe, and has led to talk of a future G2, in which the United States and China will effectively jointly determine the fate of the world. It need not happen. As the UK's foreign secretary, David Miliband, said in a speech in Warsaw in June 2009:[3]

> The question for all Europeans is whether we want to be players or spectators in the new world order. Whether we want to support the US in promoting our shared values – of freedom and liberty, peace and prosperity – or stand asideand let others shape our 21st century for us ... If we want to avoid a so-called G2 world, shaped by the US-China relationship, we need to make G3 co-operation – US, China and the EU – work.

This will require the EU member states to work much more closely together than in the past – at least in the international sphere – and a disciplined curbing of both national and personal egos. The peoples of Europe should expect nothing less.

Notes

1 Nicu Popescu, Mark Leonard and Andrew Wilson, *Can the EU Win the Peace in Georgia?*, London, European Council on Foreign Relations, 2008.
2 Charles Grant, *Is Europe doomed to fail as a power?*, London, Centre for European Reform, 2009.
3 Quoted in Grant, *op. cit.*

APPENDICES

1 Basic statistics of the member and candidate states

The following table, which has been compiled mostly from information supplied by the EU's Statistical Office (Eurostat), contains comparative data on the 27 member states and on 4 candidate members, as well as Switzerland and Norway, which belong to EFTA or the EEA. The figures refer to 2008, unless stated otherwise.

	Pop. ('000)	Total area (km²)	GDP per head PPS (% of EU average)	Real growth rate (%)	Unemployment rate[a] (%)	Employment rate (%)	Inflation[a] (%; 2005 = 100)
Austria	8,318	83,858	123.1	2.0	4.7	72.1	107.9
Belgium	10,666	30,518	114.0	1.0	8.0	62.4	109.0
Bulgaria	7,640	110,994	40.5	6.0	7.6	64.0	132.4
Cyprus	789	9,251	96.2	3.6	5.9	70.9	109.5
Czech Republic	10,381	78,865	80.1	2.5	7.0	66.6	111.8
Denmark	5,475	43,098	118.7	-0.9	6.5	78.1	108.8
Estonia	1,340	45,227	68.2	-3.6	15.2	69.8	123.5
Finland	5,300	338,150	116.1	1.0	8.6	71.1	109.2
France	63,982	549,087	107.4	0.4	10.0	64.9	106.9
Germany	82,217	357,031	116.1	1.3	7.6	70.7	107.1
Greece	11,213	131,957	93.9	2.0	9.2[b]	61.9	112.9
Hungary	10,045	93,034	62.8	0.6	9.7	56.7	125.2
Ireland	4,401	70,295	136.6	-3.0	12.9	67.6	106.5
Italy	59,619	301,323	100.6	-1.0	7.8	58.7	109.2
Latvia	2,270	64,589	55.8	-4.6	19.7	68.6	137.9
Lithuania	3,366	65,300	61.2	2.8	13.8[b]	64.3	126.8
Luxembourg	483	2,586	271.5	0.0	6.5	63.4	110.9
Malta	410	316	75.5	2.1	7.2	55.3	111.8
Netherlands	16,405	35,518	135.0	2.0	3.7	77.2	106.4
Poland	38,115	312,685	57.6	5.0	8.2	59.2	113.1
Portugal	10,617	91,909	75.6	0.0	10.1	68.2	107.1
Romania	21,528	238,391	45.8	6.2	6.4[b]	59.0	127.6
Slovakia	5,400	49,033	71.8	6.2	12.0	62.3	111.0
Slovenia	2,010	20,373	90.7	3.5	5.9	68.6	113.3
Spain	45,283	504,890	103.4	0.9	19.1	64.3	110.4
Sweden	9,182	449,974	121.0	-0.2	8.7	74.3	109.3
United Kingdom	61,933	244,101	117.2	0.6	7.8	71.5	111.5
EU-27	**498,388**	**4,322,353**	**100.0**	**0.8**	**9.2[b]**	**65.9**	**109.8**
Croatia	4,446	58,594	63.1	2.4	9.6	57.8	–
Iceland	315	103,000	119.8	1.3	–	83.6	145.3
Macedonia	2,045	25,713	32.6	4.9	–	41.9	–
Norway	4,737	323,895	189.8	1.8	3.1	78.0	110.0
Switzerland	7,593	41,293	141.6	1.8	–	79.5	103.3
Turkey	70,586	769,604	45.7	0.9	13.2[b]	45.9	139.1

a September 2009.
b July 2009.

2 Presidents of the High Authority, the Commission and the European Council

Presidents of the High Authority of the European Coal and Steel Community (ECSC)
(merged with the European Commission on July 1st 1967)

1952 Jean Monnet
1955 René Mayer
1958 Paul Finet
1959 Piero Malvestiti
1963 Dino Del Bo

Presidents of the Commission of the European Atomic Energy Community (Euratom)
(merged with the European Commission on July 1st 1967)

1958 Louis Armand
1959 Etienne Hirsch
1962 Pierre Chatenet

Presidents of the European Commission
(and since 1967 of the combined European Communities)

1958	Walter Hallstein	**1981**	Gaston Thorn
1967	Jean Rey	**1985**	Jacques Delors
1970	Franco-Maria Malfatti	**1995**	Jacques Santer
1972	Sicco Mansholt	**1999**	Romano Prodi
1973	François-Xavier Ortoli	**2004**	José Manuel Barroso
1977	Roy Jenkins		

President of the European Council

2009 Herman Van Rompuy

3 The European Commission, 2010–15

José Manuel Barroso (Portugal)	President
Joaquin Almunia (Spain)	Competition, Vice-President
Catherine Ashton (UK)	Foreign Affairs High Representative, Vice-President
Michel Barnier (France)	Internal Market and Services
Olli Rehn (Finland)	Economic and Monetary Affairs
Dacian Clolos (Romania)	Agriculture
John Dalli (Malta)	Health and Consumer Policy
Karel De Gucht (Belgium)	Trade
Stefan Füle (Czech Republic)	Enlargement
Connie Hedegaard (Denmark)	Climate Action
Maire Geoghegan-Quinn (Ireland)	Research and Innovation
Janusz Lewandowski (Poland)	Budget/Financial Programming
Guenther Oettinger (Germany)	Energy
Janez Potocnik (Slovenia)	Environment
Neelie Kroes (Netherlands)	Digital Agenda, Vice-President
László Andor (Hungary)	Employment, Social Affairs and Inclusion
Maria Damanaki (Greece)	Maritime Affairs and Fisheries
Johannes Hahn (Austria)	Regional Policy
Kristalina Georgieva (Bulgaria)	International Co-operation, Humanitarian Aid and Crisis Response
Siim Kallas (Estonia)	Transport, Vice-President
Cecilia Malmström (Sweden)	Home Affairs
Andris Piebalgs (Latvia)	Development
Viviane Reding (Luxembourg)	Justice, Fundamental Rights and Citizenship, Vice-President
Algirdas Šemeta (Lithuania)	Taxation and Customs Union
Antonio Tajani (Italy)	Industry and Entrepreneurship, Vice-President
Androulla Vassiliou (Cyprus)	Education, Culture, Multilingualism and Youth
Maros Sefcovic (Slovakia)	Interinstitutional Relations and Administration, Vice-President

4 The Directorates-General and Services of the Commission

The administration of the commission is currently organised in 41 different services and directorates-general, as listed below.

Policies

Agriculture and Rural
  Development
Competition Economic and
  Financial Affairs
Education and Culture
Employment, Social Affairs and
  Equal Opportunities
Energy and Transport
Enterprise and Industry
Environment
Executive Agencies
Health and Consumers
Information Society and Media
Internal Market and Services
Justice, Freedom and Security
Maritime Affairs and Fisheries
Regional Policy
Research
Taxation and Customs Union

External relations

Development
Enlargement
EuropeAid – Co-operation Office
External Relations
Humanitarian Aid
Trade

General services

Communication
European Anti-Fraud Office
Eurostat
Joint Research Centre
Publications Office
Secretariat General

Internal services

Budget
Bureau of European Policy
  Advisers
Informatics
European Commission Data
  Protection Officer
Infrastructures and Logistics –
  Brussels
Infrastructures and Logistics –
  Luxembourg
Internal Audit Service
Interpretation
Legal Service
Office for Administration and
  Payment of Individual
  Entitlements
Personnel and Administration
Translation

5 Addresses of main EU institutions and specialised agencies

Institutions

European Parliament
Secretariat
Centre Européen, Plateau du Kirchberg
L-2929 Luxembourg
Tel. +352 43001
Website: www.europarl.eu.int

Council of the European Union
General Secretariat
Rue de la Loi 175
B-1048 Brussels
Belgium
Tel. +32 2 2856111
Website: ue.eu.int

European Commission
Rue de la Loi 200
B-1049 Brussels
Belgium
Tel. +32 2 2991111
Website: europa.eu.int/comm

Court of Justice of the European Communities
Boulevard Konrad Adenauer
L-2925 Luxembourg
Tel. +352 43031
Website: www.curia.eu.int

European Court of Auditors
12 rue Alcide de Gasperi
L-1615 Luxembourg
Tel. +352 43981
Website: www.eca.eu.int

Economic and Social Committee
Rue Belliard 99
B-1040 Brussels
Belgium
Tel. +32 2 5469011
Website: www.esc.eu.int

Committee of the Regions
Rue Belliard 101
B-1040 Brussels
Belgium
Tel. +32 2 2822211
Website: www.cor.eu.int

European Investment Bank
100 boulevard Konrad Adenauer
L-2950 Luxembourg
Tel. +352 43791
Website: www.eib.org

European Central Bank
(formerly European Monetary Institute)
Kaiserstrasse 29
D-60311 Frankfurt am Main
Germany
Tel. +49 69 13440
Website: www.ecb.int

European Ombudsman
1 avenue du Président-Robert-Schuman
BP 403 FR
F-67001 Strasbourg Cedex
France
Tel. +33 3 8817 2313
Website: www.euro-ombusdman.eu.int

European Data Protection Supervisor
Rue Wiertz 60
B-1047 Brussels
Belgium
Tel. +32 2 2831900
Website: www.edps.eu.int

Agencies

European Centre for the Development of Vocational Training (Cedefop)
123 Europe
GR-55001 Thessaloniki
Greece
Tel. +30 2310 490111
Website: www.cedefop.eu.int

European Foundation for the Improvement of Living and Working Conditions (Eurofound)
Wyattwille Road
Loughlinstown
Dublin 18
Ireland
Tel. +353 1 2043100
Website: www.eurofound.eu.int

European Environment Agency (EEA)
Kongens Nytorv 6
DK-1050 Copenhagen K
Denmark
Tel. +45 33 367100
Website: www.eea.eu.int

European Training Foundation (ETF)
Villa Gualino
Viale Settimio Severo 65
I-10133 Turin
Italy
Tel. +39 011 6302222
Website: www.etf.eu.int

European Monitoring Centre for Drugs and Drug Addiction (EMCDDA)
Rua da Cruz de Santa Apolónia 23–25
P-1149-045 Lisbon
Portugal
Tel. +351 218 113000
Website: www.emcdda.eu.int

European Agency for the Evaluation of Medicinal Products (EMEA)
7 Westferry Circus
Canary Wharf
London E1 4HB
UK
Tel. +44 20 7418 8400
Website: www.emea.eu.int

Office for Harmonisation in the Internal Market (OHMI)
Apartado de Correos 77
E-03080 Alicante
Spain
Tel. +34 96 5139100
Website: oami.eu.int

European Agency for Safety and Health at Work (EU-OSHA)
Gran Via 33
E-48009 Bilbao
Spain
Tel. +34 94 4794360
Website: agency.osha.eu.int

Community Plant Variety Office (CPVO)
3 boulevard Maréchal-Foch
F-49100 Angers Cedex 02
France
Tel. +33 2 4125 6400
Website: www.cpvo.eu.int

Translation Centre for the Bodies of the European Union (CdT)
Bâtiment Nouvel Hémicycle
1 rue du Fort Thungen
L-1499 Luxembourg
Tel. +352 42 17111
Website: www.cdt.eu.int

European Union Agency for Fundamental Rights (FRA)
Schwarzenbergplatz 11
A-1040 Vienna
Austria
Tel. +43 1 580306 99
Website: fra.europa.eu

European Agency for Reconstruction (EAR)
Egnatia 4
GR-54626 Thessaloniki
Greece
Tel. +30 2310 505100
Website: www.ear.eu.int

European Food Safety Authority (EFSA)
Largo N. Palli 5/A
43121 Parma
Italy
Tel.: +39 0521 036 111
Website: www.efsa.eu.int

European Judicial Co-operation Unit (Eurojust)
Satumusstraat 9
2516 AD 's-Gravenhage
Netherlands
Tel.: +31 070 4125000
Website: www.eurojust.europa.eu

European Maritime Safety Agency (AESM)
Rue de Genève 12
B-1049 Brussels
Belgium
Tel. +32 2 7020200
Website: www.emsa.eu.int

European Aviation Safety Agency (AESA)
Postfach 101253
D-50452 Cologne
Germany
Tel. +49 221 89990 0000
Website: www.easa.eu.int

European Network and Information Security Agency (ENISA)
Rue Belliard 7, B-7 02/56
B-1040 Brussels
Belgium
Tel. +32 2 296374
Website: www.enisa.eu.int

6 Party groups in the European Parliament

The Euro-elections have been contested in each member state by the main national political parties. Within the Parliament, however, the elected members have joined together in transnational groups, and they sit in these groups rather than in national delegations, inside the chamber. As described in Chapter 7 there are currently seven of these, as well as some 27 MEPs who have declined to join any group and who sit as independents.

In early 2010 their membership was as follows:

European People's Party (EPP)	265
Socialists and Democrats (S&D)	184
Alliance of Liberals and Democrats for Europe (ALDE)	84
Greens/European Free Alliance (Greens/EFA)	55
European Conservatives and Reformists (ECR)	54
European United Left/Nordic Green Left Group (GUE/NGL)	35
Europe of Freedom & Democracy (EFD)	32
Unattached members (NI)	27

The table overleaf shows the breakdown of group membership by member state.

Political groups in the European Parliament, January 2010

	EPP	S&D	ALDE	Greens	ECR	GuE/ NGL	EFD	NI	Total
Austria	6	4	–	2	–	–	–	5	17
Belgium	5	5	5	4	1	–	–	2	22
Bulgaria	6	4	5	–	–	–	–	2	17
Cyprus	2	2	–	–	–	2	–	–	6
Czech Republic	2	7	–	–	9	4	–	–	22
Denmark	1	4	3	2	–	1	2	–	13
Estonia	1	1	3	1	–	–	–	–	6
Finland	4	2	4	2	–	–	1	–	13
France	29	14	6	14	–	5	1	3	72
Germany	42	23	12	14	–	8	–	–	99
Greece	8	8	–	1	–	3	2	–	22
Hungary	14	4	–	–	1	–	–	3	22
Ireland	4	3	4	–	–	1	–	–	12
Italy	35	21	7	–	–	–	9	–	72
Latvia	3	1	1	1	1	1	–	–	8
Lithuania	4	3	2	–	1	–	2	–	12
Luxembourg	3	1	1	1	–	–	–	–	6
Malta	2	3	–	–	–	–	–	–	5
Netherlands	5	3	6	3	1	2	1	4	25
Poland	28	7	–	–	15	–	–	–	50
Portugal	10	7	–	–	–	5	–	–	22
Romania	14	11	5	–	–	–	–	3	33
Slovakia	6	5	1	–	–	–	1	–	13
Slovenia	3	2	2	–	–	–	–	–	7
Spain	23	21	2	2	–	1	–	1	50
Sweden	5	5	4	3	–	1	–	–	18
United Kingdom	–	13	11	5	25	1	13	4	72
Total	**265**	**184**	**84**	**55**	**54**	**35**	**32**	**27**	**736**

7 Overseas links with the EU

The 79 ACP states

African

Angola
Benin
Botswana
Burkina Faso
Burundi
Cameroon
Cape Verde
Central African
  Republic
Chad
Comoros
Congo (Brazzaville)
Congo (Kinshasa)
Côte d'Ivoire
Djibouti
Equatorial Guinea
Eritrea
Ethiopia
Gabon
The Gambia
Ghana
Guinea
Guinea Bissau
Kenya
Lesotho
Liberia
Madagascar
Malawi
Mali
Mauritania
Mauritius
Mozambique
Namibia
Niger
Nigeria
Rwanda
São Tomé & Príncipe
Senegal
Seychelles
Sierra Leone
Somalia
South Africa[a]
Sudan
Swaziland
Tanzania
Togo
Uganda
Zambia
Zimbabwe

Caribbean

Antigua & Barbuda
Bahamas
Barbados
Belize
Cuba[a]
Dominica
Dominican Republic
Grenada
Guyana
Haiti
Jamaica
St Kitts & Nevis
St Lucia
St Vincent & The
  Grenadines
Suriname
Trinidad & Tobago

Pacific

Cook Islands
Federal States of
  Micronesia
Fiji
Kiribati
Marshall Islands
Nauru
Niue
Palau
Papua New Guinea
Solomon Islands
Timor Leste
Tonga
Tuvalu
Western Samoa
Vanuatu

a Qualified membership.

Overseas Countries and Territories (OCTs)

Denmark
Special relationship
Greenland

France
Territorial collectives
Mayotte
St Pierre & Miquelon
Overseas territories
New Caledonia & dependencies
French Polynesia
French Southern & Antarctic Territories
Wallis & Futuna Islands

Netherlands
Overseas countries
Netherlands Antilles (Bonaire, Curaçao, St Martin, Saba, St Eustace)
Aruba

UK
Overseas countries and territories
Anguilla
British Antarctic Territory
British Indian Ocean Territory
British Virgin Islands
Cayman Islands
Falkland Islands
Southern Sandwich Islands & dependencies
Montserrat
Pitcairn Island
St Helena & dependencies
Turks & Caicos Islands

8 The Maastricht, Amsterdam and Nice treaties

The **Treaty on European Union** was approved at the Maastricht meeting of the European Council on December 9th and 10th 1991, and signed in Maastricht on February 7th 1992. After ratification by the 12 national parliaments, it came into force on November 1st 1993.

The treaty, which is divided into six parts, and a long list of annexes and protocols, consists principally of amendments to the Rome treaty, in whose text it has been incorporated. The main provisions of the Maastricht Treaty are as follows:

1 The commitment of the Community to the achievement of economic and monetary union, including a single currency administered by a single independent central bank. This was to be achieved in three stages. The third stage, to start no later than January 1st 1999, but perhaps as early as January 1st 1997, committed those countries which fulfilled four specific criteria – relating to inflation, budget deficits, exchange rates and interest rates – to proceed to the adoption of a common currency. A protocol provided that the UK would not be obliged to enter the third stage of EMU without a separate decision to do so by its government and parliament.

2 The development of common foreign and defence policies, with defence issues initially subcontracted to the Western European Union, whose membership would be opened to all EC member states.

3 The introduction of union citizenship, defining the rights and obligations of nationals of the member states. These include freedom of movement, right of residence, the right to vote and stand as a candidate at municipal and European elections, and shared diplomatic protection outside the union.

4 EC powers in areas such as education and vocational training, trans-European networks, industry, health, culture, development co-operation and consumer protection were confirmed or extended.

5 The establishment of a Cohesion Fund to transfer resources from the richer to the poorer member states.

6 The strengthening of judicial, immigration and police co-operation between member states, largely on an inter-governmental basis.

7 An agreement by 11 member states, excluding the UK, to use EC machinery to implement measures arising from the Social Charter of 1989 concerning the protection of workers' health and safety, working conditions, information and consultation of workers, equal opportunity and treatment, and the integration of persons excluded from the labour market.

8 Institutional changes, including an extension of the legislative powers of the European Parliament, the increase in the commission's term of office from four to five years and the granting to the Court of Justice of the right to impose fines on member states for failing to implement its judgments.

The **Treaty of Amsterdam** was approved at the Amsterdam meeting of the European Council on June 16th and 17th 1997, and was signed, also in Amsterdam, on October 2nd 1997. It is divided into six sections and 19 chapters, with a substantial number of protocols, annexes and declarations. It consists mainly of amendments to the previous treaties, and was incorporated in the text of the Rome Treaty when it was ratified by the European Parliament and the 15 member states. It came into effect on May 1st 1999 following the receipt of the last instrument of ratification. Its main provisions are as follows:

1 Free movement of persons, asylum, immigration, the crossing of external borders and judicial co-operation in civil matters are brought within the Community framework (i.e. transferred from Pillar Three to Pillar One).

2 The Schengen Agreement, on opening of internal borders, is also brought within the Community framework.

3 The Protocol on Social Policy (the Social Chapter) is incorporated into the treaty and will apply to the United Kingdom and to all future entrants.

4 An employment chapter is added to the Treaty.

5 The provisions for a common foreign and security policy are strengthened, the Secretary-General of the Council of Ministers will become the high representative for the CFSP and will form a "troika" with the presidents of the Council and the commission.

6 The European Parliament's powers are extended, giving it the right to co-decision with the Council over the majority of EU legislation.

7 Qualified majority voting in the Council of Ministers is extended to

include research, employment, social exclusion, equal opportunities and public health.

8 The role of the president of the commission is upgraded. His appointment will need to be approved by the European Parliament and his assent will be needed for the appointment of the other members of the commission.

9 A new "flexibility" clause is added, enabling groups of member states to use the EU institutions to co-operate more closely on specific areas not within the exclusive competence of the EU.

The **Treaty of Nice** was approved at the Nice meeting of the European Council on December 11th 2000 and was signed, also in Nice, on February 26th 2001. Its main purpose was to provide for institutional changes within the EU to pave the way for the expected adhesion of a substantial number of member states during the first decade of the 21st century. Parts of the treaty were due to come into effect only in 2005, with the remainder following ratification by the 15 member states and the European Parliament. A referendum in Ireland on June 7th 2001 resulted in a "no" vote of 53.87% compared with 46.13% "yes". A further referendum in Ireland, in October 2002, reversed this verdict by 62.89% to 37.11%, enabling the treaty to come into effect on February 1st 2003. Its main provisions are as follows:

1 A reweighting of votes in the Council of Ministers to strengthen the position of the larger member states when new members, which are mostly small, join the Union.

2 The larger member states will give up their right to a second member of the commission. When EU membership reaches 27 or more, member states will no longer have an automatic right to nominate commissioners, who will be allocated on a rotation system in which all states, large or small, will be treated equally.

3 The number of seats in the European Parliament, both for the existing member states and for the 12 countries currently negotiating membership, is determined, giving a total maximum number of MEPS of 732. Membership numbers for other EU institutions are also agreed.

4 Qualified majority voting in the Council of Ministers is extended to over 30 more Articles of the Treaty of Rome, including notably the appointment of the president of the commission. The European Parliament's powers of co-decision are extended to ten more Articles.

5 Minor changes are made to the powers of the Court of Justice and the European Central Bank.
6 The scope of the "flexibility" clause of the Amsterdam treaty is extended.
7 There are new provisions to facilitate the implementation of the European Security and Defence Policy.

9 The Treaty of Lisbon

The Treaty of Lisbon came into force on December 1st 2009. It was designed to replace the Treaty establishing a Constitution for Europe (TCE), which had been approved by the European Council in June 2004 and would have come into force on November 1st 2006, had it not been rejected in referendums in France and the Netherlands in May and June 2005. The Lisbon treaty incorporates most of the provisions of the TCE but is a much less coherent document, as it consists of a long series of amendments to the Treaty of Rome and other European treaties. A summary of its main provisions was published by the commission in July 2009, from which the following paragraphs have been extracted.

More democracy, more openness

The Treaty gives you a stronger voice in decision-making.
A new **Citizens Initiative** means that one million people – out of the EU's population of 500 million – from a number of member states can petition the European Commission to bring forward new policy proposals.

This gives you a direct say in the EU's lawmaking for the first time.

To improve information about how the EU reaches decisions, the Council of Ministers will now have to meet in public when it is considering and voting on draft laws.

The Treaty increases the number of areas where the **European Parliament** shares decision-making with the **Council of Ministers**. That means that the MEPs you elect directly will have much more say in lawmaking and the EU budget.

At home, the **national parliaments** will have greater opportunities to make a direct input into EU decision making.

A new early warning system gives national parliaments the right to comment on draft laws and to check that the EU does not overstep its authority by involving itself in matters best dealt with nationally or locally.

Faster, more efficient decision making

The Lisbon Treaty streamlines the EU's decision-making procedures.
In the Council of Ministers, qualified majority voting, instead of unanimous decisions, will be extended. This will help to make action faster and more efficient.

Qualified majority voting means that, from 2014, decisions of the Council of Ministers will need the support of 55% of the Member States, representing at least 65% of the European population. This system gives double legitimacy to decisions.

Strict rules will apply to any proposals to move new policy areas to majority voting. Every Member State must agree to any such change and the national parliaments will have a right of veto.

But important policy areas such as taxation and defence will continue to require a unanimous vote.

Modernising the EU's institutions

A key aim of the Lisbon Treaty is to modernise the institutions that run the EU's business and makes them more democratic.

A new position of **High Representative for Foreign and Security Policy/Vice-President of the Commission** will be created in order to promote the EU action on the international scene and to be better able to defend its interests and values abroad.

To drive forward its work on a continuous and consistent basis, the European Council will elect a **President of the European Council** for a maximum of five years. This will make the EU's actions more visible and consistent.

The President of the Commission will be "elected" by the European Parliament, on proposal from the European Council.

The Lisbon Treaty reaffirms and updates many of the economic provisions included in earlier EU treaties. It also adds a number of important new fields. They are mentioned in the following points.

Economic policy

The Lisbon Treaty confirms the commitment to achieving economic and monetary union with the euro as the EU's currency.

The euro is now the currency of 16 Member States.

Economic and monetary union is a core objective of the EU. It is a vital force to ensure that Europe returns to prosperity and jobs. The EU and the Member States have together committed €200 billion in funding to stimulate the EU's economy in the current financial crisis.

The Lisbon Treaty formalises the position of the European Central Bank by making it an institution of the European Union.

The European Union in the world

The EU pledges to promote the values of the EU in the world by contributing to:

- peace and security;
- sustainable development of the Earth;
- solidarity and mutual respect among peoples;
- free and fair trade;
- eradication of poverty;
- protection of human rights;
- respect for and enhancement of international law as defined, in particular, in the United Nations Charter.

The EU is the world's strongest commercial power and the biggest aid donor to the developing world.

The aforementioned creation of a High Representative for Foreign and Security Policy/Vice-President of the Commission will lend greater consistency to the EU's external actions and will enable the European Union to speak with one voice abroad. He or she will be assisted by a dedicated External Action Service.

Security and defence

The Lisbon Treaty spells out more clearly the EU's role in the area of common foreign and security policy. Decisions on defence issues will continue to need unanimous approval of the 27 EU Member States.
Missions which the EU has undertaken outside its own territory have been for the purpose of peacekeeping, conflict prevention and strengthening international security in the context of the United Nations Charter.

The Lisbon Treaty extends the EU's role to include disarmament operations, military advice and assistance, and helping to restore stability after conflicts.

It also creates the possibility of enhanced cooperation between Member States that wish to work together more closely in the area of defence.

The Lisbon Treaty provides that Member States will make available to the EU the civil and military capability necessary to implement the common security and defence policy and sets out the role of the European Defence Agency.

It introduces a solidarity clause (of a voluntary nature) when a Member State is the victim of a terrorist attack or a natural or man-made disaster.

Justice and crime

The Lisbon Treaty contains important new provisions strengthening the EU's ability to fight international cross-border crime, illegal immigration, trafficking of people, arms and drugs.

The simplification proposed by the Lisbon Treaty means that greater transparency is brought to bear in this area, the roles of the European Parliament and the Court of Justice are strengthened and decision-making will be speeded up via more qualified majority voting.

The new provisions, amongst others, should enable the Union and Member States to ensure a more effective protection of the financial interests of the Union and the fight against cross-border crime.

These new provisions express respect for the different legal systems and traditions of Member States. They foresee, for example, an "emergency break" enabling a Member State not to participate in a new measure if it considers that this would affect fundamental aspects of its criminal justice system.

Exceptionally for Ireland and the United Kingdom, with their common law system and standing outside the border control scheme of Schengen, they will have a special arrangement allowing them to decide on a case by case basis whether to participate in legislation in this area.

Social policy

The Lisbon Treaty steps up the EU's social objectives. It provides that, in all its policies and actions, the EU will take into account the promotion of a high level of employment.

The key role of economic services such as public transport, telecommunications, postal services, gas and electricity supply is recognised.

The EU's role in these areas is limited, with Member States having much room for manoeuvre to supply, operate and organise services so as to respond effectively to needs at home.

The EU is to refrain from any action that would detract from the Member States' role in providing services of general interest such as health, social services, police and security forces, state schools.

Pay, right of association and the rules for taking strike action remain a matter for Member States.

New areas of cooperation

The Lisbon Treaty has important provisions in a number of new policy areas reinforcing the EU's ability to fight international cross-border crime, illegal immigration, trafficking of women and children, drugs and arms.

Two other areas are especially relevant in today's world.

Climate change: The Treaty gives priority to the EU's objective of prioritising sustainable development in Europe, based on a high level of environmental protection and enhancement.

The Treaty pledges to promote, at an international level, measures to tackle regional and global environmental problems, in particular climate change.

Strengthening the EU's rote on climate change will mean that Europe continues to take the lead in combating global warming.

Energy: The Treaty has new provisions ensuring that the energy market functions well, in particular with regard to energy supply, and that energy efficiency and savings are achieved, as well as the development of new and renewable energy sources.

For all Member States, security of energy supply is a key challenge for the future.

The Lisbon Treaty affirms the EU's commitment to a united European policy on sustainable energy.

It also provides a new basis for cooperation between Member States in sport, humanitarian aid, civil protection, tourism and space research.

Human rights

The Lisbon Treaty recognises the rights, freedoms and principles set out in the Charter of Fundamental Rights and makes the charter legally binding.

The Member States signed the charter in 2000. Now it becomes legally binding.

This means that when the EU proposes and implements laws it must respect the rights set down in the charter – and Member States must do so too when implementing EU legislation.

Rights which everyone should enjoy include personal data protection, the right to asylum, equality before the law and non-discrimination, equality between men and women, the rights of children and elderly people and important social rights such as protection against unfair dismissal and access to social security and social assistance.

The Lisbon Treaty will also allow the EU to accede to the European

Convention on Human Rights. The convention, and the European Court of Human Rights which oversees it, are the foundations of human rights protection in Europe.

Who does what

The Lisbon Treaty clarifies:

- which powers belong to the EU,
- which powers belong to the Member States,
- which powers are shared.

It sets out the **limits on the EU's powers** more clearly than before.

A basic rule is that the EU will only be able to exercise those powers that have been conferred on it by the Member States. It must respect the fact that all other powers rest with the Member States.

- The EU has exclusive charge over areas such as competition rules, monetary policy of the euro area and the common commercial policy.
- Member States have primary responsibility in fields such as health, education and industry.
- The EU and the Member States share competence in areas such as the internal market, agriculture, transport and energy.

Other provisions

The Lisbon Treaty affirms the EU's **respect for the equality of the Member States** and their national identities, including local and regional autonomy. It pledges to protect Europe's diverse cultures and languages.

For the first time there is a provision for a **Member State to withdraw from the European Union** if it wishes and sets out the arrangements which will apply in that event.

New powers for national parliaments

For the first time, national parliaments will have a direct input into the European decision-making process.

Under the Lisbon Treaty, all proposed EU laws will have to be sent to national parliaments.

An early warning system will be in place and any national parliaments will have eight weeks to argue the case if it feels a proposal is not appropriate for EU action.

If enough national parliaments object, the proposal can be amended or withdrawn.

This early warning system gives national parliaments an important role in ensuring that the EU does not overstep its authority by involving itself in matters that can best be dealt with at national, regional or local level.

Find out more

Inevitably the Lisbon Treaty is a lengthy document – over 300 pages in the consolidated form, including annexes and protocols. It includes many provisions of earlier EU treaties, amended and updated.

You can download the full text of the Lisbon Treaty and the consolidated versions of the treaties as amended by the Lisbon Treaty and find out more about it at europa.eu/lisbon_treaty/full_text/index_en.htm.

10 Chronology of major events concerning the European Union

1945	May	End of second world war in Europe.
1947	June	United States launches Marshall Plan to aid European reconstruction.
1948	April	Creation of the Organisation for Economic Co-operation (OEEC) to co-ordinate Marshall Plan assistance.
1949	April	North Atlantic Treaty signed, creating NATO.
1950	May	French foreign minister, Robert Schuman, proposes the pooling of French and West German coal and steel resources in a community open to other West European nations.
1951	April	Belgium, France, Italy, Luxembourg, the Netherlands and West Germany sign the Treaty of Paris, setting up the European Coal and Steel Community (ECSC).
1952	May	The same six countries sign a treaty to establish a European Defence Community (EDC), with a common European army.
	August	The ECSC established, with its headquarters in Luxembourg.
1954	August	French parliament refuses to ratify the EDC treaty, which is immediately abandoned.
1955	June	Negotiations begin at Messina for the creation of a European Common Market.
1957	March	Two treaties signed in Rome, setting up the European Economic Community and Euratom, by the six member states of the ECSC.
1958	January	The EEC and Euratom treaties come into effect. The EEC Commission is established, with its headquarters "provisionally" in Brussels.
1960	January	The Stockholm Convention established the European Free Trade Association (EFTA), linking the UK with Austria, Denmark, Norway, Portugal, Sweden and Switzerland.

	December	The OEEC is wound up and replaced by the Organisation for Economic Co-operation and Development (OECD), based in Paris.
1961	May	EFTA established, with its headquarters in Geneva.
	July	The EEC signs an association agreement with Greece. Ireland applies for EEC membership.
	August	Denmark and the UK also apply for membership.
	November	Membership negotiations open in Brussels.
1962	April	Norway applies for EEC membership.
1963	January	President de Gaulle vetoes UK membership; the other applicant states suspend their applications. Franco-German Treaty of Co-operation signed.
	July	Yaoundé Convention, providing for economic aid and trade concessions to 17 African states, formerly colonies of the EEC countries, is signed in the capital of Cameroon.
	September	The EEC signs an association agreement with Turkey.
1964	July	Common Agricultural Policy (CAP) comes into effect.
1965	June	Crisis in the EEC as France begins seven-month boycott of its meetings, refusing to be out-voted on issues it considers of great importance.
1966	January	France resumes its active membership, after negotiation of the "Luxembourg compromise", under which important issues are, in effect, to be decided by unanimity, irrespective of the provisions of the Rome treaty.
1967	May	Denmark, Ireland, Norway and the UK make second application to join the EEC. In view of de Gaulle's continued hostility, the applications are left on the table.
	July	The EEC is merged with the ECSC and Euratom to form a single European Community (EC).
1968	July	All internal tariffs removed within the EC, which establishes a common external tariff (CET).
1969	December	France's President Pompidou agrees with other EC leaders at a "summit" meeting in The Hague to consider an enlargement of EC membership.

1970	June	Membership negotiations open in Brussels with the four applicant states.
1972	January	Treaties of Accession signed between the EC and Denmark, Ireland, Norway and the UK.
	July	Free trade agreements signed with the six EFTA states which did not apply to join the EC.
	September	Norway turns down EC membership in a referendum (46% for, 54% against).
1973	January	Denmark, Ireland and the UK become full members of the Community.
	May	Norway signs free trade agreement with the EC.
1974	April	At request of the new UK Labour government, a "renegotiation" of the membership terms begins.
1975	February	First Lomé Convention, replacing the Yaoundé Convention of 1963, is signed, giving economic aid and trade concessions to 46 African, Caribbean and Pacific (ACP) states.
	June	Referendum in the UK shows a 2:1 majority in favour of staying in the EC. Greece applies for EC membership.
1977	March	Portugal applies for membership.
	July	Spain applies for membership.
1979	March	European Monetary System (EMS) established.
	June	First direct elections to the European Parliament.
	December	Row over UK budget contribution to the EC at the Dublin summit, when Mrs Thatcher demands "our money back".
1980	May	Provisional solution to UK budget problem, intended to last for three years.
1981	January	Greece becomes member of the EC.
1984	June	Second direct elections to European Parliament. At Fontainebleau summit agreement reached on reducing the UK budget contribution and on increasing the financial resources of the EC.
1985	January	Jacques Delors becomes president of the European Commission.
	June	At Milan summit agreement is reached on seven-year timetable to remove 300 barriers to the internal market, according to a programme devised by a British commissioner,

		Lord Cockfield. An inter-governmental conference is also appointed to consider amendments to the Rome treaty.
	December	The inter-governmental conference produces the Single European Act, a series of treaty amendments designed to speed up decision-making, especially on internal market measures. It is signed by all member states.
1986	January	Spain and Portugal become members of the EC.
1987	April	Turkey applies to join the EC.
	July	The Single European Act comes into force.
1988	February	Delors I package, which sets the guidelines for expanding EC budgets, but with tighter control over agricultural spending, over the five years 1988–92, agreed.
1989	June	Third direct elections to European Parliament. Austria applies to join the EC.
	July	G7 summit asks EC to co-ordinate western aid to Poland and Hungary. This aid is subsequently extended to other east European countries, and negotiations follow to conclude trade and association agreements with the former Soviet "satellites".
	November	Breach of the Berlin Wall heralds the collapse of communism in eastern Europe.
	December	Negotiations begin between the EC and the EFTA states to form a European Economic Area (EEA).
1990	July	Capital movements liberalised throughout the Community. Madrid summit conference approves in principle a plan to introduce economic and monetary union in three stages, with Mrs Thatcher reserving the UK position. Cyprus and Malta apply for EC membership.
	October	German unification: territory of former East Germany joins EC, as integral part of West Germany.
	December	Two inter-governmental conferences, on economic and monetary union and on political union respectively, begin work.

		Rome EC summit approves programmes of food aid and technical assistance to the Soviet Union.
1991	July	Sweden applies for EC membership.
	September	Following the failed Soviet coup, EC mission visits the former Soviet Union and the newly independent Baltic states to discuss an enhanced aid programme. EC-sponsored peace conference opens on Yugoslavia.
	November	Agreement reached to set up EEA on January 1st 1993.
	December	At Maastricht summit, agreement is reached on the Treaty on European Union. This includes detailed arrangements for EMU, with a single currency, to be in force no later than 1999, with an opt-out provision for the UK, and for gradual progression towards a common foreign and security policy.
1992	February	Delors II package proposes increasing EC budget by 30% over five years.
	March	Finland applies for EC membership.
	May	Switzerland applies for EC membership.
	June	Denmark narrowly rejects Maastricht treaty in referendum; Jacques Delors is reappointed for two more years, from January 1993, at Lisbon summit; reform of CAP narrowly agreed by Council of Ministers.
	November	Blair House agreement aligns EC and US proposals on the agricultural sector of the Uruguay round of the GATT negotiations.
	December	Switzerland turns down EEA in a referendum; Edinburgh summit adopts reduced Delors II budget package, spreading it out over seven years instead of five, and approves establishment of European Investment Fund.
1993	February	Negotiations begin on accession of Austria, Finland and Sweden.
	April	Negotiations begin on accession of Norway.
	May	In second referendum the Danish people vote in favour of the Maastricht treaty.

	July	Adoption of the TACIS programme to provide technical assistance to the independent states of the former Soviet Union.
	August	After many delays, the UK finally ratifies the Maastricht treaty.
	October	Germany, the last state to do so, deposits its ratification of the Maastricht treaty after a court challenge fails.
	November 1	Maastricht treaty comes into force: the European Community becomes the European Union.
	December	Brussels summit approves an action plan based on the European Commission's white paper on growth, competitiveness and employment.
	December	Uruguay round negotiations successfully concluded in Geneva.
1994	**January**	EEA agreement comes into force, linking the EU and five member states of EFTA, but excluding Switzerland and, temporarily, Liechtenstein.
	March	Accession negotiations successfully completed with Austria, Finland, Norway and Sweden.
	June	Fourth direct elections to the European Parliament. Partnership and Co-operation Agreement signed with Russia at Corfu summit. The UK vetoes nomination of Jean-Luc Dehaene as president of the European Commission.
	July	Jacques Santer nominated as commission president to succeed Jacques Delors.
	November	Norway rejects EU membership in referendum.
	December	Essen summit gives go-ahead for first 14 priority projects for Trans-European Networks.
1995	**January**	Austria, Finland and Sweden join the EU. New commission under Jacques Santer takes office. Pact on Stability in Europe between the EU and the states belonging to the Organisation on Security and Co-operation in Europe (OSCE) signed in Paris.
	April	Liechtenstein accedes to the EEA.
	May	Commission produces white paper on steps that the countries of central and eastern Europe should take to prepare for membership of the EU.

	July	EU member states sign convention establishing Europol (the European Police Office). First EU ombudsman, Jacob Söderman, elected.
	November	Euro-Mediterranean ministerial conference at Barcelona adopts declaration regulating future relations, including financial aid and progress towards free trade areas, between the EU and 12 Mediterranean states.
	December	EU and the United States sign a new transatlantic agenda and joint action plan. Customs union between Turkey and the EU approved by European Parliament. Madrid summit confirms introduction of a single currency (euro) on January 1st 1999.
		During the year Bulgaria, Estonia, Latvia, Lithuania, Romania and Slovakia apply for membership of the EU.
1996	**January**	Czech Republic applies for EU membership.
	March	Inter-governmental conference to review the Maastricht treaty and to prepare for further enlargement opened in Turin. EU bans UK beef exports, but offers financial aid to help combat BSE outbreak. The UK begins systematic policy of non-co-operation in effort to secure the lifting of the ban.
	June	The UK ends non-co-operation after EU stipulates conditions for the eventual lifting of the ban. Slovenia applies for EU membership.
	October	EU emphatically rejects the extra-territorial provisions of the Helms-Burton Act regarding trade with Cuba, and threatens counter-measures against the United States.
	December	Dublin summit agrees on stability pact to impose economic and financial disciplines on member states joining the single currency, reinforcing confidence that EMU would be successfully launched in January 1999.
1997	**May**	Newly elected Labour government in UK announces "fresh start" in relations with EU, and ends British opt-out from the Social Chapter.

	June	Signing of the Amsterdam Treaty, containing modest amendments to the Rome and Maastricht treaties.
	July	Commission adopts "Agenda 2000" policy statement, preparing the ground for further EU enlargement, and setting long-term targets for financial and agricultural reforms.
	December	At Luxembourg summit the way is cleared for membership negotiations to begin in March 1998 with Cyprus, the Czech Republic, Estonia, Hungary, Poland and Slovenia.
1998	**May**	Agreement is reached at special Brussels summit for 11 member states to participate in a single currency, under EMU, from January 1st 1999. Wim Duisenberg is appointed as the first president of the European Central Bank. At EU–US summit President Clinton agrees to ask the US Congress to exclude the EU from sanctions under the Helms-Burton Act.
	September	Malta reactivates its application for EU membership.
	December	European Parliament refuses to approve final accounts of the 1996 budget, precipitating a crisis with the commission.
1999	**March**	Entire Santer Commission resigns in anticipation of being censured by the Parliament. At Berlin summit Romano Prodi is nominated as successor to Santer. The summit also approves budgetary perspectives for 2000–06.
	May	Treaty of Amsterdam comes into force. Foreign ministers propose a stability pact for south-east Europe, following the Kosovo conflict.
	September	New commission, led by Romano Prodi, takes over, following its approval by the European Parliament.
	October	Special summit meeting on justice and home affairs calls for the creation of an area of "freedom, justice and security" within the EU.
	December	Helsinki summit decides to open accession negotiations with Bulgaria, Latvia, Lithuania, Malta, Romania and Slovakia.

2000	March	Special Economic Summit in Lisbon inaugurates a ten-year programme to make the EU "the most competitive and dynamic knowledge-based economy in the world".
	September	Denmark votes in referendum by 53.3% to 46.7% not to adopt the euro.
	October	Convention draws up a draft Charter of Fundamental Rights for the EU.
	December	European Council in Nice agrees treaty amending the Union's institutional provisions to facilitate the admission of up to 12 new member states.
2001	January	Greece becomes the 12th country to join the euro.
	June	Irish referendum rejects the Nice treaty by 53.87% to 46.13%.
	December	Laeken summit adopts wide-ranging proposals to combat terrorism in the wake of the September 11th attacks on the United States. It also establishes a Convention on EU reform in preparation for the 2004 IGC.
2002	January–February	Euro notes and coins replace national currencies in the 12 member states of the euro zone.
	July	The treaty establishing the European Coal and Steel Community expires, after 50 years. The ECSC's residual duties and obligations are transferred to the EU.
	October	A second Irish referendum accepts the Nice treaty by 62.89% to 37.11%.
	December	Copenhagen summit completes accession negotiations with ten candidate countries, paving the way for a 25-member EU from May 1st 2004. It agrees target dates for Bulgaria and Romania for 2007, and that the question of opening negotiations with Turkey should be decided in December 2004.
2003		Nine candidate countries approve their membership terms by referendums, while Cyprus ratifies its accession treaty by a unanimous parliamentary vote. Sweden rejects the introduction of the euro by 56% to 44% in a referendum.

	February	Nice treaty comes into effect. Croatia applies for EU membership.
	June	Convention on a European constitution completes its work and presents a draft to the Thessaloniki summit, which passes it on to an inter-govenmental conference.
	December	The IGC presents a revised draft of the constitution to a summit which fails to agree, largely because of disagreement about the proposed voting weights in the Council of Ministers.
2004	**February**	The Commission adopts financial perspectives for 2007–13.
	March	Former Yugoslav Republic of Macedonia applies for EU membership.
	May	Ten new countries – Cyprus, the Czech Republic, Estonia, Hungary, Latvia, Lithuania, Malta, Poland, Slovakia and Slovenia – join the EU, bringing the membership up to 25.
	June	European Council approves the draft Treaty establishing a Constitution for Europe (TCE). José Manuel Barroso nominated as president-designate of the commission.
	November	The Barroso Commission takes over from Romano Prodi's team, to hold office until January 2010.
2005	**March**	Summit meeting agrees to ease the provisions of the Stability and Growth Pact, redefine the objectives of the Lisbon strategy and water down the proposed directive to liberalise the provision of cross-border services.
	May–June	French and Dutch voters reject the TCE in referendums, by respectively 55% to 45% and 62% to 38%.
	December	European Council reaches agreement on the EU's financial perspective for 2007–13.
2006	**June**	10th Economic Development Fund, covering 2007–13 and totalling €22 billion, agreed for ACP countries.
2007	**January**	Bulgaria and Romania become members of the EU.

	March	Berlin Declaration on the 50th anniversary of the signing of the Rome treaty.
	December	Treaty of Lisbon signed.
2008	June	Ireland rejects Lisbon treaty in referendum, by 53.4% to 46.6%.
	August	President Sarkozy negotiates ceasefire in Russo-Georgian war.
	December	European Council agrees to co-ordinate national measures to combat the recession. Macedonia (FYROM) applies to join the EU.
2009	April	Albania applies to join the EU.
	June	Iceland applies to join the EU.
	September	José Manuel Barroso appointed for a second five-year term as president of the commission.
	October	In second referendum, Ireland votes to ratify the Treaty of Lisbon, by 67.1% to 32.9%.
	November	Herman Van Rompuy appointed as permanent president of the European Council, and Catherine Ashton as high representative for foreign and security policy.
	December	Treaty of Lisbon comes into force. Serbia applies to join the EU.
2010	February	European Parliament approves the appointment of the second Barroso Commission to serve until January 2015.

Suggestions for further reading

There is a vast literature on the EU, much of it of a highly specialist nature. The European Commission itself produces a stream of pamphlets and documentation of various kinds, much of which is available (often free of charge) from the information offices of the EU in London, Edinburgh, Cardiff and Belfast. There are similar offices in all the major EU capital cities, as well as in other major centres including New York, Washington, New Delhi, Ottawa and Canberra.

The historical background to the creation of the Community is described in fascinating detail in Jean Monnet's memoirs and his biography, and placed in a wider context by two other well-known authors.

Duchêne, F., *Jean Monnet: The First Statesman of Interdependence*, W. W. Norton, New York and London, 1994.

Grosser, A., *The Western Alliance: European-American relations since 1945*, Macmillan, London, 1980.

Monnet, J., *Memoirs*, Collins, London, 1978.

Stirk, P.M.R., *A History of European Integration since 1914*, Continuum, London, 2001.

Among the large number of books written about particular aspects of the Community's affairs, the following may be mentioned.

Bainbridge, T. and Teasdale, A., *The Penguin Companion to European Union*, 3rd edition, Penguin Books, Harmondsworth, 2004.

Bond, M., Smith, J. and Wallace, W. (eds), *Eminent Europeans: Personalities who shaped contemporary Europe*, Greycoat Press, London, 1996.

Dinan, D., *Europe Recast: A History of European Union*, Palgrave Macmillan, Basingstoke, 2004.

Edwards, G. and Spence, D. (eds), *The European Commission*, John Harper Publishing, London, 1997.

Emerson, M., *Redrawing the Map of Europe*, Macmillan, London, 1998.

Grant, C., *Delors: Inside the House that Jacques Built*, Brealey, London, 1994.

Grant, C., *Is Europe doomed to fail as a power?*, Centre for European Reform, London, 2009.

Hix, S., *The Political System of the European Union*, 2nd edition, Macmillan, London, 2005.

Hix, S., *What's Wrong with the European Union and How to Fix It*, Polity Press, London, 2008.

Jacobs, F., Corbett, R. and Shackleton, M., *The European Parliament*, 4th edition, John Harper Publishing, London, 2003.

Jenkins, R., *European Diary 1977–1981*, Collins, London, 1989.

Leonard, D. and Leonard, M. (eds), *The Pro-European Reader*, Palgrave-Macmillan, London, 2001.

Leonard, M., *Network Europe: The New Case for Europe*, Foreign Policy Centre, London, 1999.

Leonard, M., *Why Europe Will Run the 21st Century*, Fourth Estate, London, 2005.

March Hunnings, N., *The European Courts*, John Harper Publishing, London, 1996.

Mathijsen, P.S.R.F., *A Guide to European Union Law*, 8th edition, Sweet and Maxwell, London, 2004.

Menon, A., *Europe: The State of the Union*, Atlantic Books, London, 2008.

Milton, G. and Keller-Noëllet, J., *The European Constitution*, John Harper Publishing, London, 2005.

Norman, P., *The Accidental Constitution: The Story of the European Convention*, EuroComment, Brussels, 2003.

Pinder, J., *The European Union: A Very Short Introduction*, OUP, Oxford, 2001.

Reid, T.R., *The United States of Europe: The New Superpower and the End of American Supremacy*, Penguin, Harmondsworth, 2004.

Rifkin, J., *The European Dream*, Polity Press, London, 2004.

Siedentop, L., *Democracy in Europe*, Columbia University Press, New York, 2001.

Wall, S., *A Stranger in Europe: Britain and the EU from Thatcher to Blair*, OUP, Oxford, 2008.

Wallace, H. and Wallace, W. (eds), *Policy-making in the European Union*, OUP, Oxford, 2000.

Westlake, M., *The Council of the European Union*, 2nd edition, John Harper Publishing, London, 2004.

Young, H., *This Blessed Plot: Britain and Europe from Churchill to Blair*, Macmillan, London, 1998.

Index

Numbers in *italics* indicate figures; those in **bold** type indicate tables.